Hands to WORK
Hearts to GOD

RECIPES FROM THE

Maurice 1st Reformed Church

MAURICE, IOWA

Our Standard Abbreviations

tsp.	-	teaspoon	**sm.**	-	small
T.	-	tablespoon	**med.**	-	medium
c.	-	cup	**lg.**	-	large
oz.	-	ounce or ounces	**pt.**	-	pint
lb.	-	pound or pounds	**qt.**	-	quart
sq.	-	square	**doz.**	-	dozen
ctn.	-	carton or container	**bu.**	-	bushel
pkg.	-	package(s)	**env.**	-	envelope(s)
btl.	-	bottle(s)	**pkt.**	-	packet(s)
liter	-	liter	**mg**	-	milligram(s)
approx.	-	approximately	**gm**	-	gram(s)
temp.	-	temperature	**gal.**	-	gallon(s)

Printed
October 2000

Printed by:

JUMBO JACK'S COOKBOOKS
AUDUBON MEDIA CORPORATION
301 BROADWAY • AUDUBON IA 50025
1-800-798-2635

Dedication

We have crossed the threshold into the new millennium - year 2000 has brought some changes, and retained many of the same, familiar patterns of life we find comfortable.

The life of our church is also experiencing change - we are growing "inside and out"! In spite of this, we also want to retain the important, basic beliefs we hold dear -- our love of God and the desire to serve Him, and share His love with others.

We dedicate this cookbook to the efforts to upgrade and expand the physical building of Maurice First Reformed Church. The profits earned from this effort will help raise money for our building fund.

We wish to thank all of the men, women, young people, and boys and girls who shared their favorite recipes with us. We hope this collection will be referred to often, and that the resulting good food will provide times of sharing around the table and counting our blessings. To God be the glory!

The Cookbook Committee

We express our Thank You to John E. VanDerStelt for his artwork on the cover page and divider pages.

"It's The Love That You Add"

Cooking's an art - culinary they say,
With herbs and spices from far, far away.
Ingredients must be fresh, and just the right size
To satisfy the tongue, and look good to the eyes.
Nourishing, wholesome, or sinfully sweet,
When love's been added, it makes it a treat.
The dishes may be common, or uncommonly rare,
Paper, plastic, china or stoneware.
The table can be set in a casual way,
Or with linen and candles and a floral bouquet.
The guests can be friends, or just Mom and Dad,
What makes food real good is the love that you add!

Another scene comes to mind of a meal,
That was served out of doors to a crowd on a hill.
Jesus had taught in His wonderful way
About life and love and what would happen some day,
When all of life's troubles and cares will be o'er
And we will be safe on that beautiful shore.
When His friends came to tell Him, "These people need food."
They're hungry and fainting and getting quite rude!"
Then a boy came to Jesus and said, "I'll share my lunch!"
And Jesus said, "Divide them up by the bunch."
So He blessed it and broke it, and said to the lad,
"What makes food enough is the love that you add!"

So whether in cooking or serving or baking,
Or to a friend's house a gift you are taking.
Remember what Jesus reminded the lad,
What makes the difference is the love that you add!"

1 Corinthians 13:13 ~ "And now these three remain: faith, hope and love. But the greatest of these is love."
Marilyn Kruid

Weights & Measurements

Amount to equal 1 pound:
2 c. milk
2 c. chopped meat
6 c. rolled oats
2 2/3 c. powdered sugar
2 1/3 c. dry beans
4 c. all-purpose flour
4 c. entire wheat flour
4 1/3 c. rye meal
4 1/3 c. coffee

2 c. butter
2 2/3 c. oatmeal
2 c. granulated sugar
2 2/3 c. brown sugar
3 1/2 c. confectioners' sugar
4 1/2 c. cake flour
4 1/2 c. graham flour
1 7/8 c. rice

Weight to equal 1 cupful:
1/2 lb. sugar
1/2 lb. butter
1/2 lb. rice
1/2 lb. chopped meat

5 oz. cornmeal
6 oz. raisins
6 oz. currants
2 oz. stale bread crumbs

Units of Volume:
1 bushel .... 4 pecks
1 peck .... 8 quarts
1 gallon .... 4 quarts
1 quart .... 2 pints
1 pint .... 2 cups
1 cup .... 16 tablespoons
1/2 cup .... 8 tablespoons
1/3 cup .... 5 1/3 tablespoons
1/4 cup .... 4 tablespoons
1 jigger .... 1 1/2 ounces
2 tablespoons .... 1 ounce
1 tablespoon .... 3 teaspoons

Abbreviations used in this cookbook:
tsp. .... teaspoon(s)
T. .... tablespoon(s)
c. .... cup(s)
pkg. .... package(s)
oz. .... ounce(s)
lb. .... pound(s)
pt. .... pint(s)
qt. . ...quart(s)
doz. .... dozen
btl. .... bottle(s)

pkt. .... packet(s)
sm. .... small
med. .... medium
lg. .... large
ctn. .... carton or container(s)
sq. .... square(s)
bu .... bushel(s)
pk. .... peck(s)
env. .... envelope(s)

v

Where to Look in the Bible

When ...
Anxious for dear ones . Ps. 121; Luke 17
Business is poor .... Ps. 37, 92; Eccl. 5
Discouraged .... Ps. 23, 42, 43
Everything seems going from bad to
    worse .... II Tim. 3; Heb. 13
Friends seem to go back on you
    .... Matt. 5; I Cor. 13
Sorrow overtakes you ... Ps. 46; Matt. 28
Tempted to do wrong ... Ps. 15, 19, 139;
    .... Matt. 4; James 1
Things look "blue" .... Ps. 34, 71; Isa. 40
You seem too busy .... Eccl. 3:1-15
You can't go to sleep ...... Ps. 4, 56, 130
You have quarreled ..... Matt. 18; Eph. 4;
    .... James 4
You are weary .... Ps. 95:1-7; Matt. 11
Worries oppress you ...... Ps. 46; Matt. 6

If you ...
Are challenged by opposing
    forces .... Eph. 6; Phil. 4
Are facing a crisis .... Job 28:12-28;
    .... Prov. 8; Isa. 55
Are jealous .... Ps. 49; James 3
Are impatient .... Ps. 40, 90; Heb. 12
Are bereaved 1Cor. 15;
    ..... 1 Thess. 4:13-5:28; Rev. 21, 22
Are bored .... II Kings 5; Job 38;
    .... Ps. 103, 104; Eph. 3

To find ...
The Ten Commandments .... Exo. 20;
    .... Deut. 5
The Shepherd Psalm .... Ps. 23
The Birth of Jesus ..... Matt. 1, 2; Luke 2
The Beatitudes .... Matt. 5:1-12
The Lord's Prayer .... Matt. 6:5-15;
    .... Luke 11:1-13
The Sermon on the Mount .. Matt. 5, 6, 7
The Great Commandments
    .... Matt. 22:34-40
The Great Commission .. Matt. 28:16-20
The Parable of the Good Samaritan
    .... Luke 10
The Parable of the Prodigal Son
    .... Luke 15
The Parable of the Sower .... Matt. 13;
    .... Mark 4; Luke 8
The Last Judgment .... Matt. 25
The Crucifixion, Death and Resur-
    rection of Jesus ...... Matt. 26, 27, 28;
    .... Mark 14, 15, 16; Luke 22, 23, 24;
    .... John, chapters 13 to 21
The Outpouring of the Holy Spirit Acts 2

When ...
Desiring inward peace   John 14; Rom. 8
Everything is going well ... Ps. 33:12-22;
    .... 100; I Tim. 6;
    .... James 2:1-17
Satisfied with yourself Prov. 11; Luke 16
Seeking the best investment ...... Matt. 7
Starting a new job .... Ps. 1; Prov. 16;
    .... Phil. 3:7-21
You have been placed in a position
    of responsibility .... Joshua 1:1-9;
    .... Prov. 2; II Cor. 8:1-15
Making a new home .. Ps. 127; Prov. 17;
    .... Eph. 5; Col. 3;
    .... I Peter 3:1-17; I John 4
You are out for a good time
    .... Matt. 15:1-20;
    .... II Cor. 3; Gal. 5
Wanting to live successfully
    with your fellowmen .... Rom. 12

If you ...
Bear a grudge . Luke 6; II Cor. 4; Eph. 4
Have experienced severe losses
    .... Col. 1; I Peter 1
Have been disobedient .... Isa. 6;
    .... Mark 12; Luke 5
Need forgiveness .... Matt. 23;
    .... Luke 15; Philemon
Are sick or in pain ...... Ps. 6, 39, 41, 67;
    .... Isa. 26

When you ...
Feel your faith is weak ..... Ps. 126, 146;
    .... Heb. 11
Think God seems far away
    .... Ps. 25, 125, 138; Luke 10
Are leaving home ..... Ps. 119; Prov. 3, 4
Are planning your budget .... Mark 4;
    .... Luke 19
Are becoming lax and indifferent
    .... Matt. 25; Rev. 3
Are lonely or fearful .... Ps. 27, 91;
    .... Luke 8; I Peter 4
Fear death .... John 11, 17, 20;
    .... II Cor. 5; I John 3; Rev. 14
Have sinned .... Ps. 51; Isa. 53;
    .... John 3; I John 1
Want to know the way of prayer
    .... I Kings 8:12-61;
    .... Luke 11, 18
Want a worshipful mood Ps. 24, 84, 116;
    .... Isa. 1:10-20; John 4:1-45
Are concerned with God in national life .
    .... Deut. 8;
    .... Ps. 85, 118, 124;
    .... Isa. 41:8-20; Micah 4, 6:6-16

Table of Contents

Appetizers, Snacks & Beverages 1-16

Bars & Cookies 17-64

Breads, Rolls, Muffins & Breakfast 65-84

Cakes, Frostings & Candies 85-108

Casseroles & Meats 109-160

Ethnic 161-172

Desserts & Pies 173-220

Salads, Dressings & Vegetables 221-260

Sandwiches & Soups 261-274

Kids 275-288

Miscellaneous & This 'n That 289-294

Index 295-304

FAVORITE RECIPES
FROM MY COOKBOOK

Recipe Name	Page Number

Appetizers, Snacks & Beverages

Appetizers

Crab Appetizers

1/2 lb. processed cheese
3/4 c. butter or margarine
1 lb. crabmeat, shredded
1 (4 oz.) can mushrooms, chopped fine
2 pkg. English muffins, toasted lightly

Melt cheese and butter. Add crabmeat and mushrooms. Spoon onto muffins. Place under broiler until slightly browned. Cut into fourths and serve.
Kari Van Klompenburg

Deviled Eggs

6 eggs
1/4 c. Miracle Whip
1 tsp. vinegar
1 tsp. mustard
1/2 tsp. salt
Dash of pepper

Put eggs in saucepan; fill with water to 1 inch above eggs. Bring to a boil. Remove from heat and cover. Let stand for 18 minutes. Rinse eggs with cold water; peel and cut in half lengthwise. Remove yolks and mix the yolks with above ingredients. Mix well and spoon mixture into eggs. Sprinkle with paprika. Chill well.
Chris Van Beek

Low-Fat Pimento Cheese Spread

4 oz. lite or fat-free cream cheese
1 c. lite or fat-free sour cream
1 c. reduced-fat mild shredded Cheddar cheese
1 c. reduced-fat shredded Mozzarella cheese
1/2 c. sliced green olives
1/4 c. (or 1 sm. jar) diced red pimentos

Cream together the cream cheese and sour cream. Once blended and smooth, fold in the shredded Mozzarella and Cheddar cheeses, pimentos and green olives.
Goes great with Wheat Thins!
Jen Vlietstra

Cheese Puffs

1 1/3 c. flour
1/2 c. butter, softened
1 tsp. paprika
1/2 tsp. salt
2 c. (8 oz.) shredded medium natural Cheddar cheese
48 stuffed olives

Preheat oven to 400°. In a 1 1/2-quart mixer bowl, combine all ingredients, except olives. Beat at low speed, scraping sides of bowl often until well mixed, 1 to 2 minutes. Cover each olive with 1 teaspoon of mixture, making sure olive is covered with dough. Place 1 inch apart on a greased cookie sheet. Bake near center of oven at 400° for 10 to 15 minutes, or until lightly browned. Yield: 4 dozen.

Wanda Hofmeyer

Cheesy Bacon Bites

3 oz. cream cheese, softened
1/4 c. real bacon bits
2 T. chopped onion
1/8 tsp. pepper
1 (8 oz.) pkg. refrigerated crescent rolls

Preheat oven to 350°. Combine cream cheese, bacon, onion and pepper. Separate crescent rolls into 2 rectangles. Pinch seams together. Spread cheese mixture on each rectangle. Roll up, starting at longest side, and seal. Cut each roll into 16 slices. Place slices, cut-side down, on baking stone or cookie sheet. Bake for 15 minutes, or until golden brown. Serve warm.

Cheryl Van Wyk

Ham-Pickle Roll-Ups

1 jar whole pickles (dill)

Drain pickles on paper towels for 1 hour. Spread each one with cream cheese at room temperature. Wrap slice of corned beef or ham around. Let stand in refrigerator for an hour or until chilled. Slice in 1/4- to 1/2-inch slices.

Emily Maassen

Oyster Crackers

2 bags oyster crackers
1 pkg. Hidden Valley Ranch mix
1 T. dill weed
3/4 c. oil

Heat oil in microwave for 1 minute. Add seasonings. Pour over crackers. Mix well, then let stand 1/2 hour. Store in airtight container.

Michelle Bomgaars

Puppy Chow

1 box Crispix cereal
1 stick oleo
1 c. chocolate chips
3 1/2 c. powdered sugar
1/4 c. peanut butter

Melt oleo in microwave. Stir in chocolate chips. Microwave 2 minutes. Stir. Microwave until mixture is smooth (chocolate chips will burn). Stir in peanut butter. Pour cereal in bowl. Pour chocolate mixture over cereal. Stir. Pour powdered sugar over cereal. Stir or shake.

Note: I transfer Puppy Chow to a new container. All the powdered sugar does not mix in.

Ritz Cracker Snacks

2 c. dates, cut up
1 c. chopped walnuts
2 cans sweetened condensed milk

Cook ingredients over low heat in a double boiler until thick and spread on Ritz crackers. Bake for 6 to 8 minutes at 350°. Cool a little.

FROSTING:
1/2 c. butter
1 tsp. vanilla
3 to 4 c. powdered sugar
Enough milk to make frosting spread easily

Spread frosting on top of each cracker. Yield: over 100. Freezes well.

Barb Oldenkamp

Grandma Lisa's Cheese Ball

1 (8 oz.) pkg. cream cheese (soft)
1/2 c. sour cream
1 T. butter, melted
2 T. Knox vegetable soup mix, crushed
1/2 tsp. garlic salt
1/4 tsp. pepper
2 T. dry onion flakes

Mix all ingredients well. Chill for at least 2 hours. When chilled, roll with buttered hands into a ball. Roll in chopped pecans or walnuts. Serve with crackers.
Freezes well.

Chris Van Beek

Taco Cheese Ball

1 (16 oz.) ctn. sour cream
12 oz. cream cheese
3/4 lb. hamburger
1 1/2 tsp. taco seasoning
3/4 c. grated Cheddar cheese

Mix together cream cheese and sour cream until smooth. Brown hamburger and add taco seasoning. Simmer together. Mix these two together and add Cheddar cheese. Serve with the chips of your choice.

Barb Oldenkamp

Taco Tartlets

1 lb. ground beef
2 T. taco seasoning mix
2 T. ice water

FILLING:
1 c. sour cream
2 T. taco sauce
1 c. chopped black olives
3/4 c. crushed tortilla chips
1 c. shredded Cheddar cheese

Preheat oven to 425°. Mix beef, taco seasoning and ice water in a bowl. Press into mini muffin pan and press out. Prepare filling. Spoon into mini muffin pan. Meat mixture is your shell. Bake for 7 to 8 minutes.

Carolyn De Jager

Walking Taco

1 (8 oz.) pkg. cream cheese
1 (16 oz.) jar taco sauce
1 (16 oz.) ctn. sour cream

Mix together; put into a 9x13-inch pan.
Top with:
Black olives
Diced onion
Diced tomatoes
2 c. shredded Cheddar cheese
Lettuce (opt.)

Carolyn De Jager

Tidbit Smokies

1 pkg. brown gravy mix
1/2 c. grape jelly
2 T. catsup
1 pkg. smokies

Mix all ingredients together. Microwave for 7 to 8 minutes. Serve with toothpicks.

Tammy Sneller

Vegetable Pizza

2 (8-count) pkg. crescent rolls
1 pkg. dry original Hidden Valley Ranch dressing
3/4 c. Miracle Whip
2 (8 oz.) pkg. cream cheese

Press crescent rolls into jellyroll pan that has been sprayed with Pam. Bake for 8 to 12 minutes, or until lightly browned. Cool.

Mix the next 3 ingredients and spread on crescent rolls. Add small, cut-up pieces of any vegetable (broccoli, tomatoes, peppers, carrots, cauliflower, radishes). Sprinkle with bacon bits and Cheddar cheese. Refrigerate.

Karen Leusink

Snacks

Caramel Corn

8 qt. popped corn
2 sticks oleo
1/2 c. white corn syrup
2 c. brown sugar

Cook all ingredients, except popcorn, for 5 minutes on slow heat. Remove from heat; add 1/2 teaspoon baking soda and a pinch of cream of tartar. Stir in popcorn, then spread onto 2 cookie sheets. Place coated popcorn in oven and bake for 1 hour at 200°. Cool and break apart.

B. Duane De Jager

Old Dutch Caramel Corn

1 (8 oz.) bag "Old Dutch Puff Corn Curls"

Place corn curls in a large roaster pan.

CARAMEL SAUCE: In a 2-quart saucepan, cook together for 2 minutes:
1/2 lb. butter (not oleo)
1 c. brown sugar
1/2 c. light corn syrup

Add 1 teaspoon baking soda to mixture. This will cause mixture to foam, so 2-quart saucepan is necessary. Pour caramel mixture over corn curls and stir until mixed. Place in a 250° oven for 45 minutes. Stir at least every 10 to 15 minutes. Remove from oven and pour onto waxed paper. Break apart. Enjoy.

Wanda Hofmeyer

Microwave Caramel Corn

16 c. (4 qt.) popped corn
1 c. brown sugar
1/2 c. butter or margarine
1/4 c. light corn syrup
1/2 tsp. salt
1/2 tsp. baking soda

Mix brown sugar, oleo, syrup and salt in a 2 1/2-quart casserole. Microwave, uncovered. Bring to a boil; stir. Cook on FULL POWER for 2 minutes, and then add baking soda. Pour over popped corn in a large brown bag; close bag and shake well. Put into microwave again on FULL POWER for 1 1/2 minutes; shake well and put in oven again on FULL POWER for 1 1/2 minutes. Stir until cooled, in a large bowl.

*Priscilla Jansma, Mildred Reinking,
Marietta VanDer Weide, Jonna Wierda*

Caramel Chex Mix

2 c. Cheerios
3 c. Crispix
3 c. Wheat Chex
3 c. Corn Chex
1 c. peanuts
2 c. pretzels
1 c. oleo
Dash of salt
1 1/2 c. brown sugar
4 T. white syrup

Pour cereal, peanuts and pretzels into a large brown grocery bag. Heat oleo, salt, sugar and syrup on HIGH in microwave for 6 minutes, or until good rolling boil, stirring at least once. Pour over cereal and stir well. Microwave on HIGH for 4 minutes, stirring every minute. Pour out and spread on countertop to cool. Store in covered container.

Donna J. Muilenburg

"Sweet and Chewy" Chex Mix

2 boxes Rice Chex
1 lb. butter
3 c. brown sugar
3/4 c. white Karo syrup
1 1/2 tsp. vanilla
2 tsp. baking soda
M&M's
Peanuts (opt.)

Put Rice Chex in paper bag. Bring to a boil, the following, for 3 minutes: butter, brown sugar and Karo syrup. After removed from heat, add vanilla and baking soda. Pour over Chex mix and shake. Cook in microwave 2 minutes at a time, 3 times. Stir and shake between each 2 minutes. Dump out onto waxed paper; add M&M's and peanuts.

Jennifer (De Jager) Leusink

Easy Bean Dip

16 oz. refried beans
1 pkg. taco seasoning
8 oz. sour cream
1 jar salsa
1 (8 oz.) bag cheese
Jalapeños (opt.)

Mix the beans with the taco seasoning. Put in the bottom of pie pan. Top with sour cream, salsa and cheese. Add jalapeños. Heat in oven or microwave until cheese melts. Serve with chips.

Dorene Vander Zwaag

Hamburger-Cheese Dip

1 lb. hamburger
1 lb. Velveeta cheese
1/2 c. water
2 c. tomato soup

Dice Velveeta. In a bowl, mix Velveeta and water. Microwave until cheese is melted, stirring every 2 minutes. Stir in soup until smooth. Add browned and drained hamburger. Warm in small crock-pot. Serve with tortilla chips, Doritos, or corn chips.

Mexican Dip

1 lb. hamburger
1 jar salsa
1 cube Velveeta cheese

Brown hamburger. Melt cheese with salsa in the crock-pot.

Marci Jager

Mexican Dip

1 lb. ground beef, browned
1 chopped green pepper
1 sm. can tomato paste
1 c. water
1 (3 oz.) pkg. cream cheese
1 pkg. chili seasoning

Brown meat and add the rest of the ingredients. Simmer until melted together. Serve hot, with tortilla chips.

Pam Sandbulte

Nacho Cheese Dip

1 T. oil
1 onion, chopped fine
1 can chopped green chilies
1 sm. tomato, chopped fine
2 T. milk
1 lb. Velveeta cheese

Sauté onion, chilies and tomato in oil, on medium heat. When onions are soft, turn to low heat; add milk and cheese (cut into strips). Stir until melted.

Angela Van Ommeren

Nacho Dip

8 oz. cream cheese
8 oz. salsa (medium)
2 c. shredded Cheddar cheese

Blend cream cheese and salsa in blender. Stir in cheese. Refrigerate. Serve with chips.

Kari Dykstra

Dip for Nachos

1 lb. hamburger
Onion, to taste

Brown and drain.
Add:
1 lb. Velveeta cheese
1 (8 oz.) jar Pace picante sauce (mild)

Put into microwave-safe bowl and microwave until melted. Delicious with nacho chips.

Winova Van Regenmorter

Pizza Dip

11 oz. cream cheese
1/4 c. minced onion
2 T. mayonnaise
1 T. Worcestershire sauce
Garlic salt, to taste
6 oz. chili sauce
Your choice of topping (cocktail shrimp, crab, chopped pepperoni, dried beef)
Mozzarella cheese
Dried oregano
Dried parsley

Blend together cream cheese, onion, mayonnaise, Worcestershire sauce and garlic salt. Divide in half and spread over 2 regular-size plates. Cover with chili sauce. Sprinkle over your choice of meat topping. Top with Mozzarella cheese, oregano and dried parsley. Serve with crackers.

This freezes well. Serve one and freeze one for later.

Karen Bos

Salsa Dip

8 oz. cream cheese
8 oz. sour cream
8 oz. thick salsa
Lettuce
8 oz. Cheddar cheese
1 pkg. taco seasoning

Mix the cream cheese and sour cream together. Stir in the taco seasoning. Spread on a plate. Spread the salsa on top of the first layer. Cover with shredded lettuce. Cover with Cheddar cheese. Refrigerate at least 4 hours before serving. May put lettuce and cheese on just before serving.

Cindy VanDer Weide

Taco Dip

8 oz. cream cheese
16 oz. sour cream
1 lb. hamburger
Lettuce
Cheddar cheese
2 T. taco seasoning (1 pkt.)

Mix cream cheese, sour cream and 2 tablespoons taco seasoning. Put on a plate. Brown hamburger and add the rest of the taco seasoning packet. Top with lettuce, cheese, black olives, tomatoes, salsa, or anything else you want.

Darlene Kluis

Taco Dip

1 can refried beans
8 oz. sour cream
8 oz. mayonnaise
1 pkg. taco seasoning
1 capful lemon juice
Lettuce, shredded
Tomato, diced
Cheese, shredded
Black olives
Onions, chopped

Mix together sour cream, mayonnaise, lemon juice and taco seasoning. Set aside. On a serving plate, layer refried beans, then sour cream mixture. Next, spread lettuce, tomatoes, cheese, olives, onions, and other desired toppings. Refrigerate. Serve with corn chips.

Suzanne Haverdink

Caramel Apple Dip

8 oz. cream cheese, softened
1/2 c. brown sugar
1/4 c. powdered sugar
2 tsp. vanilla

Beat cream cheese until smooth. Add sugars and flavoring; serve with apple slices.

Michelle Bomgaars

Creamy Caramel Fruit Dip

8 oz. cream cheese, softened
3/4 c. brown sugar
1 c. sour cream
2 tsp. vanilla
2 tsp. lemon juice
1 c. cold milk
1 sm. pkg. instant vanilla pudding

Slowly blend cream cheese and brown sugar with electric mixer until smooth. Add the remaining ingredients, one at a time, beating well after each addition. Cover and chill for at least 1 hour.

Sandy Muilenburg

Dip for Apple Slices

3 lb. Kraft light caramels
1 pt. whipping cream
3 c. mini marshmallows

Place in crock-pot (on low) for 4 to 5 hours. Stir about every 45 minutes.

Edith Van Roekel

Fruit Dip

8 oz. cream cheese
3/4 c. brown sugar
1/4 c. white sugar
2 tsp. vanilla
1/2 c. chopped pecans

Beat cream cheese, sugars and vanilla together. Stir in pecans. Refrigerate. Serve with apple slices.

Tammy Sneller

Beverages

Brunch Punch
(Nice for Christmas brunches)

1 qt. eggnog
1 qt. vanilla ice cream
1 (6 oz.) can orange juice concentrate
1 (2-liter) btl. 7-Up

Combine the first 3 ingredients and add 7-Up immediately before serving.

Dee Ann Cleveringa

Easy Party Punch

2 pkg. Kool-Aid (any flavor)
2 c. sugar
2 qt. water
1 (46 oz.) can pineapple juice
1 qt. ginger ale

Mix Kool-Aid, sugar and water. Add pineapple juice. Chill. Add ginger ale just before serving. For extra-special punch, pour over 2 to 3 pints sherbet. Use raspberry sherbet with red punch, and pineapple or lemon sherbet with green punch.

Dawn Beukelman

Elegant Punch

1 (11.5 oz.) can frozen white grape juice
3 cans water
1 (2-liter) btl. lemon-lime soda

Mix juice and water. Add soda. Serve cold.

Michelle Bomgaars

Golden Fruit Punch

1 (30 oz.) can fruit cocktail
1 (20 oz.) can crushed pineapple
1 (29 oz.) can peaches

Purée in blender.
Add:
4 med. bananas
2 c. sugar
2 c. water

Process until smooth. Add purée to 1 (12-ounce) can frozen orange juice (thawed) and 2 tablespoons lemon juice. Cover and freeze.

Remove from freezer 2 hours before serving. Just before serving, mash mixture and combine 1/4 cup mixture with 3/4 cup lemon-lime soda. Yield: 64 (1-cup) servings.

Note: Can freeze in smaller containers, if you can't use it all in one serving. Very refreshing.

Diane Munro

Grape Punch

2 cans grape juice
6 cans water
1 (46 oz.) can pineapple juice
1 (2-liter) btl. 7-Up, cooled
1 (2-liter) btl. ginger ale, cooled

Mix the grape juice, water and pineapple juice. Add the 7-Up and ginger ale right before serving.

Arla Korver

Grape Slush Punch

1 (12 oz.) can grape juice concentrate
1 (12 oz.) can lemonade concentrate
1 (46 oz.) can pineapple juice
1 (3 oz.) box lemon Jello
6 c. water
4 c. sugar
2 (2-liter) btl. 7-Up or ginger ale

Boil water and sugar together until dissolved. Add Jello and stir well. Add the remaining juices and freeze in a 5-quart ice cream bucket. Thaw 2 to 3 hours before serving, and add 7-Up immediately before serving.

*Dee Ann Cleveringa,
Evonne Wielenga, Kathy Dykstra*

MOC-FV Purple Punch

1 (32 oz.) can Welches grape juice
1 (6 oz.) can frozen grape juice concentrate
1 (6 oz.) can frozen lemonade concentrate
2 pkg. grape Kool-Aid
1 c. sugar
6 c. water
1 qt. ginger ale

Mix all except gingerale and chill. Add ginger ale just before serving.

Emily Maassen

Pineapple-Banana Punch

1 (12 oz.) can frozen lemonade concentrate
1 (12 oz.) can frozen orange juice concentrate
1 (46 oz.) can pineapple juice
1 c. sugar
2 bananas
2 qt. water
1 (1-liter) btl. ginger ale

Mix lemonade, orange juice, pineapple juice and sugar. Mash (or blend) 2 bananas with a little of the juice. Stir into the rest of the juice mixture and add 2 quarts of water. Freeze in smaller Zip-loc bags. Will keep in freezer for several weeks. Thaw mixture approximately 2 to 3 hours before serving. Put mixture in punch bowl; add 1 liter of ginger ale. (should be slushy.) If too strong, add a little more water and/or sugar.

Dawn Beukelman

Punch

2 pkg. raspberry powdered drink mix (Kool-Aid)
3/4 c. lemon juice (ReaLemon)
3 c. pineapple juice
1 (12 oz.) can frozen orange juice concentrate
4 scant c. sugar
2 qt. water
1 (2-liter) btl. 7-Up or ginger ale

Mary Ann Winchell

Raspberry Punch

1 pkg. raspberry Kool-Aid
1 c. sugar
4 c. water
10 oz. frozen raspberries, mashed
6 oz. frozen lemonade
1 (2-liter) btl. lemon-lime soda

Combine all, but soda. Chill both mixture and soda. Combine right before serving. Yield: 1 gallon.

Michelle Bomgaars

Fizzy Ice Cream Drinks

8 to 10 scoops of vanilla ice cream
1 tsp. unsweetened Kool-Aid
1 c. ginger ale or 7-Up

Put ice cream, Kool-Aid and 7-Up in a blender. Blend together.

Janene Van Gorp

Frozen Slush Drink

Tropicana Orange-Cranberry
  Twister
9 c. water
2 c. sugar
7-Up (regular or diet)

In a large pan, boil water and sugar for 15 minutes. Remove and put into empty 5-quart ice cream container. Add Tropicana Twister and gently stir. Freeze. To serve, scoop into glasses and add 7-Up.

Linda Van Regenmorter

Lemonade

3 c. cold water
1 c. lemon juice (about 4 lemons)
1/2 c. sugar, or to taste

Combine and serve over ice.
Variation: For pink lemonade, add 2 tablespoons grenadine syrup.

Michelle Bomgaars

Fresh Lemonade

8 to 10 lemons
1 1/2 c. sugar
1 1/2 c. very hot water (not boiling)

Squeeze lemons to make 1 1/2 cups. Set aside. Mix sugar and water until sugar dissolves. Add lemon juice and refrigerate at least 1 1/2 to 2 hours. To make each serving, measure 1/4 to 1/3 cup syrup and pour over ice cubes in 10- to 12-ounce glass. Stir in 3/4 to 1 cup cold water. Garnish with lemon slices and serve. Enjoy!

Lynn Herzog

Orange Julius

1 (6 oz.) can frozen orange juice
  concentrate
1 c. milk
1 c. water
1/2 c. sugar
1/4 to 1/2 tsp. vanilla
12 to 14 ice cubes

Put ingredients in a blender and mix until ice cubes are all crushed.
Orange Smoothie: Use all milk instead of water.
Note: This also is good using fresh oranges or peaches in place of orange concentrate.

Loren Dykstra,
Carmen Hofmeyer, Stefan Maassen

Orange Julius

12 oz. frozen orange juice
concentrate
1 c. milk
1 c. water
1/2 c. sugar
1/2 tsp. vanilla
Ice cubes

Combine in blender: frozen orange juice, milk, water, sugar and vanilla. Fill the rest of the blender with ice cubes. Cover and blend until smooth. Serve immediately.

Cindy VanDer Weide

Non-Alcoholic Strawberry Daiquiri

2 c. lime-lemon soda (diet)
1 (4-serving-size) pkg. sugar-free Jello (strawberry)
2 T. lemon juice
2 T. lime juice
1 (16 oz.) pkg. frozen, unsweetened strawberries, thawed

Place all of the ingredients in a blender. Blend until smooth. Pour into cooled goblets and enjoy.

Raymond De Jager

Eggnog

2 c. milk
2 eggs
1 T. to 1/4 c. sugar
1 tsp. vanilla

Process in blender on high until foamy. Pour into glasses. Garnish with nutmeg, if desired.

Michelle Bomgaars,
DeeAnn Cleveringa

Amaretto Hot Chocolate Mix

11 c. dry milk
4 c. powdered sugar
2 jars Amaretto creamer
2 3/4 c. Quik
11 oz. Coffee-mate

Mix all together with a whisk. Yield: a large batch.
Use 4 heaping teaspoons per cup.

BJ De Weerd

Cappuccino Mix

1 c. instant creamer or flavored creamer
1 c. instant hot cocoa mix
2/3 c. instant coffee
1/2 c. sugar
1/2 tsp. cinnamon (opt.)
1/4 tsp. nutmeg (opt.)

Mix all together. Add 3 tablespoons to cup of hot water. Store in airtight container.

Marcia Cleveringa

Cappuccino Mix

1 c. powdered creamer
1 1/3 c. sugar
1 c. instant coffee

Process in blender on "Liquefy" until well blended and fine-textured. Store in airtight container.
Variations: For optional flavors, add the following before processing.

MOCHA:	6 T. baking cocoa
VIENNESE:	1 1/2 tsp. cinnamon
ORANGE:	1 piece of orange hard candy
BAVARIAN MINT:	6 T. cocoa 6 hard candy peppermints
VANILLA:	2 tsp. vanilla extract
AMARETTO:	2 tsp. almond extract

Michelle Bomgaars

Instant Cocoa Mix

1 lb. Nestlé Quik
1 (8 qt.) box powdered milk
1 (6 or 7 oz.) jar powdered cream
1 c. powdered sugar

Mix ingredients thoroughly and store in an airtight container.
Use 3 tablespoons mix per cup of boiling water.

Jonna Wierda

Bars & Cookies

Bars

Almond Bars

1/2 c. butter
1/2 c. lard
2 c. flour
3/4 tsp. salt
5 T. water, to moisten

Let rest while making filling.

FILLING:
4 egg yolks
1/2 c. milk
6 T. flour
2 c. sugar
Dash of salt
5 T. almond flavoring

Roll out 1/2 of dough. Put into a 9x13-inch pan with 1 inch up sides. Pour filling over dough and cover with other half of rolled-out dough. Pinch top and bottom crusts together. Prick crust and brush with milk; sprinkle with a little sugar. Bake at 425° until golden brown, around 25 to 30 minutes.

Joyce Baker

Almond Bars

3/4 c. shortening
3 T. sugar
1 1/2 c. flour
4 beaten eggs
2 c. white sugar
2 c. coconut
3 T. almond flavoring

Mix shortening, 3 tablespoons sugar and flour. Pat into a 9x13-inch pan. Bake for 20 minutes at 350°. Mix eggs, 2 cups of sugar, coconut and almond flavoring. Spread on top and bake for 30 minutes. Do not overbake!

Joyce Baker

Almond Bars

BARS:
1 c. butter, melted & cooled
4 eggs
2 c. sugar

1/4 tsp. salt
2 c. flour
2 T. almond extract

FROSTING:
Powdered sugar
Butter

Milk
Almond extract, to taste

Beat eggs and sugar. Add cooled butter and other ingredients. Mix well. Bake at 350° for 25 minutes in a greased 9x13-inch pan. Do not overbake.
Frosting: Mix ingredients until smooth. Frost bars.

Denise Dekker

Almond Bars

CRUST:
1 c. margarine
1 c. brown sugar

1/2 tsp. baking soda
2 1/2 c. oatmeal
2 c. flour

FILLING:
4 egg yolks
2 c. sugar

4 tsp. almond extract
8 T. milk
6 T. flour

Crust: Mix ingredients until crumbly. Press half in a 9x13-inch pan.
Filling: Beat filling ingredients together and pour over crust. Crumble remaining crust mixture on top. Bake for 30 to 35 minutes at 325°.

Diane Munro

Almond Bars

1 c. cake flour
1 c. sugar
1/4 tsp. baking powder

1/2 c. melted butter
2 eggs, beaten
2 tsp. almond extract

Mix together--do not overbeat. Pour into an 8x8-inch greased glass pan. Sprinkle with 1 to 2 teaspoons sugar and 1/4 cup sliced almonds.

Carmen (Winchell) Woeltge

Almond Tarts

CRUST:
1 1/2 sticks oleo
1 1/2 c. flour
6 oz. cream cheese

Mix like dough. Divide dough into 48 greased mini muffin cups.

FILLING:
2 c. almond paste (1/2 lb. = 1 c.)
1 c. sugar
1 egg

Mix with hands. Divide filling into 48 pieces and place in muffin cups. Bake at 350° for 20 minutes.

TOPPING:
1 c. powdered sugar
2 T. water
1 T. almond flavoring

Frost while still warm.
Tip: Divide dough and filling into fourths, and each fourth into twelfths.

Marietta VanDer Weide,
Winova Van Regenmorter

Dutch Treats

CRUST:
1 c. butter (no substitute), softened
2 (3 oz.) pkg. cream cheese
2 c. flour

FILLING:
3 eggs
1 c. sugar
8 oz. almond paste, cut in cubes
Sliced almonds

Crust: In a mixing bowl, cream butter and cream cheese. Gradually add the flour. Cover and refrigerate for 1 hour (until easy to handle). Roll into 1-inch balls. Press dough onto bottom and up the sides of ungreased mini muffin cups; set aside.

Filling: Beat eggs in a bowl until light and fluffy. Add sugar; mix well. Beat in the almond paste. Spoon a rounded teaspoonful into each cup. Top each with 3 almond slices. Bake at 325° for 25 to 30 minutes, or until light brown and filling is set. Cool 10 minutes before removing to wire racks. Yield: approximately 10 dozen.

Evelyn De Vries

Dutch Almond Tarts

CRUST:
3/4 c. oleo
1 1/2 c. flour
6 oz. cream cheese

FILLING:
2 c. (1 lb.) almond paste, room temp.
1 c. sugar
1 egg

Crust: Mix ingredients like pie crust and divide into 4 pieces. Divide each of those into 12 pieces. (Total 48 pieces.)
Filling: Mix with hands. Divide into 48 pieces. Roll into balls. Use miniature muffin tins. Shape crust in tins. Add almond balls. Bake at 325° for 20 minutes.

FROSTING:
1 c. powdered sugar
2 T. water
1 T. almond flavoring

Drizzle over tarts while warm.

Vicki Schrock

Marla's Almond Puffs

1/2 c. butter
1 c. water
1 c. flour
3 eggs
1 1/2 tsp. almond flavoring

FROSTING:
1 c. powdered sugar
1 T. milk
1 T. butter
1 T. almond flavoring

Boil butter and water. Add flour and stir until dry. Remove from heat and transfer to a bowl. Add eggs, one at a time, and beat until smooth after each. Add flavoring and drop by teaspoonful (no larger) into greased muffin tins. (I use Pam.) Bake at 350° for 25 minutes. Frost when cool. Yield: 20 to 22 puffs.
Freezes well and thaws quickly.

Emily Maassen

Best-Ever Brownies

1/2 c. liquid shortening
1 1/2 c. brown sugar
1 egg
1/2 c. milk
1 1/2 c. flour
3 T. cocoa
1/2 tsp. baking soda in 1/2 c. hot water
1 tsp. vanilla

Mix in order given. Spray a jellyroll pan with cooking spray. Pour brownie mixture into pan. Bake at 375° for 20 to 25 minutes. Frost with your favorite chocolate frosting.

Joyce Groen

Brownies

1 stick oleo
1 c. sugar

Cream together:
Add:
4 eggs (beat in one at a time)
1 (16 oz.) can chocolate topping
1 c. flour
1 c. nuts
1 tsp. vanilla

Bake on cookie sheet at 350° for 25 to 30 minutes.

Daisy VanDer Weide,
Submitted by Marietta VanDer Weide

Brownie Pizza

1 1/3 sticks melted oleo
1/2 c. cocoa
1 c. brown sugar
1 c. white sugar
1 tsp. vanilla
3 eggs
1 1/2 c. flour
1 tsp. baking powder
1/2 tsp. salt
Mini marshmallows
Plain M&M's
Caramel topping

Mix oleo, sugars, cocoa and vanilla. Add eggs and beat. Sift in dry ingredients. Beat. Pour into a 9x13-inch pan. Bake at 350° for 20 to 30 minutes. Once baked, immediately top with miniature marshmallows and return to oven for 2 minutes, or until marshmallows puff. Top with M&M's. Glaze caramel topping on top and serve.

Kari Van Klompenburg

Brownie Pizza

1 pkg. brownie mix
Peanut butter cups, to taste
Snickers candy bars, to taste
Mini marshmallows, to taste
M&M's, to taste

Make brownie mix according to directions and bake in round, greased baking tin. Three minutes before baking time is completed, sprinkle chopped peanut butter cups and chopped Snickers on top. Also sprinkle with miniature marshmallows. Return to oven to 1 to 2 minutes. Remove from oven and sprinkle with M&M's.

Linda Van Regenmorter

Buttermilk Brownies

2 c. sugar
2 c. flour
1/2 tsp. salt
4 T. cocoa
1/2 c. margarine
1/2 c. oil
1 c. cold water
1 tsp. baking soda
1/2 c. buttermilk
2 eggs
1 tsp. vanilla

Sift sugar, flour, salt and cocoa together. Bring margarine, oil and water to a boil. Pour over dry ingredients. Mix baking soda with buttermilk. Add to batter gradually while mixing. Add eggs and vanilla. Pour into a greased and floured 10x15-inch jellyroll pan. Bake at 350° to 375° for 18 minutes. Frost while still warm.

FROSTING:
6 T. butter
6 T. milk
1 1/2 c. sugar

Boil for 1 minute and add 6 ounces chocolate chips. Beat well, until chips are melted. Pour over bars.

Kathy Dykstra,
Karen Leusink

Buttermilk Brownies

1 stick butter, melted
1 c. water
1/2 c. oil
2 c. sugar
2 c. flour
1/4 c. cocoa

2 eggs
1 1/2 tsp. baking soda, mixed into 1/2 c. buttermilk
1 tsp. vanilla
1/2 tsp. salt

Pour the first 3 ingredient over sugar, flour and cocoa. Add eggs. Add vanilla and salt to baking soda-milk mixture. Mix together brownie mixture. Bake at 350° for 25 to 30 minutes. Frost while still hot and frosting is of spreading consistency.

FROSTING:
3/4 c. sugar
4 T. milk

3 T. butter
2/3 c. chocolate chips

Boil sugar, milk and butter for 30 seconds. Take off heat and add chocolate chips.

Amy Vander Zwaag

Buttermilk Brownies

2 c. sugar
2 c. flour
4 T. cocoa
1 c. water
1/2 c. oleo or butter

1/2 c. oil
1/2 c. buttermilk
1 tsp. baking soda
2 eggs

FROSTING:
1/2 c. oleo or butter
1/3 c. buttermilk

1/4 c. cocoa
1 lb. powdered sugar
1/2 tsp. vanilla

Mix sugar, flour and cocoa. Boil water, oleo and oil. Pour over dry ingredients and beat until creamy. Add buttermilk, baking soda and eggs. Beat well. Bake in jellyroll pan for 20 minutes at 350°.
Frosting: Mix melted oleo, buttermilk, cocoa, powdered sugar and vanilla. Beat until smooth. When storing, do not cover frosting. Use a strip of plastic wrap to cover edge of cake.

Judy Vlietstra

Candy Bar Brownies

3/4 c. melted butter
2 c. sugar
4 eggs
2 tsp. vanilla
1 1/2 c. flour
1/3 c. cocoa
1/2 tsp. baking powder
1/4 tsp. salt
4 (2.07 oz.) Snickers bars, coarsely chopped
3 (1.55 oz.) plain Hershey candy bars, coarsely chopped

Combine melted butter, sugar, eggs and vanilla. Combine flour, cocoa, baking powder and salt. Set aside 1/4 cup. Add the rest of the dry ingredients to the egg mixture. Mix well. Toss the Snickers candy bar pieces into the reserved 1/4 cup flour mixture. Stir into the batter. Put into a 9x13-inch pan. Sprinkle Hershey pieces on top. Bake in 350° oven for about 30 minutes. Do not overbake.
Ruth De Koter

Chocolate Crunch Brownies

1 c. oleo, softened
2 c. sugar
4 eggs
6 T. baking cocoa
1 c. flour
2 tsp. vanilla extract
1/2 tsp. salt
1 (7 oz.) jar marshmallow creme
1 c. peanut butter
2 c. chocolate chips
3 c. Rice Krispies

In a mixing bowl, cream butter and sugar; add eggs. Stir in cocoa, flour, vanilla and salt. Spread into a greased stoneware bar pan (10x15-inch). Bake at 350° for 20 minutes, or until brownies are done. Cool. Spread marshmallow creme over brownies. In a small saucepan, melt peanut butter and chocolate chips over low heat, stirring constantly. Remove from heat and stir in cereal. Spread over marshmallow layer. Chill before cutting. Store in the refrigerator.
Cheryl Van Wyk

Cream Cheese Brownies

1 pkg. German chocolate cake mix

FILLING:
1 egg
8 oz. cream cheese
1/2 c. sugar
1/2 c. chocolate chips
1/2 c. chopped walnuts (opt.)

Preheat oven to 350°. Mix cake as directed on box. Pour 1/2 of cake batter into a greased and floured jellyroll pan. Set aside. In another bowl, mix egg, cream cheese and sugar. Drop by tablespoons onto batter in pan. Pour remaining cake batter over top. Sprinkle chocolate chips and nuts (if desired) on top. Bake at 350° for 20 to 30 minutes, or until center will spring back when touched.
Keith Probst

Crunchy Brownies

1 brownie mix
3/4 c. oatmeal
1/2 c. brown sugar
1/3 c. melted oleo
1 c. M&M's

Prepare brownie mix as directed on box. Crumble the brown sugar, oatmeal and oleo; put on top of brownies. Sprinkle with 1 cup M&M's. Bake at 350° for 20 minutes.

Vi De Jong

Disappearing Marshmallow Brownies

Melt 1 cup butterscotch chips and 1/2 cup oleo in a heavy saucepan, stirring constantly. Cool to lukewarm.
Add to butterscotch mixture:

1 1/2 c. flour
2/3 c. brown sugar
2 tsp. baking powder
1/2 tsp. salt
1 tsp. vanilla
2 eggs

Mix well.
Add:

2 c. mini marshmallows
2 c. chocolate chips

Bake for 20 to 25 minutes at 350°, in a 9x13-inch pan. Do not overbake. Center will be jiggly, but becomes firm upon cooling.

Jamie Beukelman

Easy Bars
(Brownies)

Make a box of vanilla pudding according to directions, and while still hot, add a box of chocolate cake mix. Put into a greased jellyroll pan; sprinkle with chocolate chips and nuts. Bake for 20 minutes at 350°.

Linda Mellema

Frosted Fudge Brownies

1 c. + 3 T. butter or margarine
3/4 c. baking cocoa
4 eggs
2 c. sugar

1 1/2 c. all-purpose flour
1 tsp. baking powder
1 tsp. salt
1 tsp. vanilla

FROSTING:
6 T. butter or margarine (soft)
2 2/3 c. confectioners' sugar

1/2 c. baking cocoa
1 tsp. vanilla extract
1/4 to 1/3 c. milk

In a saucepan, melt butter. Remove from heat. Stir in cocoa. Cool. In a mixing bowl, beat eggs and sugar. Combine flour, baking powder and salt; gradually add to egg mixture. Stir in vanilla and cooled chocolate mixture. Mix well. Spread into a greased 9x13x2-inch baking pan. Bake at 350° for 25 to 28 minutes, or until toothpick inserted in center comes out clean. Do not overbake. Cool on wire rack.

Frosting: In a mixing bowl, cream butter, confectioners' sugar, cocoa and vanilla. Add enough milk until frosting achieves a spreading consistency. Spread over brownies. Cut into bars. *Sharon Schelling*

Macaroon Brownies

1 c. softened butter or margarine
2 c. sugar
4 eggs
1 tsp. vanilla extract

2 c. all-purpose flour
1/2 tsp. cream of tartar
1/2 c. cocoa
1/2 c. chopped walnuts

MACAROON FILLING:
1 (14 oz.) pkg. flaked coconut

1 (14 oz.) can sweetened condensed milk
2 tsp. vanilla extract

FROSTING:
3/4 c. sugar
1/4 c. milk
2 T. butter

1 c. mini marshmallows
1 c. semi-sweet chocolate chips
1 tsp. vanilla

Bar: In a mixing bowl, cream butter and sugar. Add eggs and vanilla; mix well. Combine flour, cocoa and cream of tartar; gradually add to creamed mixture. Stir in nuts. Spread 1/2 into a greased 9x13-inch pan.

Filling: Combine coconut, condensed milk and vanilla; carefully spread over chocolate layer. Top with the remaining chocolate mixture. Bake at 350° for 40 to 45 minutes, or until a toothpick inserted near the center comes out clean. Cool.

Frosting: Combine sugar, milk and butter in saucepan; cook and stir until sugar is dissolved. Add the remaining ingredients. Cook and stir until marshmallows and chips are melted. Cool for about 25 minutes. Stir and spread over cooled brownies. Cut into bars. Yield: 4 dozen. *Ruth De Koter*

Marbled Brownies

1 c. water
1/2 c. margarine
6 T. cocoa
2 c. flour
2 c. sugar

2 eggs
1/2 c. sour cream
1 tsp. baking soda
1/2 tsp. salt
6 oz. chocolate chips (minis)

MARBLE INGREDIENTS:
8 oz. cream cheese

1/3 c. sugar
1 egg

Combine water, margarine and cocoa in a large saucepan. Bring just to a boil; remove from heat. Stir in combined flour and sugar. Add eggs, sour cream, baking soda and salt; mix well. Pour into a greased 10x15-inch jellyroll pan.

Marble: Combine softened cream cheese and sugar. Mix well, until blended; add egg. Mix well. Spoon marble mixture over brownie mixture. Cut through batter with knife several times for marbled effect. Sprinkle with chocolate chips. Bake at 375° for 20 to 25 minutes, or until toothpick comes out clean. (Also great without marbling--just frost instead.)

FROSTING:
1/2 c. margarine
1/3 c. milk
6 T. cocoa

4 1/2 c. powdered sugar
1 tsp. vanilla
1/2 c. chopped nuts (opt.)

Combine margarine, milk and cocoa in a saucepan. Bring to a boil; remove from heat. Add powdered sugar; beat until smooth. Add vanilla. Frost brownies while frosting is warm. Sprinkle with nuts. Cut into squares when cool.

Faye Vander Lugt

Milk Chocolate Brownies

1 (1 lb. 5 oz.) pkg. brownie mix
6 oz. chopped walnuts
2 eggs
1 tsp. vanilla

8 oz. whipped topping, thawed
1/2 c. chocolate chips
1/2 c. white chocolate chips

Preheat oven to 325°. Grease bottom of a 9x13-inch pan. In a large bowl, mix whipped topping, eggs and vanilla until smooth. Stir in brownie mix, just until moistened. Stir in nuts and spread mixture in pan. Sprinkle chocolate chips and white chips on top. Bake for 30 to 40 minutes, or until toothpick comes out clean. Do not overbake. Cool and slice. Yield: 10 to 12 servings.

Joyce Baker

Mom's Brownies

Beat together:
1/4 lb. butter or margarine
1 c. sugar
4 eggs (add 2 at a time)

Add:
1 tsp. vanilla
1 (1 lb.) can chocolate syrup
1 c. + 1 T. flour
1/2 tsp. baking powder
1/2 tsp. salt (opt.)

Mix well with electric mixer. Pour into a greased or sprayed pan (11x13-inch), or cookie sheet (11x15-inch). Bake at 350° for 20 to 30 minutes. Brownies are done when toothpick comes out clean. Frost while hot.

FROSTING:
6 T. butter or margarine
6 T. milk
1 1/2 c. sugar

Bring to a boil for just 30 seconds. Add 1 cup chocolate chips. Freezes well!

Carl Van Voorst

Triple-Fudge Brownies

1 sm. pkg. chocolate instant pudding
1 chocolate cake mix
2 c. chocolate chips

Mix pudding with 2 cups milk as package instructs. Stir in cake mix and chips. Bake in 10x15-inch pan at 350° for 30 to 35 minutes.

Elaine Vander Broek

Chocolate Caramel Bars

1 German chocolate cake mix
3/4 c. oleo
1/3 c. evaporated milk

Spread 1/2 of batter in a 9x13-inch pan and bake at 350° for 6 to 8 minutes.

3/4 bag chocolate chips
1/3 c. evaporated milk
14 oz. caramels

Melt the caramels and milk together. Sprinkle 3/4 of bag of chocolate chips over this. Spread over the remainder of batter and bake for 15 to 20 minutes.

Marietta VanDer Weide

Chocolate Chip Coconut Bars

1/3 c. oleo
1/2 c. white sugar
1/2 c. brown sugar, packed
1 egg
1 tsp. vanilla
2 T. water
1 c. flour
1 1/4 tsp. baking powder
1/4 tsp. salt
1/2 c. coconut
1/2 c. nuts
1 (6 oz.) pkg. chocolate chips

Cream oleo and sugars. Add beaten egg and mix well. Add vanilla and water; continue creaming until fluffy. Sift and add dry ingredients. Add coconut, chocolate chips and nuts. Press into a greased 7x11-inch pan. Bake at 350° for 25 to 30 minutes. May sprinkle powdered sugar on bars while warm, or frost with melted chocolate chips.
These freeze well.

Elvera Van Horssen

Chocolate Chip Bars

3 1/3 c. flour
1 1/2 tsp. baking soda
1 1/2 tsp. salt
1 1/2 c. soft butter
1 1/2 c. brown sugar, packed
1 1/2 tsp. vanilla
3 eggs, beaten
1 1/2 pkg. chocolate chips
1 1/2 c. nuts

Combine and bake at 375° for 20 minutes. Cool before cutting.
Note: Don't bake in AirBake pan. Put in jellyroll pan.

Linda Boone

Chocolate Chip Bar

1 c. oleo
1 1/2 c. white sugar
1 1/2 c. brown sugar
4 eggs
2 tsp. vanilla
4 c. flour
2 tsp. baking soda
2 tsp. salt
1 c. chocolate chips

Cream oleo and sugar together. Add egg and vanilla; beat well. Add dry ingredients. Stir in chocolate chips and spread in a well-greased jellyroll pan. Bake at 350° for 20 minutes. Do not overbake!
Note: Batter will be stiff!

Vi De Jong

Chocolate Marshmallow Bars

3/4 c. butter or margarine
3 eggs
1 1/3 c. flour
1/2 tsp. salt
1/2 c. chopped nuts (opt.)

1 1/2 c. sugar
1 tsp. vanilla
1/2 tsp. baking powder
3 T. cocoa
4 c. mini marshmallows

TOPPING:
1 1/2 c. chocolate chips
3 T. butter

1 c. peanut butter
2 c. crisp rice cereal

Cream butter and sugar. Add eggs and vanilla; beat until fluffy. Combine flour, baking powder, salt and cocoa. Add to creamed mixture. Stir in nuts. Spread in a greased jellyroll pan. Bake at 350° for 15 to 18 minutes. Sprinkle marshmallows over cake; return to oven for 2 to 3 minutes. Using a knife dipped in water, spread out marshmallows.

Topping: Combine chocolate chips, butter and peanut butter. Melt in microwave, then stir in rice cereal. Spread over bars. Chill.

Marcia Cleveringa

Chocolate-Oatmeal Bars

Melt in microwave:
1 (8 oz.) Hershey's milk chocolate candy bar

1 can sweetened condensed milk
2 T. butter

Add:
2 tsp. vanilla

1 c. nuts

Boil 2 1/2 minutes in microwave. Stir until melted.

BATTER:
2 1/2 c. flour
1 tsp. baking soda
1 c. oleo

2 c. brown sugar
2 eggs
5 tsp. vanilla
3 c. oatmeal

Pat 2/3 of the batter in bottom of a 9x13-inch high-sided pan. Pour on chocolate mixture. Crumble remaining batter over top. Bake for 20 minutes in 350° oven.

Joan Punt

Chocolate Revel Bars

1 yellow cake mix
1 egg
1/2 c. margarine
1 pkg. chocolate chips
1 T. margarine
1 can sweetened condensed milk

Combine cake mix, egg and margarine. Press 2/3 into a greased 9x13-inch pan. Melt chocolate chips, margarine and milk. Pour over crust. Drop the rest of cake mix by spoonfuls over chocolate. Bake at 350° for 20 minutes. Cool completely and cut into bars. *Michelle Bomgaars*

Chocolate Revel Bars

3 c. quick-cooking, rolled oats
2 1/2 c. flour
1 tsp. salt
1 c. margarine or butter
2 c. packed brown sugar
2 eggs
4 tsp. vanilla
1 (14 oz.) can sweetened condensed milk
1 1/2 c. chocolate chips
2 T. butter or margarine

Combine oats, flour, baking soda and 1/2 teaspoon salt. Beat the 1 cup margarine for 30 seconds. Add brown sugar and beat until fluffy. Add eggs and 2 teaspoons of vanilla. Beat well. Stir dry ingredients gradually into beaten mixture, until well combined. Heat together sweetened condensed milk, chocolate chips, 2 tablespoons margarine and 1/4 teaspoon salt, over low heat, stirring until smooth. Remove from heat. Stir in remaining 2 teaspoons vanilla. Pat 2/3 of oat mixture in the bottom of an ungreased 10x15x1-inch baking pan. Spread chocolate mixture over dough. Dot with remaining oat mixture. Bake at 350° for 25 to 30 minutes. Cool on a wire rack. *Priscilla Jansma*

Easy Fudge Bars

Combine:
1 yellow cake mix
1 egg
1/2 c. oleo

Pat 2/3 of mixture into greased 9x13-inch pan.

Melt together in microwave:
1 (12 oz.) pkg. milk chocolate chips
1 can sweetened condensed milk
1 T. oleo

Pour over first mixture. Crumble the remaining cake mix mixture over top. Bake at 350° for 25 minutes (do not overbake).
Winova Van Regenmorter

Fudge Bars

1 c. brown sugar
1/2 c. oleo
1/2 tsp. vanilla
1 egg

3/4 c. flour
1/2 tsp. salt
1/2 tsp. baking soda
2 c. oatmeal

Press 1/2 of crumbs in a 9x13-inch pan. Save other half.

Melt in pan:
1 (6 oz.) pkg. chocolate chips
1 T. butter
1 can sweetened condensed milk

1 tsp. vanilla
1/4 tsp. salt
1/2 c. nuts

Cook until chocolate chips melt. Remove from heat. Add nuts; pour over base. Put the remaining crumbs on top and bake at 350° for 25 minutes.

Joyce Baker,
Marietta VanDer Weide

Marshmallow Fudge Bars

3/4 c. sugar
1/2 c. oleo
2 eggs
3/4 c. flour
1/4 tsp. baking powder

1/4 tsp. salt
2 T. cocoa
1 tsp. vanilla
1/2 c. nuts

Spread into a greased 9x13-inch pan. Bake at 350° for 15 to 20 minutes. Remove from oven. Put miniature marshmallows over the top. Return to the oven for 3 minutes. Let cool and frost.

FROSTING:
1/2 c. brown sugar
1/4 c. water

2 T. cocoa
3 tsp. butter

Bring all to a boil. Add 1 teaspoon vanilla. Cool. Add 1 1/2 cups powdered sugar. Frost bars.

Caroline Smits,
Colette Hofmeyer

Napoleon Cremes

1/2 c. butter
1/4 c. sugar
1/4 c. cocoa
1 tsp. vanilla
1 egg, slightly beaten
2 c. finely-crushed graham cracker crumbs
1 c. flaked coconut

1/2 c. butter
3 T. milk
1 (3 3/4 oz.) pkg. vanilla instant pudding mix
2 c. sifted powdered sugar
1 (6 oz.) pkg. semi-sweet chocolate chips
2 T. butter

Combine first 4 ingredients in top of double boiler. Cook over simmering water until butter melts. Stir in egg; continue cooking and stirring until mixture is thick, about 3 minutes. Blend in crumbs and coconut. Press into buttered 9x9-inch pan.

Cream 1/2 cup butter well. Stir in milk, pudding mix and sugar. Beat until fluffy. Spread evenly over crust. Chill until firm. Melt chocolate and butter in top of double boiler; cool. Spread over pudding layer. Chill.

Karen Bos

Turtle Bars

32 caramels
1/4 c. evaporated milk
1 pkg. refrigerated chocolate chip cookie dough

1 c. chocolate chips
1/2 c. chopped nuts

Melt caramels and evaporated milk together and set aside. Slice cookie dough and lay in the bottom of a 9x13-inch greased cake pan. Put the cookie dough in a preheated oven at 350° for about 20 minutes, until they look light brown, being careful not to overbake. Take out and let cool for about 5 minutes. Sprinkle 1 cup of chocolate chips on top. Pour caramel mixture on next, and sprinkle 1/2 cup chopped nuts on top. Refrigerate for at least 1 hour and then cut. Keeps best in the refrigerator.

Dawn Beukelman

Caramel Bars

1 pkg. German chocolate cake mix
1 sm. can evaporated milk
3/4 c. margarine, melted

14 oz. caramels
1 c. chocolate chips

Mix together cake mix, 1/3 cup evaporated milk and melted margarine. Spread 1/2 of it in a greased 9x13-inch pan. Melt together caramels and 1/3 cup evaporated milk. Pour it over cake mixture. Sprinkle with chocolate chips. Top with remaining cake mixture. Bake for 15 to 20 minutes at 350°.

Tammy Sneller

Caramel Bars

1 c. flour	1/4 tsp. salt
3/4 c. margarine	3/4 c. margarine
3/4 c. oatmeal	1 (6 oz.) pkg. chocolate chips
1/2 c. brown sugar	32 Kraft caramels
1/2 tsp. baking soda	2/3 c. evaporated milk

Preheat oven to 350°. Combine dry ingredients. Cut in margarine until crumbly. Reserve 1 cup. Press the remaining mixture in bottom of a greased pan. Bake at 350° for 12 minutes. Take from oven. Sprinkle chips on crust. Melt caramels with milk in a covered double boiler over low heat, or microwave in bowl. Spread melted caramel mixture over the chips. Sprinkle reserved 1 cup mixture over top. Bake at 350° for 20 minutes more. Take from oven and cut into squares. Chill in refrigerator for 2 hours.

Lonna Kluis

Caramel Bars

64 caramels   10 tsp. milk

Melt together in double boiler.

CRUST:

1 c. flour	1/4 tsp. salt
1 c. oatmeal	3/4 c. brown sugar
1/2 tsp. baking soda	3/4 c. oleo

Press into a 9x13-inch pan, 1/2 of crumb mixture. Bake this for 10 minutes at 350°. Pour caramel mixture over crust and sprinkle 1/2 cup chocolate chips and 1/2 cup nuts on top, with remainder of crust mixture. Bake for 12 to 15 minutes.

Marietta VanDer Weide

The expert in anything was once a beginner.

Tackling Toffee Caramel Bars

1 pkg. yellow cake mix
1/3 c. oil
2 eggs
1 (12 oz.) pkg. semi-sweet chocolate chips
1 c. vanilla chips
3 (1.4 oz.) Skor or Heath candy bars
1/2 c. butter
32 unwrapped caramels
1 (14 oz.) can sweetened condensed milk

In a large bowl, combine yellow cake mix, oil and eggs. Blend well. Stir in semi-sweet chocolate chips, white vanilla (white chocolate) chips and the chocolate-covered Toffee candy bars (cut into pieces). Mixture will be thick. Press 1/2 of the mixture into bottom of a greased pan and bake at 350° for 10 minutes.

In a medium saucepan, combine butter, unwrapped caramels and sweetened condensed milk. Cook over medium-low heat until caramels are melted and mixture is smooth, stirring occasionally. Slowly pour caramel mixture evenly over partially-baked crust. Top with remaining cake mixture. Bake an additional 25 to 30 minutes, until top is set and edges are golden brown. Cool for 20 minutes. Run a knife around sides of pan to loosen. Cool for 40 minutes. Refrigerate for 1 hour. Cut into bars. **Jennifer Leusink**

Caramel Rice Krispie Bars

25 to 30 caramels
1 can sweetened condensed milk
2 sticks butter or oleo
8 c. Rice Krispies
10 c. mini marshmallows

Make middle layer first, so it can cool. Melt caramels, sweetened condensed milk and 1 stick butter together. Cool for 45 minutes in refrigerator.

Make one batch of Rice Krispie bars. Melt 4 cups miniature marshmallows and 1/4 cup oleo or butter. Add 4 cups Rice Krispies. Put in bottom of a 9x13-inch pan. Cool. Add middle layer when cool. Put 2 cups marshmallows on top of caramel layer. Make another batch of Rice Krispie bars. Put on top. Cool. **Cheryl Van Wyk**

Caramel Rice Krispie Bars

1/2 c. oleo
8 c. marshmallows
8 c. Rice Krispies
1 bag caramels
1 1/2 sticks oleo
1 can sweetened condensed milk

Melt 1/4 cup oleo and 4 cups marshmallows in a large microwavable bowl. Stir in 4 cups Rice Krispies. Spread in bottom of a greased jellyroll pan. Melt caramels, 1 1/2 sticks oleo and sweetened condensed milk in a microwave. Spread over Rice Krispies. Melt remaining 1/4 cup oleo and 4 cups marshmallows. Stir in remaining cereal. Spread over cooled caramel mixture. **Judy Vlietstra**

Krunch Bars

1/2 c. oleo
1 c. peanut butter
1 lg. pkg. chocolate chips
1 sm. pkg. butterscotch chips

Melt and cool.
Add:
1 pkg. mini marshmallows   4 c. Rice Krispies

Put into buttered 9x13-inch pan.

Rachel Hubers

Scotch-a-Roo Bars

1 1/4 c. white syrup
1 c. white sugar
1 1/4 c. peanut butter
6 c. Rice Krispies
5.5 oz. chocolate chips
5.5 oz. butterscotch chips

Combine sugar and syrup in a large pan. Bring to a boil until sugar is dissolved. Take off heat. Add peanut butter to mixture and stir. When thoroughly mixed, fold in Rice Krispies. Pour Rice Krispie mixture into a 9x13-inch greased pan. Spread evenly. In a separate bowl, melt chips, then pour on top of Rice Krispies. Let cool!

Adam Blom

Scotcharoos

1 c. white syrup
1 c. sugar
1 1/2 c. peanut butter
3 c. Rice Krispies

Combine white syrup, sugar and peanut butter in a saucepan. Cook on a low heat until mixture is thickened. Add to Rice Krispies. Pour into a 9x13-inch pan. Melt 1 (6-ounce) package butterscotch chips and 1 (6-ounce) package chocolate chips and spread on top of warm bars. Let harden.

Melissa De Jager

Scotcharoos

1 c. sugar   1 c. light corn syrup

Cook over medium heat until mixture begins to bubble. Remove from heat. Stir in 1 cup peanut butter. Add 6 cups Rice Krispies. Press into a buttered 9x13-inch pan.
Melt:
6 oz. chocolate chips   6 oz. butterscotch chips

Stir to blend. Spread over Rice Krispies. Chill until top is firm.

Loren Dykstra

Rice Krispie Bars

1 c. sugar
1 c. white syrup
1 1/2 c. peanut butter
3 c. Rice Krispies
1 c. chocolate chips
1 c. butterscotch chips

Bring the sugar and syrup to a boil. Add the peanut butter and Rice Krispies. Melt the chocolate and butterscotch chips together. Spread on top of Krispie mix in a 9x13-inch pan.

Arla Korver

Easy Bars

1 pkg. dry yellow cake mix
10 T. oleo
3 c. mini marshmallows
1 (12 oz.) pkg. chocolate chips
3 c. Rice Krispies
1 can sweetened condensed milk

Mix melted oleo and yellow cake mix. Press in bottom of a 10 x 15 1/2-inch jellyroll pan. Sprinkle marshmallows, chocolate chips and Rice Krispies over bottom layer. Pour milk evenly over the top. Bake for 20 to 25 minutes in a 350° oven.

Donna J. Muilenburg

Chipper Bars

2 c. oatmeal
1 c. flour
1 c. brown sugar
3/4 c. butter or oleo
1/2 tsp. baking soda
1/2 tsp. salt
1 (14 oz.) can sweetened condensed milk
1/3 c. peanut butter
1 1/2 c. M&M's (or 3/4 c. chocolate chips & 3/4 c. butterscotch chips)

Mix oatmeal, flour, brown sugar, butter, baking soda and salt until crumbly. Reserve 1 1/2 cups crumb mixture. Press the remaining crumbs in a jellyroll pan. In a small bowl, stir together condensed milk and peanut butter. Pour evenly over crumb mixture. Sprinkle with M&M's or chocolate and butterscotch chips. Pat reserved 1 1/2 cups crumb mixture into filling. Bake at 350° for 30 minutes, or until lightly browned.

Julie Leusink

M&M Bars

1 (18 1/4 oz.) pkg. yellow cake mix
2 eggs
1/4 c. brown sugar
1/4 c. butter or margarine, melted
1/4 c. water
1 1/2 c. M&M's
1 T. shortening
1/2 c. semi-sweet chocolate chips

In a mixing bowl, combine the first 5 ingredients. Beat on medium speed for 2 minutes. Stir in 1 1/2 cups M&M's. Spread in a greased 9x13-inch baking pan. Bake at 375° for 20 to 25 minutes, or until lightly browned and a toothpick inserted near the center comes out clean. Cool on wire rack.
Melt shortening and chocolate chips; drizzle over the top. Yield: about 3 1/2 dozen.

Amy Aberson

M&M Bars

2 c. oatmeal
1 c. brown sugar
1 1/2 c. flour
3/4 tsp. salt
1 tsp. baking soda
1 c. melted oleo
1 can sweetened condensed milk
1/3 c. creamy peanut butter
1 c. mini M&M's
1 1/2 c. milk chocolate chips

Combine the first 5 ingredients. Add melted oleo. Mix until moist. Reserve 1 1/2 cups of mixture. Press remaining mixture into a 9x13-inch pan. Bake in 375° oven for 12 minutes. Combine sweetened condensed milk and peanut butter. Spread over baked crust. Sprinkle with chocolate chips. Combine reserved 1 1/2 cups crust mixture with M&M's. Sprinkle on top of chocolate chips and press down. Bake in 375° oven for 20 to 22 minutes.

Brenda Oolman

Kindness is hard to give away - it keeps coming back to the giver.

Best Oatmeal Bars

Pour 1 1/2 cups boiling water over 1 cup oatmeal and 1 stick butter; let stand for 10 minutes.

Add:

1 c. white sugar	1 tsp. cinnamon
1 c. brown sugar	1/2 tsp. salt
1 1/2 c. flour	1 tsp. baking soda
2 eggs	

Beat and pour into a 9x13-inch greased and floured pan. Bake for 30 to 35 minutes at 350°.

FROSTING: Boil for 2 minutes:

3/4 c. brown sugar	3 T. milk
6 T. butter	Dash of salt

After boiling for 2 minutes, remove from heat and add 1 3/4 cups powdered sugar. Spread on hot bars.

Greg Van Beek

Cola Bars

1 c. cola	2 c. flour
1 stick oleo	3 eggs
1/2 c. oil	1/2 c. sour milk
4 T. cocoa	1 tsp. baking soda
2 c. sugar	1 tsp. vanilla

Mix cola, oleo and oil over low heat and bring almost to a boil. Remove from heat and add cocoa. Mix sugar and flour together first, and then add all above to mixture. Stir in eggs, one at a time. Dissolve baking soda in milk, with vanilla; pour into mixture. Stir. Pour into greased jellyroll pan. Bake at 350° for 25 minutes. Frost.

COLA FROSTING:

1/4 c. cola	1 stick oleo
	3 T. cocoa

Melt together. Add 2 to 3 cups powdered sugar and beat until smooth. Frost when bars are cool.

Jan Budden

Delicious Bars

1/4 c. oleo
4 c. mini marshmallows
4 c. Rice Krispies

Melt oleo and marshmallows; stir in Rice Krispies and pat into an 11x16-inch pan.
Melt:
1 (14 oz.) bag caramels
1 1/4 sticks oleo
1 (13 oz.) can sweetened condensed milk

Bring to a boil. Pour over Rice Krispie mixture and refrigerate for 30 minutes. Make another layer of oleo, Rice Krispies and marshmallows--same as first layer--and put on top of caramel layer. Keep refrigerated.

BJ De Weerd

Double Dairy Bars

CRUST:
1 c. butter
2 c. brown sugar
2 eggs
1 tsp. vanilla
1 1/2 c. flour
1 tsp. baking soda
1 tsp. salt
2 c. quick oatmeal

Cream butter and sugar. Add eggs and beat. Add vanilla, flour, baking soda, salt and oatmeal. Mix and spread in a large jellyroll pan.

FILLING:
1 (14 oz.) can sweetened condensed milk
1 tsp. vanilla
1 (8 oz.) pkg. cream cheese

Beat until smooth. Reserve 1/3 cup and spread the rest on crust. Sprinkle 1 cup chopped nuts on top. Bake at 350° for 25 minutes. While it's baking, mix 2/3 cup chocolate chips and reserved filling in a double boiler. Heat until melted. Add 2 to 3 tablespoons milk, if necessary. Drizzle on bars while still warm.

Vera Brouwer

Double-Delicious Cookie Bars

1/2 c. margarine or butter
1 1/2 c. graham cracker crumbs
1 (14 oz.) can Eagle Brand sweetened condensed milk (not evaporated milk)
2 c. (12 oz.) semi-sweet chocolate chips
1 c. peanut butter chips

Preheat oven to 350°. In a 9x13-inch pan, melt margarine in oven. Sprinkle crumbs evenly over margarine. Pour sweetened milk evenly over crumbs. Top with chips. Press down firmly. Bake for 25 to 30 minutes, or until lightly browned.
Optional Garnish: Melt 1 cup semi-sweet chocolate chips with 1 1/2 teaspoons of shortening. Drizzle over bars.

Laura Haverdink

Dump Bars

2 c. sugar
1 3/4 c. flour
1/2 c. cocoa
1/2 tsp. salt
5 eggs
1 c. vegetable oil
1 tsp. vanilla
1 c. chocolate chips
1 c. nutmeats

Dump all ingredients, except chips and nutmeats, in a bowl. Mix well. Spread in a greased and floured 9x13-inch pan. Sprinkle chips and nuts over top. Bake at 350° for 25 minutes.
This is a rich bar and needs no frosting.

Barb Oldenkamp

Peanut Butter Bars

2 sticks margarine, melted
1 3/4 c. graham cracker crumbs
1 c. smooth peanut butter
2 1/3 c. powdered sugar
2 c. milk chocolate chips

Melt margarine. Add graham cracker crumbs, peanut butter and powdered sugar. Mix by hand. Spread in a greased 9x13-inch pan. Refrigerate. Melt chocolate chips and spread over bars.

Tammy Sneller

Peanut Butter S'mores Bars

1/2 c. oleo
1/2 c. peanut butter
1/2 c. white sugar
1/2 c. brown sugar
1 egg
1/2 tsp. vanilla
1 1/2 c. flour
2 tsp. baking powder
1/2 tsp. salt
2 1/2+ c. mini marshmallows
1 c. chocolate chips
1 c. salted peanuts

Cream oleo, peanut butter and sugars until light and fluffy. Beat in egg and vanilla. Add flour, baking powder and salt; mix well. Divide dough in half. Pat 1/2 of dough in a 9x13-inch pan (flour hands to keep from sticking). Spread the marshmallows over dough. Sprinkle chocolate chips on, then the salted peanuts. Put the rest of the dough, in little pieces, over this. Bake at 350° for 20 minutes, or until lightly browned.

Edith Kuiken,
Evelyn De Vries

S'more Bars

8 to 10 graham crackers
  (2 1/2" x 5")
1 c. butter or oleo
4 sq. chocolate
2 c. sugar
4 eggs
1 1/2 c. flour
Pinch of salt
2 c. marshmallows
1 c. chocolate chips
Nuts (opt.)

Preheat oven to 350°. Arrange crackers, single layer, in a greased 9x13-inch pan. Melt butter and chocolate. Stir in sugar, eggs, flour and salt. Spread over crackers and bake at 350° for 25 to 30 minutes, until toothpick inserted in center comes out clean. Sprinkle with marshmallows, chips and nuts (optional). Place in oven for 5 more minutes. Remove and cool.

Note: Can omit crackers and make plain brownies.

Dee Ann Cleveringa

Salted Nut Bars

1 yellow cake mix
1/2 c. butter, softened
1 egg
3 c. mini marshmallows
1/4 c. butter
2/3 c. white syrup
1 (12 oz.) pkg. butterscotch chips
2 c. Rice Krispies
2 c. dry-roasted peanuts

Mix cake mix, 1/2 cup butter and egg; pat into a 9x13-inch pan. Bake at 350° for 10 to 12 minutes. Remove from oven and sprinkle marshmallows over the batter. Bake 3 minutes longer. Crust will be soft and marshmallows puffy. Remove from oven. Melt in saucepan: 1/4 cup butter with white syrup for 1/2 minute. Add butterscotch chips and stir until melted. Immediately add Rice Krispies and salted nuts. Spread over marshmallows while all is warm. Let cool completely before cutting.

Karla Hundt

♥ Sugarless Bars
(Diabetic)

1 c. dates
1/2 c. raisins
1/2 c. prunes
1 c. water
2 eggs
1/2 c. oleo
1/4 tsp. salt
1 tsp. vanilla
1 c. flour
1 tsp. baking soda

In a blender, put the water, eggs, dates, raisins and prunes. Blend until the fruits are ground smooth. Pour into mixing bowl and blend in the remaining ingredients. Bake in a 9x13-inch cake pan for 20 minutes at 350°.
Note: May be served as a dessert, with a dab of Cool Whip.

Marlene De Jager

Look upon even the rainy days as a gift, a challenge, an opportunity.

Super Party Bars
(Large Batch)

2 1/2 c. flour	2 c. brown sugar
1 tsp. baking soda	2 eggs
1/2 tsp. salt	5 tsp. vanilla
1 c. oleo	3 c. oatmeal

Mix and pat 2/3 of batter into a high-sided large cookie sheet. Melt:

1 pkg. chocolate chips	2 T. butter
1 pkg. butterscotch chips	1/4 tsp. salt
1 can sweetened condensed milk	1 tsp. vanilla

Pour over crust and crumble the remaining batter on top. Bake for 30 minutes at 350°.

BJ De Weerd

Twix Bars

1 tube sugar cookie dough	1 can sweetened condensed milk
16 caramels	1 pkg. chocolate chips
1 stick margarine	1 1/2 c. peanut butter

Press cookie dough into jellyroll pan. Bake at 350° for about 10 minutes. Melt caramels, margarine and milk. Spread over cookie layer. Let cool. Melt chocolate chips and peanut butter. Spread over caramel. Let cool. Cut into bars.

Michelle Bomgaars

Twix Bars

1 tube Pillsbury sugar cookie dough	1/2 stick (1/4 c.) oleo
14 to 16 oz. caramels	1 pkg. milk chocolate chips
1/2 can sweetened condensed milk	1/2 c. peanut butter

Spread cookie dough in a greased jellyroll pan. Bake at 350° until golden. Melt 14 to 16 ounces caramels with 1/2 can sweetened condensed milk and 1/4 cup oleo. Spread over cookie crust. Melt 1 package milk chocolate chips and 1/2 cup peanut butter. Spread over caramel layer. Place in refrigerator until firm; cut into bars. Keep in refrigerator.

Evelyn De Vries

Applesauce Bars

1 c. sugar
1 c. applesauce
1 tsp. cinnamon
1/2 tsp. salt
1 c. flour, sifted

1 egg
1/2 c. shortening
1/2 tsp. nutmeg
1 tsp. baking soda

Bake at 350° for 35 to 40 minutes.

Mrs. Anna De Jager (William)

Apple-Nut Squares

3 eggs
1 3/4 c. sugar
1 c. vegetable oil
2 tsp. vanilla
2 c. flour

1 tsp. salt
1 tsp. baking soda
1 1/2 tsp. cinnamon
4 med. apples, pared & diced
1/2 c. chopped nuts

Combine and mix eggs, sugar, cinnamon and oil. Stir in dry ingredients and mix well. Fold in vanilla, apples and nuts. Bake in a greased 9x13-inch pan for 1 hour at 325°.
Very good served with a dab of Cool Whip.

Arloa Jansma

Apple Squares

1 1/2 c. flour
1/3 c. sugar
3/4 tsp. salt
1/2 c. butter
4 c. chopped apples
2 T. lemon juice
1/3 c. sugar

1 tsp. cinnamon
1/2 c. sugar
1 egg
1/3 c. evaporated milk
1 tsp. vanilla
1 1/2 c. coconut
3/4 c. nuts

Mix together flour, 1/3 cup sugar and salt. Cut in butter to form crust. Press in pan. Mix together apples, lemon juice, 1/3 cup sugar and cinnamon. Put on crust and bake at 375° for 20 minutes. Mix the 1/2 cup sugar, egg, milk, vanilla, coconut and nuts. Spoon over apple mixture and bake for 25 to 30 minutes longer.

Dorene Vander Zwaag

Banana Bars

1/2 c. butter, softened
2 c. sugar
3 eggs
1 1/2 c. mashed bananas

1 tsp. vanilla extract
2 c. all-purpose flour
1 tsp. baking soda
Pinch of salt

FROSTING:
1/2 c. butter, softened
1 (8 oz.) pkg. cream cheese, softened

4 c. confectioners' sugar
2 tsp. vanilla extract

Cream butter and sugar. Beat in eggs, bananas and vanilla. Combine flour, baking soda and salt. Add to the creamed mixture and mix well. Pour into a greased 10x15-inch pan. Bake at 350° for 25 minutes. Cool.

Frosting: Cream butter and cream cheese in a bowl. Gradually add confectioners' sugar and vanilla; beat well. Spread over bars.

Chris Van Beek

Carrot Bars

2 c. sugar
1 c. oil
4 eggs
2 lg. jars baby food carrots
2 c. flour

2 tsp. cinnamon
Dash of nutmeg
2 tsp. baking soda
1/2 tsp. salt

Mix all together. Pour into a greased jellyroll pan. Bake for 20 to 25 minutes at 350°.

Jan Budden

Cherry Bing Bars

2 c. sugar
2/3 c. evaporated milk
Dash of salt
2 c. mini marshmallows
1 stick butter

2 c. cherry chips
1 tsp. vanilla
12 oz. chocolate chips
3/4 c. peanut butter

Bring sugar, milk, salt, marshmallows and butter to a boil over medium heat. Boil for 5 minutes. Add cherry chips and vanilla. Pour into a well-greased 9x13-inch pan. Chill until set. Melt chocolate and peanut butter. Spread evenly over cherry mixture. Chill to set. Cut into pieces and store in airtight container.

Michelle Bomgaars

Cherry Squares

1 c. margarine
1 1/2 c. sugar
4 eggs, beaten
2 c. flour
1 tsp. vanilla
1 tsp. almond extract
1 (21 oz.) can cherry pie filling
Powdered sugar

In a large mixing bowl, cream together margarine and sugar. Add eggs and flour. Mix in extracts and blend well. Spread batter in a 10 1/2 x 15 1/2 x 1-inch pan. Cut surface of batter to make 28 squares. Spoon pie filling in center of each square. During baking, batter puffs up around pie filling. Bake in a 350° oven for 40 minutes. Cut into squares. When cooled, sprinkle with powdered sugar.

Elvera Van Horssen

♥ Coconut-Pineapple Bars
(Diabetic)

3 lg. eggs
1 1/2 c. butter
1 c. pineapple juice

Beat together.
Add:
2 1/4 c. flour
1 tsp. baking soda
2 tsp. baking powder
1 tsp. cinnamon
1/4 tsp. salt

Fold in 2 cups coconut and drained pineapple from 1 (20-ounce) can. Bake in a greased 9x13-inch glass pan, in a 350° oven for 25 minutes.

Gert Sjaarda

Lemon-Coconut Squares

1 1/2 c. flour
1/2 c. powdered sugar
3/4 c. butter or oleo

Combine until crumbly. Press into the bottom of a lightly-greased 9x13x2-inch baking pan. Bake at 350° for 15 minutes.
Meanwhile, beat:

4 eggs
1 1/2 c. sugar
1/2 c. lemon juice
1 tsp. baking powder

Pour over crust; sprinkle with 3/4 cup coconut. Bake at 350° for 20 to 25 minutes, or until golden brown.
Cool on wire rack. Cut into bars.

Darlene Wichers

Raisin Bars

1 c. butter, melted
1 3/4 c. oatmeal
1 c. brown sugar
1 tsp. baking soda
1 3/4 c. flour
2 c. raisins
4 egg yolks

1 c. white sugar
3 T. cornstarch
1/4 tsp. salt
2 c. cream
1 T. butter
1 tsp. vanilla

Combine butter, oatmeal, brown sugar, baking soda and flour to make crumb mixture. Put 1/2 of these crumbs in the bottom of an 11x15-inch cookie sheet or jellyroll pan.

Cook raisins in 1/2 cup water for about 4 minutes.

In another saucepan, combine white sugar, cornstarch and salt. Beat egg yolks and cream together; add to dry ingredients. Add butter. Cook until thick. Add raisins (drained) and vanilla. Pour filling over crumbs in pan. Top with the rest of the crumbs. Bake for 15 minutes at 350°.

Karen Bos

Raisin Cream Bars

1 3/4 c. oatmeal
1 3/4 c. flour
1 3/4 c. brown sugar

1 tsp. baking soda
1 c. oleo, melted

Combine until crumbly; put 1/2 of the mixture in the bottom of a 9x13-inch pan. Set the rest aside.

4 egg yolks
1 c. sugar
3 T. cornstarch
2 c. evaporated milk

1 tsp. vanilla
2 T. oleo
2 c. raisins
1/2 c. water

Combine yolks, sugar, cornstarch, evaporated milk, oleo and vanilla. Cook until thick. Cook raisins in water. Add to filling mixture. Pour over the first layer. Crumble remaining half of crumbs over filling. Bake at 350° for 15 minutes.

Judy Vlietstra

Sour Cream Raisin Bars

1 3/4 c. flour
1 c. brown sugar
1 tsp. baking soda
1 c. oleo, melted
1 3/4 c. oatmeal

Mix until crumbly. Put 1/2 into a 9x13-inch pan.

FILLING:
2 c. raisins
1/2 c. water
3 egg yolks
2 c. sour cream
3 T. cornstarch
1 c. sugar
1/4 tsp. baking soda
1 tsp. vanilla

Cook raisins in water. Mix egg yolks, sour cream, cornstarch, sugar and baking soda. Stir in raisins. Cook until thick. Add vanilla. Pour over crumb mixture in pan. Top with remaining crumbs. Bake for 20 minutes at 350°.

Crystal Brink

Sour Cream Raisin Bars

CRUST:
1 3/4 c. oatmeal
1 3/4 c. flour
1 tsp. baking soda
1 c. margarine or butter
1 c. brown sugar

FILLING:
1/2 c. water
4 egg yolks, beaten
1 1/2 c. sugar
2 c. raisins
2 c. sour cream
3 T. cornstarch

Cream margarine and brown sugar; add baking soda, flour and oatmeal. Mix well. Pat 1/2 of mixture in the bottom of a greased 9x13-inch pan.
In a small saucepan, simmer raisins in water until all is absorbed. Mix sour cream, yolks, and combined sugar and cornstarch. Cook until thickened, stirring constantly. Add raisins. Pour over crust. Sprinkle reserved crumbs over top. Bake at 350° for 20 minutes.

Faye Vander Lugt

Cookies

"Can't Eat Just One" Chocolate Chip Cookies

1 c. brown sugar
1 c. white sugar
1 c. margarine
1 c. oil
1 egg
2 tsp. vanilla

1 tsp. salt
1 tsp. baking soda
1 tsp. cream of tartar
2 c. oatmeal
3 1/2 c. flour
6 oz. chocolate chips

Mix sugar and margarine, oil, egg and vanilla. Add dry ingredients; stir. Drop onto cookie sheet. Bake at 350° for 12 to 15 minutes.

Jeremy Wiersema

Chocolate Chip Cereal Cookies

1 c. oleo
1 c. salad oil
1 c. brown sugar
1 c. white sugar
1 egg
2 tsp. vanilla
3 1/2 c. flour

1 tsp. salt
1 tsp. baking soda
1 tsp. cream of tartar
1 c. oatmeal or rolled oats
1 c. Rice Krispies
1 (12 oz.) pkg. chocolate chips

Combine all ingredients and mix well. Drop by teaspoonfuls onto lightly-greased cookie sheet. Bake at 350° for 12 minutes.

Chris Van Beek

Chocolate Chip Cookies

1 c. lard
1 c. white sugar
1/2 c. brown sugar
2 eggs
1/2 tsp. salt

1 tsp. vanilla
1 tsp. baking soda
2 c. sifted flour (add 1 T. more flour)
1 pkg. chocolate chips
1/2 c. nutmeats

Mix lard with white and brown sugar. Add eggs. Sift flour, baking soda and salt. Add to lard mixture. Mix well. Add vanilla, chocolate chips and nutmeats. Bake in a 350° oven for 20 minutes, approximately.

Mrs. Anna De Jager (William)

Chocolate Chip Cookies

1 c. brown sugar
1 c. white sugar
1 c. Crisco (very important--lard does not work)
2 eggs
1/2 tsp. salt
1 tsp. cream of tartar
1 tsp. baking soda
1 tsp. vanilla
2 1/2 c. flour
1 1/2 c. chocolate chips

Cream sugars and Crisco; add eggs, salt, cream of tartar, baking soda and vanilla. Beat well. Add flour and chocolate chips. Bake at 300° for 12 to 15 minutes. Bake slow for crispness.
(Barb Muilenburg's recipe from orange cookbook.) *Julie Leusink*

No. 1 Chocolate Chip Cookies

1 c. white sugar
1 c. shortening
1 egg
1/2 to 1 tsp. salt
1 tsp. baking soda
3 1/2 to 4 c. flour
1/2 c. chopped walnuts (opt.)
1 c. brown sugar
1 c. cooking oil
1 T. milk
1 tsp. vanilla
1 tsp. cream of tartar
1 c. chocolate chips

Cream sugars with shortening and oil; add the next 6 ingredients. Mix; stir in flour. Add chips and nuts last. Drop with a spoon onto cookie sheets and bake for 10 to 15 minutes at 350°, until light brown. Yield: about 4 dozen.
Note: Can make into balls the size of walnuts and press down slightly. Use ungreased cookie sheet. *Amy Rensink, Gert Sjaarda, Colette Hofmeyer, Mrs. Marion Klein, Marilyn Kruid, Linda Mellema*

Cinnamon Chocolate Chip Cookies

1 1/2 c. flour
1 tsp. baking soda
1 tsp. cinnamon
1 c. butter, softened
1/2 c. brown sugar
1 c. sugar
1 egg
1 tsp. vanilla
1 1/2 c. old-fashioned oats
1 c. semi-sweet chocolate chips

Mix together flour, baking soda and cinnamon. Beat together butter, brown sugar and sugar at medium speed until light and fluffy. Beat in egg and vanilla. At low speed, beat in flour mixture until blended. Fold in oats and chocolate chips. Cover with plastic wrap; chill for 1 hour. Preheat oven to 350°. Grease cookie sheets. Shape dough into 1-inch balls and flatten each cookie slightly. Bake until lightly browned around edges, 10 to 12 minutes. Yield: 4 dozen. *Cherie Van Donkelaar*

Grandma Kate's Chocolate Chip Cookies

1 c. white sugar
1 c. brown sugar
1 c. shortening
2 eggs
1 tsp. baking soda

2 c. flour
1 tsp. vanilla
1/2 tsp. salt
Chocolate chips

Bake at 350° for 10 to 12 minutes.

BJ De Weerd

Keebler Soft Chocolate Chip Cookies

4 sticks butter
2 eggs
2 T. molasses
2 tsp. vanilla
1/3 c. water
1 1/2 c. sugar
1 1/2 c. packed brown sugar

1 tsp. baking powder
1 1/2 tsp. baking soda
1 tsp. salt
5 c. flour
1 (12 oz.) pkg. semi-sweet chocolate chips

Preheat oven to 350°. Cream butter, eggs, molasses, vanilla and water. In a large bowl, sift together sugar, flour, salt, baking soda and baking powder. Combine dry mixture and moist mixture. Add chips. Shape into 1-inch balls. Place on ungreased cookie sheet. Bake for 8 minutes, until light brown around edges.

Variations: For Pepperidge Farm Chesapeake or Sausalito cookies, use the above recipe, but omit molasses and water. For Chesapeake cookies, add 3 cups chopped pecans. For Sausalito cookies, use macadamia nuts, broken into rather large chunks. Bake at 375° for 10 to 11 minutes, for a crispier cookie.

Diane Munro

Our Favorite Chewy Chocolate Chip Cookies

1 c. shortening
1 c. sugar
1/2 c. brown sugar
2 eggs
2 tsp. vanilla

2 1/2 c. flour
1 1/2 tsp. salt
1 tsp. baking soda
12 oz. chocolate chips
1 c. nuts (opt.)

Cream shortening, sugars, eggs and vanilla until light and fluffy. Sift together dry ingredients. Stir into creamed mixture; blend well. Add chocolate chips and nuts. Drop from a teaspoon onto a lightly-greased cookie sheet. Bake at 375° for 10 minutes. Yield: 6 dozen.

Lori Van Gorp

Jordan's Cookies
(AKA: Peanut Butter Chocolate Chip Cookies)

1/2 c. butter
1/2 c. peanut butter
1/2 c. white sugar
1/2 c. brown sugar
1 egg
2 tsp. vanilla
1 1/2 c. flour
1/2 tsp. baking soda
1/2 tsp. salt
2/3 c. milk chocolate chips
2/3 c. peanut butter (Reese's) chips

Cream together butter, peanut butter and sugars. Add egg, vanilla, baking soda, salt and flour. Once blended, add in chocolate and peanut butter chips. Roll into small balls or use small scooper and place on a well-greased cookie sheet. Bake in a preheated 350° oven for 8 minutes, until golden brown.

Jen Vlietstra

Soft Batch Chocolate Chip Cookies

2 sticks margarine
1/4 c. sugar
3/4 c. brown sugar
1 (4 oz.) pkg. instant vanilla pudding
1 pkg. milk chocolate chips
2 eggs
1 tsp. vanilla
2 1/4 c. flour
1 tsp. baking soda

Beat butter, sugars, pudding, eggs and vanilla until fluffy. Mix in flour and baking soda. Stir in chocolate chips. Bake on ungreased cookie sheet at 375° for 8 to 10 minutes, or until golden brown.

Variations: Can use different combinations, like chocolate pudding with chocolate chips, chocolate pudding with white chocolate chips, butterscotch pudding with butterscotch chips.

BJ De Weerd

Sour Cream Chocolate Chip Cookies

1 c. butter-flavor Crisco
1 c. packed brown sugar
1/2 c. granulated sugar
1 egg
1/2 c. sour cream
1/4 c. honey
2 tsp. vanilla
2 1/2 c. flour
1 1/2 tsp. baking powder
1/2 tsp. salt
2 c. chocolate chips

Combine shortening, brown sugar and granulated sugar. Add egg, sour cream, honey and vanilla. Combine flour, baking powder and salt. Add to shortening mixture. Stir in chocolate chips. Drop onto greased baking sheets, 2 inches apart. Bake at 375° for 10 to 12 minutes.

Michelle Plendl

$250 Dollar Cookie Recipe

5 c. blended oatmeal
2 c. butter
2 c. sugar
2 c. brown sugar
4 eggs
2 tsp. vanilla
4 c. flour

1 tsp. salt
2 tsp. baking powder
2 tsp. baking soda
24 oz. chocolate chips
1 (8 oz.) Hershey bar
3 c. chopped nuts (your choice)

Measure oatmeal and blend in a blender to a fine powder. Cream the butter and both sugars. Add eggs and vanilla; mix together with flour, oatmeal, salt, baking powder and baking soda. Add chocolate chips, Hershey bar (grated), and nuts. Roll into balls and place 2 inches apart on a cookie sheet. Bake for 10 minutes at 375°. Yield: 112 cookies.

Emily Maassen

Melt-in-Your-Mouth Cookies

1/2 lb. Crisco
1 c. oil
1 c. brown sugar
1 c. sugar
2 eggs
4 1/2 c. flour

1 T. baking soda
1/2 tsp. salt
1 T. cream of tartar
1 to 2 c. white chocolate chips, to taste

Mix Crisco and oil. Add sugars, eggs and vanilla. Sift dry ingredients. Add to mixture. Fold in chips. Bake at 350° for 12 to 15 minutes.

Linda Van Regenmorter

Angel Cookies

1/2 c. Crisco
1/2 c. butter
1/2 c. white sugar
1/2 c. brown sugar
1 egg
2 c. flour

1 tsp. baking soda
1 tsp. cream of tartar
1/2 tsp. salt
1/2 c. nuts (opt.)
1 tsp. vanilla

Cream shortening and sugars. Add other ingredients in order given, sifting dry ingredients. Make into balls the size of a walnut and dip in water, then in sugar. Place on a greased cookie sheet, sugared-side up. Bake in moderate oven (350°) until edges turn golden, approximately 15 minutes. May put 1/2 pecan on top to decorate.

Evelyn De Vries

Bonbon Cookies

1 c. oleo
1 1/2 c. white sugar
1 egg
1/2 tsp. vanilla
1/2 tsp. almond extract

2 1/2 c. flour
1 tsp. baking soda
1 tsp. cream of tartar
Almond nut chips

Mix all together. Roll in small balls and flatten. Add almond nut chips in center of cookie. Bake at 350° for 12 to 15 minutes.

Jonna Wierda

Butter-Pecan Turtle Cookies

CRUST:
2 c. flour

CARAMEL LAYER:
2/3 c. butter

1 c. brown sugar
1/2 c. butter (no substitutes)

1/2 c. whole pecan halves
1 c. milk chocolate chips

Preheat oven to 350°.

Crust: Combine crust ingredients. Mix at medium speed for 2 to 3 minutes, or until mixed well. Pat into ungreased 9x13-inch pan. Sprinkle pecans evenly over unbaked crust.

Caramel Layer: Combine butter and brown sugar in a heavy pan. Cook over medium heat. Stir constantly until mixture begins to boil. Boil for 30 seconds to 1 minute, stirring constantly. Pour caramel layer evenly over pecans and crust. Bake for 20 minutes, or until caramel is bubbly and crust is light brown. Remove from oven. Immediately sprinkle with chips. Allow to melt slightly and swirl as they melt. <u>Do not</u> spread chips.

Wanda Kuiken

Best Butter Cookies

1 c. butter
1 c. sugar
1 3/4 c. flour

1/2 tsp. baking soda
1/2 tsp. salt
1/2 tsp. vanilla

Cream butter and sugar. Add dry ingredients. Mix well. Chill for 30 to 45 minutes. Form into small balls and press down before baking. Bake at 325° to 350° until slightly browned.

Margaret Cleveringa,
Evelyn De Vries

Best-Ever Cookies

1 c. white sugar
1 c. brown sugar
1 c. lard or butter
1 1/2 c. oil
1 egg, beaten
4 c. flour

1 tsp. cream of tartar
1 tsp. baking soda
1 tsp. salt
1 tsp. vanilla
1 c. oatmeal
1 c. crushed corn flakes

Mix as in order, and bake at 325° for 10 minutes, or until light brown.
Note: You can add chocolate chips.

Marie Maassen

Cookies

2 c. soft oleo   2 c. sugar

Beat 15 minutes, until light and fluffy, with mixer at medium speed. Add:

3 1/2 c. flour
1/2 tsp. baking powder
1 tsp. baking soda

1/4 tsp. salt
2 tsp. vanilla
1 c. nutmeats

Make in walnut-size balls or drop from spoon. Do not grease cookie sheet. Bake for 15 to 20 minutes at 300° to 325°.
Note: Press cookies down with fingers to flatten some. These are good plain, without nuts, and to make them pretty, put a pecan nut on center of cookies.

Mrs. Al Dekker

Forgotten Cookies

3 egg whites
3/4 c. sugar
1/2 tsp. vanilla

1 c. chocolate chips
1 brown paper bag

Preheat oven to 400°. Line a cookie sheet with bag. Spray bag with Pam. With a mixer, beat egg whites until stiff. Add sugar and vanilla until blended and egg whites form stiff peaks. Fold in chocolate chips. Drop onto cookie sheet by large tablespoon. Place in oven. <u>Immediately</u> turn off oven and leave in overnight. Should be light gold. Yield: 12

Bob Cleveringa

Coconut-Oatmeal Cookies

1 c. brown sugar
1 c. white sugar
1/2 c. Crisco
1/2 c. oleo
2 eggs
1 c. coconut
2 c. quick oatmeal
1 1/2 c. flour
1/2 tsp. baking powder
1 tsp. baking soda
1/8 tsp. salt
1/2 tsp. vanilla

Mix in order given. Drop from a teaspoon onto greased cookie sheet. Bake for 12 to 15 minutes at 350°.
Joyce Groen

Neiman-Marcus Cookies

Cream together:
2 c. butter
2 c. sugar
2 c. brown sugar

Add:
2 tsp. vanilla
4 eggs

Add:
4 c. flour
5 c. blended oatmeal*
1 tsp. salt
2 tsp. baking powder
2 tsp. baking soda

Mix together.
Add:
24 oz. chocolate chips
1 (8 oz.) Hershey bar, grated
3 c. nuts of your choice**

Roll into balls and place 2 inches apart on cookie sheet. Bake for 10 minutes at 375°. Yield: 112.
*Measure oatmeal and blend in blender to a fine powder. **We like 1/2 walnuts and 1/2 pecans.
Marietta VanDer Weide

No-Bake Cookies

2 c. sugar
1/2 c. milk
1 stick oleo
3 T. cocoa
2 1/2 to 3 c. oatmeal
2 tsp. vanilla
1/2 c. peanut butter

Stir the first 4 ingredients in microwave bowl or pan on stove. Bring to a boil and cook for 1 1/2 minutes at a full boil. Remove from heat and stir in remaining ingredients. Drop onto waxed paper by spoonfuls and refrigerate.
Jan Budden

No-Bake Chocolate Cookies

2 c. sugar
1/2 c. milk
1/2 c. oleo
4 T. cocoa

Boil 2 minutes. Remove from heat.
Add:
1/2 c. crunchy peanut butter
1 tsp. vanilla
3 c. oatmeal

Drop onto waxed paper. Keeps best in refrigerator.

Marietta VanDer Weide

Chocolate-Oatmeal No-Bake Cookies

FIRST MIXTURE:
3 c. oatmeal
1/2 c. coconut
3 T. cocoa
1/2 c. peanut butter

SECOND MIXTURE:
1/4 lb. butter
2 c. sugar
1/2 c. milk
1 tsp. vanilla

Cook second mixture to a rolling boil. Add to the first mixture. Drop by tablespoons onto waxed paper; let cool and eat!

Gary De Weerd

Oatmeal-Cranberry-White Chocolate Chunk Cookies

2/3 c. corn oil margarine
2/3 c. brown sugar
2 eggs
1 1/2 c. oatmeal
1 1/3 c. flour
1 tsp. baking soda
1/2 tsp. salt
6 oz. Craisins (sweetened, dried cranberries)
2/3 c. white chocolate morsels

Beat margarine and sugar until light and fluffy. Add eggs and mix well. In a separate bowl, mix dry ingredients. Add to butter mixture in several additions, mixing well after each addition. Stir in cranberries and chips. Drop by rounded teaspoonfuls onto ungreased cookie sheet. Bake for 10 to 12 minutes at 350°, until golden brown. Cool completely. Store tightly covered.

Diane Munro

Oatmeal Cookies

1 c. Crisco
2 c. brown sugar
2 eggs
1 3/4 c. flour
1 tsp. baking soda
1 tsp. salt
2 tsp. vanilla

2 c. coconut
2 c. oatmeal
2 c. powdered sugar
1/3 c. butter
1 tsp. vanilla
Milk

Combine shortening and brown sugar; add eggs. Combine flour, baking soda and salt. Add to first mixture. Add vanilla; mix well. Stir in coconut and oatmeal. Bake at 350° for 7 to 8 minutes. Let cool until just warm; frost with powdered sugar frosting.

Make frosting by combining powdered sugar, butter and vanilla. Add milk and stir to desired consistency.

Kathy Smits

Oreo Cookies

COOKIES:
2 boxes chocolate cake mix

2 sticks butter
4 eggs

FILLING:
8 oz. cream cheese

3 1/2 c. powdered sugar

First, mix filling. Spoon into frosting decorator bag or large Ziploc with one corner cut off. Set aside. Mix cookie ingredients. Make small balls that are uniform in size. Bake on a lightly-greased cookie sheet for 9 minutes at 350°. Do not overbake! Cookies will appear very soft. Cool 7 minutes. Pipe filling over back of one cookie. Top with another. Cool completely. Store in airtight container in refrigerator.

Michelle Bomgaars

Peanut Cookies

1 c. brown sugar
1 c. white sugar
1 c. Crisco (not oleo)
2 eggs
1 tsp. vanilla

1 tsp. baking soda
1 tsp. cream of tartar
2 c. flour
1 c. salted peanuts

Cream sugars and Crisco. Add the eggs and beat well. Add vanilla. Mix dry ingredients together and stir into creamed mixture. Add peanuts. Bake at 325° to 350°.

Joan Dekker

Peanut Butter Cookies

1 c. white sugar
1 c. brown sugar
1 c. oleo
1 c. peanut butter
2 eggs

1 T. milk
2 c. flour
1 tsp. baking soda
1/2 tsp. salt

Sift flour, baking soda and salt. Set aside. Cream sugars, oleo and peanut butter. Add eggs and milk. Next, add the flour mixture. Roll in small balls and flatten with a fork. Bake for 8 to 10 minutes at 375°.   **Kathy Dykstra**

Peanut Butter Cup Cookies

1 c. white sugar
1 c. brown sugar
1 c. soft butter or oleo
2 tsp. vanilla
2 eggs

2 1/2 c. flour
1/3 c. cocoa
1 tsp. baking soda
1 pkg. small-size peanut butter cups
   (may also use Rolo candy)

Beat sugars and oleo until light and fluffy. Add vanilla and eggs; beat well. Add flour, cocoa and baking soda. Blend well. Shape about 1 teaspoon of dough around 1 peanut butter cup, covering completely. Roll in sugar and place 2 inches apart. Bake at 350° to 375° for 7 to 10 minutes, until done.
   Evelyn De Vries

Peanut Butter Cup Delights

Mix together:
1 c. oleo
1 c. peanut butter

1 c. white sugar
1 c. brown sugar

Beat in:
2 eggs

1 tsp. vanilla

Stir together:
1 1/2 c. flour
1 tsp. baking powder

1 tsp. baking soda
1 tsp. salt

Gradually add to sugar mixture and stir well. Shape into 1-inch balls and roll in sugar. Place in mini muffin pans and bake at 350° for 12 minutes. Remove from oven and quickly press Reese's miniature peanut butter cups into the center of each cookie. Return to oven for 2 minutes. Remove from oven and let cool for 10 to 15 minutes before trying to remove cookies from mini muffin pans.   **Dawn Beukelman**

Chocolate Star Cookies

1/2 c. oleo
1/2 c. peanut butter
1/2 c. white sugar
1/2 c. brown sugar
1 egg
2 T. milk
1 tsp. vanilla
1 3/4 c. flour
1 tsp. baking soda
Dash of salt

Beat the first 4 ingredients until light and fluffy. Add egg, milk and vanilla; beat well. Blend dry ingredients into the rest. Make into small balls and roll in sugar. Put onto an ungreased cookie sheet. Bake for 8 minutes at 375°. Remove and put a Brach's chocolate star on; bake for 2 minutes more.

Jan Budden

Peanut Butter Star Cookies

Mix together:
1 c. oleo
1 c. peanut butter
1 c. white sugar
1 c. brown sugar

Beat together:
2 eggs
1 tsp. vanilla

Stir together:
2 1/2 c. flour
1 tsp. baking powder
1 tsp. baking soda
1 tsp. salt

Gradually add to sugar mixture and stir well. Shape into 1-inch balls and roll in sugar. Bake at 350° for 15 minutes. Remove from oven and quickly press a chocolate star in center of each. Return to oven for 1 or 2 minutes. Yield: 6 dozen.

Marietta VanDer Weide

Pecan Crispies

1/2 c. shortening
1/2 c. oleo
2 1/2 c. brown sugar
2 eggs
2 1/2 c. flour
1/2 tsp. baking soda
1/4 tsp. salt
1 c. finely-ground pecans

Cream together shortening, oleo and sugar. Add eggs, and then dry ingredients. Drop onto cookie sheet. Bake at 350° for 10 to 12 minutes.
Note: Recipe can easily be doubled.

Elvera Van Horssen

Snicker Cookies

1 c. sugar
1 c. brown sugar
1 c. oleo
2 tsp. vanilla
2 eggs
1 c. peanut butter
1 tsp. baking powder
1 tsp. baking soda
1/2 tsp. salt
3 c. flour
1 lb. bite-sized Snickers bars

Cream oleo and sugars. Beat in vanilla, eggs and peanut butter. Mix in baking powder, baking soda, salt and flour. Refrigerate for awhile. Shape dough around each unwrapped Snickers bar. Completely cover. Bake at 350° for 12 to 15 minutes. <u>Do not</u> overbake.

Jennifer (Wiersema) Probst,
Wanda Kuiken

Sand Cookies

2 c. sugar
1 c. butter or margarine
1 c. Mazola oil
3 egg yolks
1 tsp. vanilla
1 tsp. salt
4 c. flour
1 tsp. baking soda

Mix in order given. Roll in little balls and slightly flatten. Bake at 325° for about 15 to 20 minutes, until light brown.   *Marie Maassen*

Crispy Sugar Cookies

1 c. oleo
2 eggs
1 c. powdered sugar
1 tsp. cream of tartar
1 tsp. vanilla
1 c. vegetable oil
1 c. white sugar
1 tsp. baking soda
1/4 tsp. salt
4 c. flour

Mix all ingredients together. Roll in balls and dip in sugar; flatten with a glass. Bake at 350° or 375° for 8 to 10 minutes.
Note: Recipe can be cut in half.   *Lois Klein*

Old-Fashioned Sugar Cookies

1 c. sugar
2 sticks oleo or butter
1 3/4 c. flour
1/2 tsp. baking soda
1 tsp. vanilla

Cream sugar and oleo well. Mix baking soda into flour; add to creamed mixture. Add vanilla. Roll into 1-inch balls by hand and place on greased cookie sheets. With a flat-bottomed glass, dip it first in a small dish of sugar, and then flatten the cookie balls. Make sure you dip the glass into sugar each time you flatten. Bake for 12 minutes at 350°--need not be brown--just very light around edges.

Betty Jasper,
Jan Budden

Sugar Cookies

1 c. butter
1 1/2 c. sugar
1 T. vinegar
1 tsp. vanilla
1/2 c. lard
1 tsp. baking soda
3 c. flour
1/2 tsp. almond flavoring

Cream butter, lard and sugar. Add baking soda, vinegar, flour, vanilla and almond flavoring. Roll in balls the size of walnuts. Flatten with a glass dipped in sugar. Bake at 325° until light brown around edges, about 12 minutes.

Marcia Cleveringa

Grandma Dykstra's Tea Cookies

1 lb. butter
1 c. sugar
1/2 tsp. salt
1 c. chopped nuts (opt.)
4 c. flour
1 tsp. vanilla

Mix and roll into balls; press down in the center for frosting. Bake for 20 minutes at 325°. Cool and frost.
Note: I use colored powdered sugar frosting with a little almond flavoring in it.

Helen Oolman

Thumbprint Cookies

1 c. oleo, softened
1/2 tsp. salt
1/2 c. powdered sugar
1 T. vanilla
2 c. flour
1 c. nuts, chopped

Mix ingredients in order given. Form balls, 1 inch in size. Put on cookie sheet and press center with thumb. Bake at 350° for 10 to 12 minutes. Bake until bottoms are lightly browned. When cool, fill with frosting.

FROSTING:
1 1/2 c. powdered sugar
1 tsp. vanilla
1 tsp. butter
1 or 2 T. milk

Stir until smooth. Add more milk or powdered sugar to get the right consistency.

Sharon Plendl

Ten-Cup Cookies

1 c. oleo
1 c. sugar
1 c. brown sugar
1 c. peanut butter
2 eggs
1 c. flour
1 c. coconut
1 c. oatmeal
1 c. chocolate chips
1 c. raisins
1 c. chopped walnuts

Mix the first 5 ingredients, and then add the rest. Drop onto cookie sheet. Bake at 350° for 10 to 12 minutes.

Imo Mulder

Breads, Rolls, Muffins & Breakfast

Breads, Rolls, Muffins

Apple Bread

BREAD:
1 c. sugar
1/2 c. salad oil
2 c. chopped apples
2 c. flour

1/2 tsp. salt
2 eggs
2 T. sour milk
1 tsp. baking soda
1 tsp. vanilla

TOPPING:
2 T. sugar
2 T. flour

2 T. oleo
1/2 tsp. cinnamon

Mix bread ingredients together and pour into greased loaf pans. Mix topping ingredients together and sprinkle over top of breads before baking. Bake at 350° for 45 to 60 minutes, until done. Mix a small amount of milk and powdered sugar together and pour over top of baked breads as a glaze. Yield: 1 large or 2 small loaves. Toothpick must not come out clean, or it will be overbaked.
Dawn Beukelman, Pam Sandbulte, Pam Jeltema

Banana Bread

1/2 c. oleo or shortening
1 c. sugar
2 eggs
2 med.-sized bananas
2 c. flour

1 c. milk
1/2 c. nuts
1 tsp. baking soda
1/4 tsp. salt

Cream 1/2 cup shortening or oleo and 1 cup sugar. Add 2 eggs, one at a time, beating after each addition. Add 2 medium-sized bananas, which have been mashed with a fork. Sift 2 cups flour, and then resift with 1 teaspoons baking soda and 1/4 teaspoon salt. Beat in this flour alternately with 1 cup of milk. With the last addition of flour, add 1/2 cup nuts. Mix and put into a greased loaf pan. Bake for 1 hour in a 350° oven.
Sharla De Jager

Banana Bread

Cream together:
2 c. sugar   1 c. shortening

Add:
4 eggs   2 tsp. vanilla

Blend with the creamed mixture.

4 c. flour   2 tsp. baking soda
1 tsp. salt   6 lg. or 8 sm. bananas, mashed

Add the dry ingredients alternately with the mashed bananas. Divide batter into 3 large bread pans or 4 small bread pans. Bake at 350° for 50 to 60 minutes, or until done.

Wendy Heemstra

Banana Bread

1 1/2 c. sugar   1/4 tsp. salt
1/2 c. lard   1 tsp. baking soda in 5 T. sour milk
2 eggs   3 ripe bananas
2 c. flour   1/2 c. nuts (opt.)

Mix in conventional manner. Grease and flour loaf pans. Bake at 350° for 1 to 1 1/2 hours.

Karleen Smits,
Colette Hofmeyer

Banana Bread

1 yellow or white cake mix   3 bananas
1/2 c. nuts   1/4 c. water
2 eggs

Heat oven to 350°. Mash the bananas with a fork. Add 1/4 cup water, eggs, nuts and cake mix. Stir well and pour into a greased loaf pan or 2 small loaf pans. Bake for 1 hour. Let cool 10 minutes before removing from pan. Bake for 40 minutes, if in small pans.
Also makes great muffins.

Cheryl Van Wyk

Banana-Pecan Bread

1 1/2 c. flour
1 pkg. sugar-free instant banana pudding
1 tsp. baking soda
1 tsp. baking powder
1 tsp. pumpkin pie spice

2 oz. (1/2 c.) chopped pecans
2 ripe med. bananas
2 eggs
1/2 c. applesauce (no sugar added)
1/4 c. apple juice (no sugar added)

Preheat oven to 350°. In a bowl, combine flour, pudding mix, baking soda, baking powder, pumpkin pie spice and pecans. In a small bowl, mash bananas. Add eggs, applesauce and juice; blend well. Add to flour mixture. Mix gently to combine. Pour into a 4x8-inch loaf pan, sprayed with butter-flavored cooking spray. Bake for 1 hour, or until top tests done.

Sandy Holtrop

Best Banana Bread

1 1/4 c. sugar
1/2 c. butter, softened
2 eggs
1 1/2 c. mashed ripe bananas
1/2 c. buttermilk

1 tsp. vanilla
2 1/2 c. all-purpose flour
1 tsp. baking soda
1 tsp. salt

Put oven rack on lowest setting. Heat oven to 350°. Grease bottom of a 5x9x3-inch loaf pan. Mix sugar and margarine in a large bowl. Stir in eggs. Blend well. Add bananas, buttermilk and vanilla; beat until smooth. Stir remaining ingredients just until moistened. Pour into pan. Bake for 1 1/4 hours, or until wooden toothpick inserted into center comes out clean. Cool 5 minutes, then remove from pans and cool on cooling rack.

Chris Van Beek

Bran-Banana Bread

2 c. flour
1 tsp. baking powder
1/2 tsp. baking soda
1/2 tsp. salt
1 1/2 c. mashed, fully-ripe bananas

2 1/2 c. Kellogg's 40% bran flakes cereal
1/2 c. margarine or butter, softened
3/4 c. sugar
2 eggs
1/2 c. chopped nuts

Stir together flour, baking powder, baking soda and salt. Combine mashed bananas and cereal; let stand 2 minutes. In a large mixing bowl, beat margarine and sugar. Beat in eggs and cereal mixture. Stir in flour mixture and nuts. Bake in a greased 5x9x3-inch loaf pan, at 350° for about 1 hour, or until tests done.

Edith Van Roekel

Strawberry-Banana Bread

1/2 c. butter
3/4 c. sugar
1 egg
3 T. milk
1 (3 oz.) pkg. strawberry Jello
1 c. mashed bananas
1/2 tsp. baking soda
1 tsp. baking powder
2 c. flour

Cream butter; add sugar and egg (beaten). In a separate bowl, mix milk, Jello and baking soda. Add bananas. Mix together with butter mixture. Sift baking powder and flour together. Add to butter mixture. Pour into a greased pan. Bake at 350° for 40 minutes, or until done.

Wanda Hofmeyer

♥ Sugarless Banana Bread
(Diabetic)

1 3/4 c. cake flour
2 tsp. baking powder
1/4 tsp. baking soda
1/2 tsp. salt
1/4 c. melted shortening
2 eggs, well beaten
6 pkt. powdered sugar substitute
1 tsp. vanilla
2 med. bananas, mashed
2 T. unsweetened applesauce

Combine liquids; add eggs. Stir in dry ingredients. Fold in bananas. Bake at 350° for 45 to 50 minutes. Yield: 1 loaf.

Joyce Baker

Lemon Bread

1 pkg. lemon cake mix
1 (3 1/2 oz.) pkg. instant lemon pudding
1/2 c. oil
1 c. hot water
4 eggs
1/2 c. poppy seeds

Beat all above ingredients in a mixing bowl for 4 minutes. Pour into 2 loaf pans that have been sprayed. Bake for 40 minutes at 350°.

Elvera Van Horssen

Oatmeal Bread

2 c. scalded milk
1 c. oatmeal

Put oatmeal in milk and let stand for 1 hour.

1/2 c. brown sugar
1 T. oil
2 tsp. salt

Dissolve 1 package dry yeast with 1/4 cup warm water and 1/4 teaspoon sugar. Add 4 cups flour to first ingredients. Add the yeast-water mixture with spoon. You will end mixing and kneading by hand. Let rise, then knead down. Let rise again. Put into 2 loaves and let rise again. Bake in 350° oven for 40 to 50 minutes.

Wilma Vander Stelt

Peach Bread

1 1/2 c. sugar
2 eggs
1/2 c. shortening
2 c. peaches, mashed
2 c. flour
1 tsp. baking powder
Pinch of salt
1 tsp. vanilla
1 tsp. cinnamon
1 tsp. baking soda
1/2 c. nuts

Cream together sugar, eggs and shortening. Add the remaining ingredients and mix well. Sprinkle top with 1/2 cup sugar, 2 tablespoons butter and 1/2 teaspoon cinnamon. Bake in 2 greased loaf pans for 35 to 40 minutes at 350°.

Ruth Heidebrink

Pumpkin Bread

3 c. white sugar
1 c. salad oil
4 eggs
1 1/2 tsp. salt
1 tsp. nutmeg
1 tsp. cinnamon
2/3 c. water
3 1/3 c. flour
2 tsp. baking soda
2 c. (No. 303 can) pumpkin

Mix sugar and oil in a large bowl. Add eggs, one at a time, until well mixed. Mix dry ingredients together (salt, spices, flour and baking soda). Add to egg mixture alternately with the water. Add the can of pumpkin last. Bake at 350° for 1 hour. Yield: 3 greased loaves, or you can use 1 loaf pan and 5 small foil pans. Remove small pans after 50 minutes.

Betty Jasper,
Jan Budden

Pumpkin Bread

1 1/2 c. sugar
1/4 tsp. baking powder
1 tsp. baking soda
3/4 tsp. salt
1/2 tsp. cloves
1/2 tsp. cinnamon

1 2/3 c. flour
1/2 c. salad oil
1/2 c. water
1 c. pumpkin
2 eggs

Combine sugar, baking powder, baking soda, salt and spices in a large bowl. Add other ingredients in order given and mix well; place batter in one large loaf pan or 2 small ones. Bake for 1 1/2 hours at 325°.

Eunice Koopmans

Zucchini Bread

Mix:
2 c. sugar
3 eggs

5/8 c. oil

Add:
1 tsp. vanilla
1 tsp. cinnamon
1/4 tsp. baking powder
2 c. shredded zucchini

1 tsp. salt
1 tsp. baking soda
3 c. flour

Put into 2 greased loaf pans. Bake for 1 hour at 350°.

Evonne Wielenga

Boston Brown Bread

1 3/4 c. raisins
1 3/4 c. water
2 tsp. baking soda
2 T. butter
1 1/2 c. sugar

1/4 tsp. salt
2 eggs
2 1/2 c. flour
1 T. oil

Boil the raisins in the water, and then add the baking soda and soak them overnight.

The next day, mix the remaining ingredients and add the raisins. Bake for 1 hour in a 350° oven, in 4 cans or pans, floured.

Alice Vander Broek

Cornbread

3/4 c. sugar
2 eggs
2 c. flour
1 c. cornmeal (yellow)
1 T. baking powder
3/4 tsp. salt
1 1/2 c. milk
1 T. butter, melted
1 c. fresh or frozen blueberries
   (opt., but very good!)

Beat sugar and eggs until feathery. Sift dry ingredients together. Stir flour mixture into egg mixture. Beat in milk and butter. Turn into a 9x13-inch pan. Bake at 400° for 25 minutes.

Shellie Vander Schaaf

Grape-Nut Flakes Bread

1 1/2 c. flour
2 1/2 tsp. baking powder
1/2 tsp. salt
1 c. Grape-Nut flakes
1 c. 2% milk
2/3 c. packed brown sugar
1 egg
1/4 c. honey
2 T. margarine, melted

Heat oven to 350°. Mix flour, baking powder and salt in a large bowl. Mix cereal and milk in another bowl; let stand 5 minutes, then stir in sugar, egg, honey and melted margarine. Add to the flour mixture; stir just until moistened. (Batter will be lumpy.) Pour into loaf pan, which has been sprayed with no-stick cooking spray. Bake for 55 to 60 minutes. Cool 10 minutes; remove from pan and cool entirely on a wire rack.

Chris Van Beek

Eight Dozen Buns

2/3 c. lukewarm water
1 T. sugar
2 pkg. dry yeast
18 c. flour, warmed
1 c. sugar
1 c. oleo
1 T. salt
1 egg, beaten
2 qt. warm water

Warm the flour in a large bowl. Combine 1 tablespoon sugar, lukewarm water and yeast; let stand until bubbly. Make a well in the center of flour; add 1 cup sugar, soft oleo, salt and beaten egg. Stir in warm water and yeast. Mix and knead (not quite as stiff as for bread). Let rise until double in size. Knead and let rise again. Make into buns. Let rise until double in size. Bake for 20 to 25 minutes at 350°. Put a little butter over them when you take them out of the oven. Cover until cool.

These freeze well.

Mrs. Al Dekker

White Bread

1/2 c. warm water
2 pkg. dry yeast
3 1/2 c. warm water
1/4 c. sugar

2 T. salt
1/4 c. shortening or oleo, melted
11 to 12 c. flour

Soak yeast in 1/2 cup water until it rises. Combine liquid with sugar, salt and shortening. Beat in yeast mixture with 4 cups flour until smooth. Knead. Add more flour until it leaves the side of the bowl. Let rise until double in size. Punch down and let rise again. Divide dough into 4 pieces. Put into greased bread pans and cover. Put into a warm place to rise until double in size. Bake in 400° oven for 15 minutes, and then at 350° for 30 minutes. Yield: 4 loaves.

Mrs. Al Dekker

Southern-Style Biscuits

2 1/2 c. flour
1/4 c. sugar
1 1/2 T. baking powder

3/4 c. margarine or oleo (cool)
1 c. cold milk

Mixture will be stiff. Put in muffin tins, greased. Bake at 400° for 20 minutes.

Sadie Van Peursem

Bubble Bread

2 loaves frozen bread dough
1/2 c. butter
1 c. brown sugar

1 lg. or 2 sm. pkg. vanilla
  or butterscotch pudding (not
  instant)
1/4 c. milk
1/2 tsp. cinnamon

Thaw bread dough. (Do not allow to rise.) Grease a 9x13-inch pan. Tear one loaf into 1-inch pieces and drop into pan. Melt butter and add the rest of the ingredients. Beat until smooth. Pour over the pieces of bread dough in pan. Tear the second loaf into 1-inch pieces and place on top. Let rise until double in size. Bake at 350° for 25 minutes.

Evonne Wielenga,
Vicki Schrock, Linda Van Regenmorter

Monkey Bread

3/4 c. sugar
1 T. cinnamon
4 tubes buttermilk biscuits

1 c. sugar
1 1/2 tsp. cinnamon
3/4 c. oleo

Combine 3/4 cup sugar and 1 tablespoon cinnamon in a large mixing bowl or paper bag. Cut (or pull) biscuits into fourths. Place in mixture and shake. Drop into a greased bundt or tube pan and sprinkle with nuts. Bring the other sugar, oleo and cinnamon to a boil. Pour over biscuits. Bake at 350° for about 1/2 hour.

Karla Hundt

Mini Cinnamon Rolls

2 (8 oz.) cans refrigerated crescent rolls
1/2 c. butter, softened

1/4 c. sugar
1 tsp. cinnamon

GLAZE:
1 c. powdered sugar

2 T. milk

Preheat oven to 350°. Separate rolls into rectangles; press perforations. Spread with butter. Combine sugar and cinnamon. Sprinkle mixture over rectangles. Roll up each rectangle from short end. Cut each roll into 5 slices. Place slices, cut-side down, in a greased 9x13x2-inch baking dish. Bake for 20 to 25 minutes, or until golden brown. Yield: 40 mini rolls.

Mix glaze. Drizzle on top of warm rolls.

Carol Kleyer

Caramel Topping for Rolls

6 T. margarine
1/3 c. cream

1/4 c. white syrup
1 1/2 c. packed brown sugar

Heat until margarine is melted and all is well blended. Pour into a 9x13-inch pan. Pecans may be added. Top with frozen cinnamon roll dough, or your own roll recipe.

Diane Munro

Orange-Caramel Sauce
(For Cinnamon Rolls)

2 T. butter
1/2 c. brown sugar
1 T. grated orange rind
1 tsp. ground cinnamon
2 T. white sugar
1/2 c. orange juice

Mix all the ingredients in a heavy saucepan and bring to a boil. Pour into a 9x13-inch pan with cinnamon rolls.

Jen Vlietstra

Cream Cheese Rolls

1 c. brown sugar
1/4 c. melted oleo
1/3 c. maple syrup
8 oz. cream cheese
2 T. butter
1/2 c. powdered sugar
2 pkg. refrigerated biscuits

Combine brown sugar, melted oleo and maple syrup; put into the bottom of an 8x12-inch glass pan. Cream the cream cheese, butter and powdered sugar together. Flatten biscuits and place 1 rounded teaspoon of cream cheese mixture on each one. Roll up. Place open-side down. Bake for 30 minutes at 350°. Cool. Turn over onto foil.

Denise Vander Stelt

Honey Buns

1 (8 oz.) tube crescent rolls
5 T. butter
2/3 c. powdered sugar
3 T. honey
1 tsp. vanilla

Preheat oven to 375°. Grease muffin pan. Heat butter and sugar in microwave, or over low heat until blended. Do not boil. Stir in honey and vanilla. Open dough. Do not unroll. Slice the roll into 12 pieces. Spoon 1 tablespoon honey mixture into each muffin cup. Place crescent slice over. Bake for 10 to 12 minutes. Invert onto serving platter.
Makes neat, light, and delicious rolls for breakfast/brunch.

Dee Ann Cleveringa

Banana Crumb Muffins

1 1/2 c. all-purpose flour
1 tsp. baking soda
1 tsp. baking powder
1/2 tsp. salt

3 lg. ripe bananas, mashed
3/4 c. sugar
1 egg, lightly beaten
1/3 c. butter or margarine, melted

TOPPING:
1/3 c. packed brown sugar
1 T. all-purpose flour

1/8 tsp. ground cinnamon
1 T. cold butter or margarine

In a large bowl, combine dry ingredients. Combine bananas, sugar, egg and butter; mix well. Stir into dry ingredients, just until moistened. Fill greased or paper-lined muffin cups 3/4-full. Combine the first 3 topping ingredients; cut in butter until crumbly. Sprinkle over muffins. Bake at 375° for 18 to 20 minutes, or until muffins test done. Cool in pan 10 minutes before removing to a wire rack. Yield: about 1 dozen.

Clarine Van Klompenburg

Morning Glory Muffins

2 1/2 c. sugar
4 c. flour
4 tsp. cinnamon
4 tsp. baking soda
1 tsp. salt
1 c. shredded coconut
1 c. raisins

4 c. shredded carrots
2 apples, shredded
1 c. pecans
6 eggs
2 c. vegetable oil
1 tsp. vanilla extract

Sift dry ingredients into a large bowl. Add coconut, fruit and nuts; mix well. Add eggs, oil and vanilla, stirring only until combined. Spoon batter into cupcake tins and bake at 375° for 20 minutes. Muffins should ripen for 24 hours for flavors to blend properly. Yield: about 30 to 36 muffins.

Note: You can substitute applesauce in place of oil, but may need to use more for moisture.

B. Duane and Goldie De Jager

Strawberry Muffins

2 c. flour
1/2 c. sugar
2 tsp. baking powder
1/2 tsp. baking soda
1/2 tsp. salt

2 eggs
1 (6 oz.) ctn. strawberry yogurt
1/2 c. vegetable oil
1 c. chopped fresh strawberries

Combine the first 5 ingredients in a bowl. In another bowl, beat eggs; add yogurt, oil and strawberries. Stir together. Stir this mixture into the dry ingredients, just until moistened. Put into muffin tins sprayed with cooking oil. Bake at 375° for 19 to 21 minutes. Yield: 12 large muffins, or 15 smaller muffins.
Note: Egg substitute can be used in place of eggs.

Marilyn Kruid

Biscuit Bites

1/4 c. butter or margarine, melted
2 T. grated Parmesan cheese
1 T. dried, minced onion

1 1/2 tsp. parsley flakes
1 (12 oz.) pkg. refrigerated biscuits

In a bowl, combine butter, cheese, onion and parsley. Cut biscuits into quarters; roll in butter mixture. Place in a greased 10x15x1-inch baking pan; let stand for 15 minutes. Bake at 400° for 8 minutes, or until lightly browned. Yield: 40 pieces.

Beth Zeutenhorst

Cheese Biscuits
(Like Red Lobster's)

1 1/4 lb. Bisquick
3 oz. shredded Cheddar cheese

11 oz. cold water

GARLIC SPREAD:
1/2 c. melted butter
1 tsp. garlic powder

1/4 tsp. salt
1/8 tsp. onion powder
1/8 tsp. dried parsley

To cold water, add Bisquick and cheese until dough is firm. Using a small scoop, place dough on baking pan lined with baking paper. Bake at 375° for 10 to 12 minutes, until golden brown. While biscuits bake, combine garlic spread ingredients. Brush baked biscuits with the topping.

Jennifer Vander Schaaf

Cheesy Garlic Bread

1 loaf French bread
1/2 c. soft margarine
2 c. white cheese (Parmesan, Romano, Mozzarella or a combo)
1 c. mayonnaise
1 bunch green onion tops, chopped
2 tsp. garlic powder

Cut loaf in half horizontally. Mix rest of ingredients in a bowl. Spread on loaves. Place on cookie sheet and bake at 350° for 7 minutes. Broil 3 minutes more. Cut and serve.
Michelle Bomgaars

Cheesy Garlic Bread

1 loaf French bread
1/2 c. softened margarine
1/3 to 1/2 c. Miracle Whip or salad dressing
1/2 to 1 tsp. garlic salt
Parmesan cheese
Paprika
Parsley

Slice loaf lengthwise. Whip margarine, Miracle Whip and garlic salt. Spread over both halves of bread. Sprinkle cheese, paprika and parsley on top. Bake, uncovered, for 10 minutes at 350°.
Joan Dekker,
Mary Ann Winchell

Bread Machine Garlic Bread

1 c. warm water
1 T. melted butter
1 T. dry milk powder
1 T. sugar
1 1/2 tsp. salt
4 1/2 tsp. parsley
2 tsp. garlic powder
3 c. bread flour
2 tsp. yeast

Place ingredients in bread machine pan in order. Select "Basic White Bread" setting and start.
Michelle Bomgaars

Garlic Bubble Loaf

1/4 c. butter or margarine, melted
1 T. dried parsley flakes
1 tsp. garlic powder
1/4 tsp. garlic salt
1 (1 lb.) loaf frozen white bread dough, thawed

In a bowl, combine butter, parsley, garlic powder and garlic salt. Cut dough into 1-inch pieces; dip into butter mixture. Layer in a greased 5x9x3-inch loaf pan. Cover and let rise until double, about 1 hour. Bake at 350° for 30 minutes, or until golden brown. Yield: 1 loaf.
Mary Ann Winchell

Herb Bread

1 unsliced loaf Vienna or French bread
1 c. soft oleo
1 T. parsley flakes
1/4 tsp. oregano
1/4 tsp. dill weed
1 shake garlic powder

Mix all ingredients, but bread. Cut bread into thick slices. Spread mixture on bread (both sides is great!) Wrap in foil and bake in 375° oven for 15 minutes. Great with steak or spaghetti.
Also works to make it on top shelf of grill.

Teresa Jasper

Olive Garden Breadsticks

1 loaf frozen bread dough, thawed, or 1 batch white bread dough from bread machine
Cooking spray
Garlic powder
Dry oregano (opt.)

Divide dough in 8 to 10 pieces and roll into cigar-shape. Place 3 inches apart on cookie sheets. Let rise for 1 1/2 hours, or until double in size. Lightly spray tops of sticks with cooking spray. Dust with garlic powder and oregano. Bake at 375° for 15 to 20 minutes, or until golden brown.

Michelle Bomgaars

Outback Bread

1 1/2 c. warm water
2 T. butter, softened
1/2 c. honey
2 c. bread flour*
1 2/3 c. wheat flour*
1 T. cocoa
1 T. sugar
2 tsp. instant coffee
1 tsp. salt
2 1/4 tsp. (1 pkg.) yeast

*Also works with all white or all wheat flour.

Step 1: If using a bread machine, put all ingredients in order and set on "Knead". When cycle is done, remove from pan and go to Step 3.

Step 2 (By Hand): Combine dry ingredients. Make a well in the center and add the rest. Slowly mix with spoon until you can handle the dough. Combine by hand, kneading at least 10 minutes. Set dough in covered bowl in a warm place to rise for 1 hour.

Step 3: Punch down and divide into 6 even portions. Form into tubular loaves. (Be sure to use plenty of flour to prevent sticking.) Place loaves in miniature bread pans or on greased cookie sheets. Cover with plastic wrap and set in a warm location to rise for 1 hour, or until doubled.

Step 4: Preheat oven to 350°. Uncover dough to bake for 20 to 24 minutes. Cool 5 minutes and remove from pans. Best when served with lots of butter.

Michelle Bomgaars

Pepperoni Pizza Bread

1 3/8 c. water
3 c. bread flour
2 T. powdered milk
2 T. sugar
1 1/2 tsp. salt
2 T. butter
1/2 c. chopped pepperoni
1/3 c. shredded Mozzarella cheese
1 T. Parmesan cheese
1/3 c. mushrooms
1/4 c. dried, chopped onion
3/4 tsp. garlic powder
2 1/2 tsp. yeast

Place ingredients in bread machine pan. Select "Basic White Bread" setting (usually No. 1). Start.

Michelle Bomgaars

Pretzels

1 (11 oz.) pkg. refrigerated bread sticks
2 T. sugar
1/4 tsp. cinnamon
1 T. margarine or butter

Preheat oven to 350°. Grease a cookie sheet with shortening. Gently pull or roll each breadstick on the countertop to make a rope of dough. Shape each rope into a pretzel. Place pretzels on baking sheet, about 2 inches apart. Baste pretzels with melted margarine and sprinkle with cinnamon and sugar. Bake for 15 to 18 minutes.
Note: Also good with garlic salt.

Janene Van Gorp

Breakfast

Breakfast Oatmeal Snack

1/2 c. melted butter or oleo
3/4 c. brown sugar
2 beaten eggs
3 c. oatmeal
2 tsp. baking powder
1 c. milk

Mix all together. Put into a greased 9x13-inch pan. Bake at 350 for 30 minutes. Serve warm, with syrup.

Julie Leusink

Ranch Granola

8 c. oatmeal
1 c. bran
2 c. almond slices
2 c. coconut
1 c. wheat germ
1/2 c. sesame seeds

1/2 c. brown sugar
1 tsp. cinnamon
2 tsp. vanilla
1 1/4 c. oil
1 1/4 c. honey

Mix the first 8 ingredients together in a large bowl. Stir together the vanilla, oil and honey. Pour the wet ingredients over the dry ingredients and "knead" together with your hands. Pour into a large pan and bake at 250° for 2 hours, stirring occasionally.
Note: I also like to bake it overnight in a 100° oven for breakfast.

Paulette Maassen

Orange French Toast

4 eggs
2/3 c. orange juice
1/3 c. milk
1/4 c. sugar

1 tsp. vanilla
1/8 tsp. nutmeg
8 slices French or Italian bread
1/4 c. butter or oleo

Beat the first 6 ingredients. In a 9x13-inch pan, arrange bread slices. Pour egg mixture over bread and cover. Refrigerate 2 to 24 hours.

To bake, place butter in a 10x15x1-inch pan and place in a preheated oven, just until butter melts. Place bread in a single layer on melted butter. Bake for 20 minutes. Serve immediately, with orange syrup.

Orange Syrup: In a saucepan, combine 1/2 cup butter or oleo, 1/2 cup sugar and 1/3 cup frozen orange juice concentrate. Heat--don't boil. Cool for 10 minutes and beat until slightly thick.

Darlene Kluis

Popeye Toast

Butter a slice of bread on both sides. Cut a circle from the slice with the top of a drinking glass. Place on hot, buttered skillet over low heat. Drop an egg into center. Cook slowly, until egg is set and underside of bread is brown. Turn. Brown other side. Don't forget to brown the cut-out circle.

Emily Maassen

Egg and Broccoli Quiche

6 slices whole-grain bread
2 c. diced ham
3/4 lb. Colby cheese
10 eggs
1 head broccoli
1/2 c. chopped onion
8 oz. Portabello mushrooms, chopped
2 3/4 c. milk
A good squirt of mustard
1 1/4 tsp. salt
4 T. melted butter

Butter an 8x12-inch baking dish. Cube bread and ham; chop up broccoli. Add mushrooms. Combine eggs, milk, salt and mustard. Pour over top of bread mixture. Melt butter and pour over eggs. Bake at 325° for 1 hour. Let stand 10 minutes.

Sandy Holtrop

Egg and Sausage Casserole

6 eggs, slightly beaten
6 slices bread, cubed
1 c. shredded Cheddar cheese
1 tsp. salt
1 tsp. dry mustard
1 (12 oz.) pkg. pork sausage links (or smokies), cooked & cut into pieces
2 c. milk

Mix all ingredients together in a 2-quart casserole. Refrigerate for 4 to 6 hours, or overnight. Cover with plastic wrap or lid. Cook in microwave oven, covered, on 70% POWER LEVEL for 15 to 20 minutes, or until knife inserted in center comes out clean. Serve immediately. Yield: 4 to 6 servings.

Colette Hofmeyer

Buttermilk Pancakes

1 c. flour
1 tsp. baking powder
1/2 tsp. baking soda
1/4 tsp. salt
1 c. buttermilk
1 egg
3 T. vegetable oil

Preheat griddle to 375°. Blend the first 4 ingredients with a wire whisk. (Mixing in a 2-quart measuring pitcher works well.) Add the remaining 3 ingredients. Do not overmix--some small lumps are okay. Fry until bubbles begin popping. Do not press down when frying, or they will lose their fluffiness.

Dee Ann Cleveringa

Chocolate Pancakes

1/2 c. Bisquick
2 T. cocoa
1 T. sugar
1 egg
1/3 c. milk
1 T. vegetable oil

Combine and mix well, until almost smooth. Cook like you would regular pancakes, and serve.
Note: For a unique dessert, top one pancake with a dip of ice cream and drizzle with chocolate syrup. *Michelle Bomgaars*

Great Pancakes

1 c. milk
1 egg, beaten
1/2 tsp. salt
2 T. baking powder
2 T. cooking oil
1 c. sifted flour
2 T. sugar

Mix egg, oil and milk. Sift the dry ingredients and add to the liquids. Add 2 more tablespoons milk and fry on a hot griddle. *Henrietta De Jager, Eunice Koopmans*

Swedish Oatmeal Pancakes

4 c. old-fashioned rolled oats
1 c. flour
2 tsp. baking soda
1/2 tsp. cinnamon
1/4 c. sugar
2 tsp. baking powder
Pinch of salt

Blend in:
1 qt. buttermilk
4 eggs, beaten
1/2 c. melted butter
1 scant T. vanilla

Mix well. Let batter stand for 30 to 45 minutes. Will be thick. Butter griddle; turn when pancake is full of air bubbles and browned lightly.
Carmen (Winchell) Woeltge

Belgian Waffles

2 eggs
2 c. flour
1/4 c. vegetable oil
1 3/4 c. milk
1 T. brown sugar

1 T. white sugar
4 tsp. baking powder
1/4 tsp. salt
2 tsp. vanilla

Beat eggs on high until airy. Add in white sugar, brown sugar, salt, vanilla, oil and milk. Slowly add in the flour and baking powder. Beat on high until smooth.

Jen Vlietstra

Everyday Waffles

1 3/4 c. flour
1/2 tsp. salt
3 tsp. baking powder
2 beaten egg yolks

1 1/4 c. milk
1/2 c. oil
2 beaten-stiff egg whites

Sift dry ingredients. Combine egg yolks, milk and oil; stir into dry ingredients. Fold in stiffly-beaten egg whites. Bake in hot waffle iron. When steam no longer appears, the waffle is done. Yield: approximately 8 waffles.

Evelyn De Vries

Waffles

2 eggs
2 c. milk
2 tsp. sugar
2 c. flour

2 tsp. baking powder
1 tsp. salt
2 T. melted butter

Beat all ingredients together. Pour into waffle iron.

Marcia Cleveringa

Waffles

Sift together:
3 c. flour	1 tsp. salt
4 tsp. baking powder	2 tsp. sugar

Add:
2/3 c. oil	2 c. milk
4 eggs	

Stir by hand until all ingredients are mixed. Will be lumpy. Transfer to a blender and blend on high until all lumps are gone. Bake in preheated waffle iron. Yield: 5 to 6 full-size, 4-section waffles.

Eunice Koopmans

Cakes, Frostings & Candies

Cakes

Good Old-Fashioned Angel Food Cake

1 2/3 c. egg whites
1 c. + 2 T. sifted cake flour
3/4 c. sifted sugar
1/2 tsp. salt
1 1/2 tsp. cream of tartar
1 tsp. vanilla
3/4 tsp. almond extract
1 c. sifted sugar

    Have egg whites at room temperature. Sift cake flour with 3/4 cup sugar 5 times. Beat the egg whites and salt in a large mixer bowl at high speed until foamy. Add cream of tartar; beat until whites are stiff and stand in peaks. Rapidly sprinkle, while beating, the 1 cup sugar. Beat only until sugar is blended; scrape bowl toward beaters, then up and over with rubber spatula. Add extracts. Turn mixer speed to low. Sprinkle in sifted flour evenly and quickly, beating just to blend. <u>Gently</u> push into ungreased angel food pan. Cut through batter with spatula. Bake at 350° for 35 minutes. Remove from oven and immediately invert on a funnel for 1 hour.

Lori Van Gorp

Apple Dump Cake

2 eggs, beaten
1 c. oil
2 c. sugar
2 c. flour
1 c. raisins
1 c. chopped nuts
2 tsp. baking soda
1 tsp. cinnamon
1 tsp. salt
1 tsp. vanilla
1 can apple pie filling

    Dump all ingredients into a large bowl and beat well (it will be thick). Fold in one can apple pie filing. Bake in a greased and floured 9x13-inch pan for 1 hour at 350°. Serve with Cool Whip or ice cream.

Edith Kuiken

Carrot Cake

2 c. flour
2 1/2 tsp. baking soda
2 tsp. cinnamon
1 tsp. salt
1 c. oil
2 c. sugar
3 eggs
1 (8 oz.) can crushed pineapple in juice
2 c. grated carrot
1 c. flaked coconut
1/2 c. chopped nuts

Mix flour, baking soda, cinnamon and salt. Beat oil, sugar and eggs thoroughly. Add dry ingredients. Beat until smooth. Add pineapple, carrots, coconut and nuts. Pour into a greased 9x13-inch pan. Bake at 350° for 50 to 60 minutes. Cool.

FROSTING: Blend:
1 (3 oz.) pkg. cream cheese
3/4 stick oleo
1 tsp. milk
1 tsp. vanilla
1 3/4 c. powdered sugar

Beat until smooth and creamy. Put on cake.

Diane Munro

Creamy Coconut Cake

1 box yellow cake mix
2 eggs, beaten
1/2 c. oil
1 1/2 c. water
1 1/2 c. coconut
3/4 c. cream of coconut, or 1/2 can (found in liquor department of store)

FROSTING:
1 (8 oz.) ctn. Cool Whip
1 c. coconut

Mix cake mix, eggs, oil, water and coconut. Pour into a greased 9x13-inch pan. Bake at 350° for 30 minutes, or until cake springs back when touched in the center. Poke holes on top of cake (wooden spoon handle works good) and pour cream of coconut over cake. Let cool. Frost with Cool Whip and coconut mixture. Refrigerate leftovers, or freeze.

Joyce Baker,
Gert Sjaarda

Dump Cake

1 can crushed pineapple
1 can applesauce
1 pkg. yellow cake mix
1/2 c. brown sugar
3/4 c. melted oleo
1 c. nutmeats

Grease a 9x13-inch pan. Put pineapple in the bottom of pan, then applesauce over that. Sprinkle 1/2 cup brown sugar over fruit. Add the yellow cake mix. Pour the melted oleo over the cake mix and sprinkle with chopped nuts. Bake at 350° for 30 to 35 minutes.

Gert Sjaarda

Earthquake Cake

1 1/2 c. pecans, chopped
3 oz. coconut
1 pkg. German chocolate cake mix
1/2 c. butter
1 (8 oz.) pkg. cream cheese
1 lb. powdered sugar

Grease a 9x13-inch pan. Sprinkle pecans in bottom of pan. Sprinkle coconut over pecans. Prepare cake mix according to directions. Pour over pecans and coconut. Melt butter and cream cheese together. Add powdered sugar; mix well. Pour mixture over cake batter. Bake at 350° for 45 minutes, or until done.

Joyce Baker

Easy Cake
(Diabetic)

1 (1-Step) Pillsbury angel food cake mix
1 (20 oz.) can crushed pineapple, undrained

Oil the bottom of a 9x13-inch pan. In a large bowl, mix the cake mix and pineapple, juice and all, with a wire whip. Pour into pan. Bake for 40 minutes in a 350° oven. Check and make sure a toothpick in the center comes out clean. Serve with lite Cool Whip.

Gert Sjaarda

Lemon Cake Supreme

1 white cake mix
1 can lemon pie filling
1 ctn. Cool Whip

Mix and bake white cake mix, as directed on the package. When cool, spread with 1 can lemon pie filling. Top with Cool Whip. Keep refrigerated.

Elvera Van Horssen

Luscious Lemon Delight Cake

1 box lemon cake with pudding mix
1 1/2 c. confectioner's sugar
1 (6 oz.) can frozen lemonade

ICING:
1 (3 oz.) box lemon instant pudding
1 lg. can crushed pineapple
1 (8 oz.) ctn. whipped topping, or
1 c. heavy cream, whipped

Bake lemon cake according to package directions. Combine confectioners' sugar with thawed lemonade concentrate. When cake is done, remove from oven and poke holes all over cake with a fork. Pour lemonade mixture over cake and bake an additional 5 minutes.

Icing: When cake has cooled, combine lemon instant pudding powder with crushed pineapple and juice. Fold in whipped cream. Ice cake and keep refrigerated until served. Garnish with lemon zest, if desired.

Clarine Van Klompenburg

Mandarin Orange Cake

1 white or yellow cake mix
4 eggs
1/2 c. vegetable oil
1 can mandarin oranges & juice

ICING:
1 (No. 16) can crushed pineapple
1 lg. pkg. instant vanilla pudding mix
1 (8 oz.) ctn. whipped topping, or
1 c. heavy cream, whipped

Preheat oven to 350°. Grease 2 (9-inch) cake pans. Combine cake ingredients (you may want to cut up mandarin oranges); bake for 40 minutes, or until cake tests done. Cool on a rack.

Icing: Combine crushed pineapple and juice with pudding mix. Fold in whipped topping. Ice cake and refrigerate until used.

Clarine Van Klompenburg

Moon Cake

1 c. water
1/2 c. butter
1 c. flour
4 eggs
2 sm. pkg, vanilla instant pudding

8 oz. cream cheese
Chocolate sauce
Chopped nuts
Whipped cream

Mix water and butter. Bring to a boil. Add flour, all at once, and stir rapidly on low heat until mixture forms a ball. Will take about 3 minutes. Remove from heat and cool 5 minutes. Beat in eggs, one at a time, beating well with a spoon or mixer. Spread on ungreased 11x15-inch cookie sheet. Bake at 400° for 28 to 30 minutes. Cool. Will look like moon's surface. Do not prick- -leave. Cool as is.

Mix pudding according to directions. Beat in cream cheese. Blend well and spread on crust. Refrigerate for 20 minutes. Top with whipped cream. Drizzle with chocolate sauce. Sprinkle with chopped nuts.

Marietta VanDer Weide

Bundt Pudding Cake

NUT MIXTURE:
1/4 c. sugar

1/2 c. nuts
1 tsp. cinnamon

Combine and set aside.

1 box yellow cake mix with
   pudding in the mix (or add
   instant vanilla pudding)
3/4 c. oil

4 eggs
1 tsp. butternut extract
3/4 c. water
1 tsp. vanilla

Grease bundt pan. Combine cake mix, oil and water. Mix well. Add eggs, one at a time. Beat for 8 minutes and stir a few times. Add flavoring toward end of beating period. Layer batter and nut mixture, beginning and ending with batter. Bake at 350° for 35 to 40 minutes. Cool and add glaze.

GLAZE:
1 c. powdered sugar
1/2 tsp. butternut flavoring

3 T. milk
1/2 tsp. vanilla

Lois Klein

Blueberry Coffeecake

2 boxes blueberry muffin mix
1 (12 oz.) can crushed pineapple
2 eggs
1 c. coconut
1/2 c. brown sugar
2 T. flour
4 T. melted butter

Mix together dry blueberry muffin mix; add 2 eggs and crushed pineapple with the juice. Spread in a greased 9x13-inch cake pan. In a bowl, mix together coconut, brown sugar, flour and melted butter. Top the cake with the crumble mixture and bake according to temperature and time directions on box.

Jen Vlietstra

Butterbrickle Coffeecake

2 c. brown sugar
2 c. flour
1/4 c. oleo
1 slightly-beaten egg
1 c. buttermilk
1 tsp. baking soda
Pinch of salt
1 tsp. vanilla
1/2 c. nuts (opt.)

Combine sugar, flour and oleo. Mix until crumbly. Reserve 1 cup of this. Add the remaining ingredients to egg and mix with first mixture. Pour into a greased 9x13-inch pan. Sprinkle with 1 cup of topping (reserved crumbs). Break up 5 or 6 butterbrickle bars. Sprinkle over top (also nuts, if using). Bake at 350° for 30 minutes.

Elaine Vander Broek,
Marietta VanDer Weide

Coffeecake

1 butter pecan cake mix
8 oz. instant vanilla pudding
4 eggs
3/4 c. oil
3/4 c. water
1 tsp. vanilla

TOPPING:
2 T. soft butter
1/2 c. brown sugar
1 tsp. cinnamon
2 T. flour

Beat cake mixture 2 minutes and put into a 9x13-inch pan. Mix topping and crumble on top of cake. Bake for 30 to 35 minutes at 350°. Serve warm or cold, topped with whipped cream.

Helen Oolman

Coffeecake

1 c. sugar
2 c. flour
1 can pie filling
1 tsp. baking powder
1/4 tsp. salt
1 c. cooking oil
4 eggs

Cream sugar, oil and eggs. Add flour, baking powder and salt. Put 1/2 of batter into a greased 9x13-inch pan, then pie filling and the rest of batter. Sprinkle with sugar and cinnamon. Bake for 40 minutes in 325° oven. When done, drizzle with powdered sugar frosting.

Dawn Beukelman

Coffeecake

1 1/2 c. brown sugar
1 c. chopped nuts
1 tsp. cinnamon
2 c. flour
1 c. sugar
2 tsp. baking powder
1 tsp. salt
1 pkg. instant vanilla pudding
4 eggs
1 pkg. instant butterscotch pudding
1 c. water
3/4 c. oil
1 tsp. vanilla

Mix brown sugar, nuts and cinnamon; set aside. In a large bowl, mix all of the rest of the ingredients. Beat for 2 minutes. Put 1/2 into a 9x13-inch greased pan, then 1/2 of topping; repeat. Bake at 350° for 40 minutes, plus.

Jonna Wierda

Coffeecake and Glaze

1 c. brown sugar
2 T. flour
2 tsp. cinnamon
2 T. soft oleo
1/2 c. nuts, chopped

GLAZE:
1 c. powdered sugar
1 T. oil
2 eggs
1 yellow cake mix (no pudding in mix)
1 (16 oz.) can vanilla pudding

1 T. white corn syrup
1 T. + 2 tsp. hot water
1/4 tsp. vanilla

Mix the first 5 ingredients until crumbly. Set aside. Beat eggs very well. Set aside. Beat cake mix and pudding for 2 minutes. Add beaten eggs slowly and mix well. Put 1/2 of batter into a greased 9x13-inch pan. Sprinkle about 2/3 of crumbly mix on top. Add remaining cake batter and sprinkle the rest of crumbly mixture on top. Bake at 350° for 30 to 35 minutes. Cool; mix ingredients of glaze and pour over cake.

Darlene Kluis

Coconut Coffeecake

1 white cake mix without pudding
1 sm. pkg. coconut pudding (instant)
1 c. water
1/2 c. oil
1 egg
1 tsp. vanilla
1 tsp. butter flavoring (opt.)

Put all ingredients in a mixing bowl and beat for 8 minutes. Put 1/2 of batter into a greased 9x13-inch pan.
Sprinkle with the following mixture:

1/2 c. sugar
1/2 tsp. cinnamon
1/2 c. chopped pecans

Top with the remaining batter and sprinkle with remaining sugar mixture. Bake for 30 minutes at 350°. Cool and drizzle with powdered sugar icing.

Linda Van Regenmorter

Melissa's Coffeecake

1 yellow cake mix
1 sm. pkg. instant vanilla pudding
2 T. vegetable oil
1 1/3 c. water
2 eggs

STREUSEL:
1 c. flour
1 c. brown sugar
4 tsp. cinnamon
6 T. butter, melted

Preheat oven to 350°. Grease a 9x13-inch pan. In a large bowl, beat the first 5 ingredients at medium speed for 2 minutes. Spread 3/4 of batter into a greased 9x13-inch pan. Sprinkle with 2/3 of streusel. Spread remaining batter and sprinkle remaining streusel. Bake at 350° for 40 to 50 minutes.

Teresa Jasper

Raspberry Coffeecake

2 c. Bisquick
1 (3 oz.) pkg. cream cheese
1/4 c. margarine
1/3 c. milk
1/2 c. raspberry jam

Cut margarine and cream cheese into Bisquick; stir in milk. Knead dough 8 to 10 strokes. On waxed paper, roll out to an 8x12-inch rectangle. Turn onto a greased cookie sheet. Spread jam down the center of dough. Make 2 1/2-inch-long cuts at 1-inch intervals on each side of jam. Fold strips crisscross over filling. Press to seal. Bake at 425° for 12 to 15 minutes. Drizzle with powdered sugar icing while warm.

Tammy Sneller

Rhubarb Coffeecake

1/2 c. shortening
1 1/2 c. shortening
1 egg
2 c. flour

1/2 tsp. baking soda
1 c. buttermilk or sour milk
1 1/2 c. rhubarb

Cream shortening and sugar. Beat in egg. Mix dry ingredients together and add alternately with buttermilk. Beat well and fold in rhubarb. Bake at 350° for 30 minutes in a 9x13-inch pan. Drizzle with powdered sugar frosting while warm.

Pam Jeltema

Rhubarb Coffeecake

1 1/2 c. packed brown sugar
1/2 c. oil
1 egg
2 c. flour

1 tsp. baking soda
1/2 tsp. salt
1 c. sour cream
1 1/2 c. chopped rhubarb

TOPPING:
1/4 c. sugar
1/4 c. brown sugar

1/2 c. chopped walnuts
1 T. oleo or butter
1 tsp. cinnamon

Cream brown sugar and oil. Add egg. Add flour, baking soda, salt and sour cream. Fold in rhubarb. Spread in a 9x13x2-inch greased pan.
Combine all topping ingredients. Sprinkle over batter. Bake at 350° for 45 to 50 minutes. Cool on wire rack.

Darlene Wichers

Strawberry-Rhubarb Coffeecake

1 pkg. Betty Crocker SuperMoist
  yellow cake
1 c. packed brown sugar
3/4 c. chopped walnuts (pecans)
2 T. oleo

2 eggs
1 c. sour cream
2 c. chopped rhubarb
2 c. sliced strawberries

Heat oven to 350°. Take 2/3 cup dry cake mix, brown sugar, walnuts and oleo; mix together until crumbly. Set aside. Beat eggs slightly in a large bowl with a fork. Add sour cream, then add remaining dry cake mix. Mix together and add rhubarb--batter will be thick. Spread 1/2 of batter into a 9x13-inch pan (grease and flour); put sliced strawberries, then the rest of batter on top. Sprinkle reserved topping over this. Bake for 40 to 50 minutes. Drizzle with your favorite glaze while warm.

Darlene Kluis

Sour Cream Coffeecake

TOPPING:
1/3 c. packed brown sugar
1/4 c. sugar
2 tsp. ground cinnamon

CAKE:
1/2 c. butter, softened
1 c. sugar
1 c. sour cream
1 tsp. vanilla
2 Eggs
2 c. flour
1 tsp. baking powder
1 tsp. baking soda
1/4 tsp. salt

Combine topping ingredients; set aside. For cake, cream butter and sugar in a mixing bowl. Add eggs, sour cream and vanilla; mix well. Combine flour, baking powder, baking soda and salt. Add to creamed mixture; beat until combined. Pour 1/2 of the batter into a 9x13-inch baking pan. Sprinkle with 1/2 of topping. Add remaining batter and sprinkle with remaining topping. Bake at 325° for 35 minutes.

Priscilla Jansma

Chocolate Cheese Cupcakes

1 1/2 c. flour
1 c. sugar
1/4 c. cocoa
1/4 tsp. salt
1 tsp. baking soda

1 c. water
5 T. oil
1 T. vinegar
1 tsp. vanilla

FILLING:
8 oz. cream cheese
1/3 c. sugar
16 oz. chocolate chips
1 egg

Sift together dry ingredients. In a different bowl, beat water, oil, vinegar and vanilla. Add liquids to dry ingredients, mixing until smooth. Fill 18 paper-lined cupcake tins 1/2-full. Top each with 1 tablespoon of filling. Bake at 350° for 25 minutes.

Dorene Vander Zwaag

Cupcakes

8 oz. cream cheese
1 egg
1/3 c. sugar
1/8 tsp. salt
1 c. semi-sweet chocolate chips
2 1/4 c. flour
3/4 tsp. salt
1 1/2 c. sugar
1 1/2 tsp. baking soda
6 T. cocoa
1 1/2 tsp. vanilla
1/2 c. oil
1 1/2 c. water
1 1/2 tsp. vinegar

Mix cream cheese, egg, 1/3 cup sugar and salt. Add chocolate chips. In a separate bowl, mix the remaining ingredients. Fill cupcake papers just over half-full with chocolate mixture. Drop 1 teaspoon of the first mixture into batter. Bake at 350° for 25 minutes. Yield: 2 dozen.

Judy Vlietstra

Chocolate Swirl Cake

1 pkg. chocolate cake mix
1 (8 oz.) pkg. cream cheese
1 egg
1/2 c. sugar
1/2 c. chocolate chips

Preheat oven to 350°. Grease a jellyroll pan. Prepare cake mix as directed on box. Pour into pan. Mix cream cheese, egg and sugar. Drop by spoonful onto batter. Cut through batter with a knife for a marble effect. Sprinkle with chocolate chips. Bake for 25 to 30 minutes. Cool. Frost with chocolate frosting.

BJ De Weerd

Fudge Marble Pound Cake

1 pkg. Duncan Hines Deluxe fudge marble cake mix
1 (4-serving) pkg. vanilla instant pudding
1/3 c. Crisco oil
1 c. water
4 eggs

Preheat oven to 350°. Generously grease, and then flour 2 loaf pans. Blend all ingredients, except small packet, in a large bowl; beat at medium speed for 2 minutes. Pour 3/4 of batter into baking pan. Blend contents of small packet into remaining batter. Spoon dark batter here and there over light batter. Pull knife through batter in wide curves. Bake at 350° for 45 minutes. Check cake with a toothpick.

Linda Mellema

Never-Fail Chocolate Cake

1/4 c. oleo
1/4 c. Crisco
1/2 c. cocoa
2 tsp. baking soda
2 c. flour
3/4 c. hot water
1 tsp. vanilla
2 eggs
1 c. sour milk

Cream all together with mixer, in order given. Bake in 3 layer pans, or a 9x13-inch greased pan, for 35 minutes in 350° oven.
Note: Milk can be made sour with a little vinegar.
If I make layers, I use this for filling and frosting:

WHIPPED CREAM FROSTING:
3/4 c. oleo
3/4 c. Crisco
1 1/2 c. sugar
2 egg yolks
1 tsp. vanilla

Takes an electric mixer. <u>Slowly</u> add 1/2 to 3/4 cup milk. This cake will need to be kept in the refrigerator.
Wilma Vander Stelt

Microwave Chocolate Cake

1/2 c. sugar
1 sm. egg
Scant 1/4 c. oil
1/8 c. cocoa
Scant 1/4 c. milk
1/2 + 1/8 c. flour
1/2 tsp. baking soda
1/8 tsp. salt
1/8 tsp. vanilla
1/4 c. hot water

Bake at FULL POWER for 4 minutes in a 5 1/2 x 7 x 2-inch ungreased pan, in microwave. First bake for 2 minutes; turn pan 1/4-way. Bake for 1 minute. Turn another 1/4-way, and bake 1 more minute. It will be very uneven and moist on top. Cool and frost.
It's ugly looking, but it tastes delicious.
Darlene Wichers

Red Earth Cake

1/2 c. butter
2 c. sugar
2 c. flour
2 eggs, beaten
1/2 c. buttermilk
3 T. cocoa
1 tsp. salt
1 tsp. baking soda
1 c. boiling water
3 T. red food coloring

Cream butter and sugar. Add eggs and buttermilk. Sift dry ingredients and add to other mixture. Dissolve baking soda in boiling water. Add food coloring and mix well. Pour into a 9x13-inch pan. Bake at 350° for 35 minutes.
Marietta VanDer Weide

Snack-Attack Chocolate Cake

2 c. flour
2 c. sugar
1 c. butter
4 T. cocoa
1 c. water

1/2 c. buttermilk
2 eggs, slightly beaten
1 tsp. baking soda
1 tsp. vanilla

FROSTING:
1/2 c. butter
4 T. cocoa
5 T. buttermilk

4 c. powdered sugar
1 tsp. vanilla
1 c. walnuts (opt.)

Preheat oven to 400°. Grease a 9x13-inch pan. Sift flour and sugar. In a saucepan, over high heat, bring butter, cocoa and water to a boil. Pour over sugar and flour mixture. Mix well. Add buttermilk, eggs, baking soda and vanilla to flour mixture; mix well. Bake for 25 minutes at 400°.
Frosting: Bring butter, cocoa and buttermilk to a boil. Remove from heat. Add sugar, vanilla and walnuts; beat. While frosting is still warm, spread on cooled cake.

Helen Oolman

Strawberry Cream Cake Roll

4 eggs
1 tsp. vanilla
3/4 c. sugar

3/4 c. sifted cake flour
1 tsp. baking powder
1/4 tsp. salt

CREAM FILLING:
1 c. whipping cream
1/4 c. sugar
1/2 tsp. vanilla

2 c. frozen or fresh strawberries
Additional strawberries & whipping cream

In a mixing bowl, beat eggs with vanilla on high speed with an electric mixer for 5 minutes, or until lemon-colored. Gradually add sugar, beating until dissolved. Combine flour, baking powder and salt. Fold gently into egg mixture, just until combined. Pour into a greased and waxed-paper-lined jellyroll pan. Spread batter evenly over pan. Bake at 375° for 10 to 12 minutes, or until light brown. Turn out onto a cloth that has been sprinkled with powdered sugar. Peel paper off cake; roll up cloth and cake. Cool.
Filling: Whip cream, sugar and vanilla. Unroll cake and spread filling over it. Sprinkle with strawberries. Roll up cake and chill 2 hours before serving. Sprinkle with powdered sugar. Garnish with strawberries and whipped cream.

Jennifer (De Jager) Leusink

Texas Sheet Cake

2 c. flour
2 c. sugar
1 stick oleo
4 T. cocoa
1/2 c. Crisco
1 c. water
2 eggs
1 tsp. vanilla
1/2 c. sour milk or buttermilk
1 tsp. baking soda

Mix flour and sugar in a bowl. In a saucepan, mix oleo, cocoa, Crisco and water; bring to a boil. Pour over flour and sugar. Mix baking soda with sour milk; add to other ingredients, along with eggs and vanilla. Pour into a greased 12 x 18-inch pan; bake for 20 minutes in 400° oven. Mix frosting before cake is done; frost immediately when cake is out of the oven.

FROSTING:
1/3 c. milk
1/2 c. oleo
3 T. cocoa

Mix and bring to a boil. Take off heat.
Add:
2 1/2 c. powdered sugar   1 tsp. vanilla

Note: Coconut or nuts may be added.

Marlene Van Beek

Wacky Cake

3 c. flour
2 c. sugar
2 tsp. baking soda
1 tsp. salt
6 T. cocoa
3 T. vinegar
3/4 c. oil
2 c. cold water
2 tsp. vanilla

Sift dry ingredients together and make 3 wells in the top. Mix oil and vinegar together; pour into holes. Pour water and vanilla over top. Beat by hand until smooth. Bake in a greased 9x13-inch pan at 350° for 35 minutes. Frost.

Jan Budden

Yellow Cake with Pineapple Frosting

1 box yellow or white cake mix
   (one without pudding in it)
1 box instant vanilla pudding mix
1 c. water
1/2 c. oil
3 eggs

Mix for 4 minutes and bake at 350° for 45 to 50 minutes, in a 9x13-inch pan. Cool.

TOPPING:
1 (8 3/4 oz.) can crushed pineapple
1 pkg. vanilla pudding (cook type)
2 egg yolks
2 T. sugar
1 1/4 c. pineapple juice (or use juice & water to make amount)
1/2 c. coconut (opt.)

Combine sugar and pudding. Add juice and water and egg yolks; bring to a full boil. Remove from heat; add pineapple and coconut. Cool, then add 1 1/2 cups of Cool Whip. Sprinkle with a little more coconut.

Edith Kuiken

Jelly Roll Deluxe

1 c. flour
1 tsp. baking powder
3 eggs
1/4 tsp. salt
1 c. sugar
1 tsp. vanilla
2 T. shortening
1/3 c. hot milk

FILLING:
2 c. powdered sugar
1/4 c. flour
1 tsp. vanilla
3 T. cocoa
1/2 c. Crisco
1/4 c. milk
Pinch of salt

Beat eggs with salt until fluffy. Add sugar and vanilla. Fold in flour and baking powder. Melt shortening in hot milk and blend quickly into first mixture. Pour into a well-greased jellyroll pan. Bake at 375° for 15 minutes. Invert onto towel sprinkled with powdered sugar. Cool a few seconds and roll up.
Filling: Mix all ingredients well and beat on medium speed until fluffy and smooth. If too thick, add a little more milk. Unroll cake; spread on filling and reroll cake.

Tammy Sneller

Easy Rhubarb Cake

1 yellow cake mix
5 c. rhubarb, chopped
1 1/3 c. sugar
1 c. cream

Mix cake according to package directions. Pour into a greased 9x13-inch pan. Mix together rhubarb and sugar; place over cake mixture. Pour cream over all. Bake at 350° for 55 minutes.

Lynn Herzog

Rhubarb Cake

1 yellow cake mix
3 c. cut-up rhubarb
1 1/2 c. sugar
1 pt. whipping cream (2 sm. ctn.)

Mix cake mix according to directions. Put into a greased and floured 9x13-inch pan. Spread rhubarb on top. Sprinkle sugar on top. Pour cream over the top. Bake at 350° for 1 hour. Top with Cool Whip or ice cream.

Wanda Hofmeyer

Rhubarb Cake

4 c. rhubarb
1 c. sugar
1 (3 oz.) box strawberry Jello
1 box cake mix (white)
1/3 c. melted butter
1 c. water

Place rhubarb in a 9x13-inch pan. Sprinkle sugar over rhubarb. Sprinkle dry Jello over rhubarb. Spread dry cake mix over rhubarb. Pour melted butter over cake mix. Pour water over mixture. Bake for 45 to 60 minutes at 350°.

Wanda Hofmeyer

♥ Sweet, Tart Rhubarb Cake
(Diabetic)

1 box yellow cake mix*
1 box vanilla pudding* (sugar-free for less sugar)
4 c. rhubarb, cut up

*Or use extra-moist yellow cake mix.

Mix cake mix according to recipe on box, with vanilla pudding mix, in a large bowl. Stir in rhubarb. Put into a 9x13-inch glass cake pan. (Glass if going to be in pan more than one day.) Bake at 325° for 45 to 60 minutes, or until golden.

David Koopmans

Confetti Cake

1 1/4 c. flour
3/4 c. sugar
1 1/4 tsp. baking powder
1/4 tsp. salt
2 T. multi-colored decorating candies
3/4 c. milk
1/3 c. softened margarine or butter
1 tsp. vanilla
1 egg

Preheat oven to 375°. Put flour, sugar, baking powder and salt in a large bowl and mix. Add milk, margarine, vanilla and egg; mix. Add decorating candies. If making cupcakes, bake for 20 minutes. If making a 9x9-inch cake, bake for 25 to 30 minutes.

Janene Van Gorp

Lazy Daisy Cake

1 c. sugar
2 eggs
1 c. flour
1 tsp. baking powder
1/4 tsp. salt
1/2 c. milk
1 T. butter

Whip sugar and eggs; add flour and baking powder. Heat milk and butter; add to above mixture. Bake at 350°, in a 9x13-inch pan.

Mary Stallbaum

♥ Poke-and-Pour Cake
(Diabetic)

1 pkg. white cake mix
1 (4-serving-size) pkg. sugar-free strawberry Jello
1 (8 oz.) ctn. Cool Whip

Mix cake according to package directions. Pour into a 9x13-inch pan. Bake according to directions. While cake is baking, make the Jello according to package directions. When cake is done, immediately poke holes in cake, about every inch, using the handle of a wooden spoon. Pour Jello all over cake. Cool cake and frost with Cool Whip.

Ronald De Jager

Scripture Cake

1 c. Judges V:25
3 c. I Kings IV:22
3 c. Jeremiah VI:20
2 c. I Samuel XXV:12
2 c. I Samuel XXX:12
1 c. Genesis XXIV:17

1 c. Genesis XVIII:11
6 Isaiah X:14
1 T. Exodus XVI:21
Pinch of Leviticus II:13
I Kings X:10, to taste

Method: Proverbs XXIII:14.

Note: Use the ingredients found in the scripture passages. This recipe was originally published in the American Reformed Church Cookbook, Maurice, IA (1907-1945). It was later published in a Maurice First Reformed Cookbook in the 1950's.

John E. Vander Stelt

♥ Sugarless Cake
(Diabetic)

2 c. water
1 c. dates, cut up

1 c. prunes, cut up
1 1/2 c. raisins

Bring to a boil; stir and let cool.
Add:

1 c. oleo
6 eggs
2 tsp. baking soda
1 c. nutmeats
1/2 c. vegetable oil

2 tsp. vanilla
1/2 tsp. salt
1 tsp. cinnamon
2 c. flour
1/2 c. crushed pineapple & juice

Mix all well and bake on a cookie sheet at 350° for 20 to 25 minutes. Watch very closely. <u>Do not</u> overbake, as it will get very dry.

Edith Kuiken

Frostings

Easy Caramel Frosting

1/2 c. butter
1 c. brown sugar

1/4 c. milk
1 3/4 to 2 c. powdered sugar

Melt butter; add firmly-packed brown sugar. Cook over low heat for 2 minutes, stirring constantly. Add 1/4 cup milk and continue to cook and stir until mixture boils. Remove from heat. Cool and add powdered sugar gradually, until right thickness to spread.

Mary Stallbaum

Never-Fail Frosting

3 1/2 c. powdered sugar
1/2 c. oleo
2 egg whites
Pinch of salt
1 tsp. vanilla

Cream together 1/2 cup powdered sugar and oleo; beat egg whites. Add egg whites and the remainder of sugar to the vanilla. Beat until smooth.

Mrs. Al Dekker

Candies

Almond Toffee Crunch

1 1/3 c. sugar
1 c. margarine or butter
1 T. light corn syrup
1 tsp. vanilla
1/2 c. semi-sweet chocolate pieces
1/4 c. slivered almonds, finely chopped

In a heavy 2-quart pan over medium heat, beat sugar, margarine, corn syrup, vanilla and 2 tablespoons water to boiling, stirring constantly. Continue stirring frequently, until mixture reaches 300°, about 20 minutes. Immediately pour evenly onto an ungreased, large cookie sheet. Sprinkle chocolate pieces over; spread as it melts. Sprinkle with almonds; let cool. Break in pieces.

Emily Maassen

Chocolate Mints

1 can Sweetened condensed milk
2 (7.3 oz.) Hershey's milk chocolate bars
2 sq. unsweetened chocolate
1 tsp. peppermint extract
1 T. margarine

Melt milk and chocolates over medium heat. Remove from heat; stir in extract and margarine. Drop by teaspoon onto waxed paper and refrigerate.

Marlys Lenters

Caramels

2 c. white sugar
2 c. white corn syrup
Pinch of salt
2 c. whipping cream
1/4 lb. real butter
1 tsp. vanilla

Combine sugar, syrup and salt. Bring to a fast boil and cook to 245° on candy thermometer. Slowly pour in cream, and add butter, a small amount at a time. Do not let mixture boil. After adding cream and butter, heat to 242° and add vanilla. Remove from stove and pour into a buttered 9x14-inch glass pan. Do not scrape pan when pouring into glass pan. After sugar and syrup boils, <u>do not</u> stir mixture again.

Linda (Baker) Boone

Coconut Candy

1/2 c. oleo, softened
1 lb. powdered sugar
1/2 c. sweetened condensed milk
14 oz. coconut
1 tsp. vanilla

Mix together and flatten in a 9x13-inch pan. Refrigerate. When chilled, cut into squares (or make into balls), and dip in melted chocolate chips with a little paraffin wax added.

Dawn Beukelman

The glory of every morning is that it offers us a chance to begin again.

Chocolate-Caramel Snicker Candy

FIRST LAYER:
1 c. (6 oz.) milk chocolate chips
1/4 c. butterscotch chips
1/4 c. creamy peanut butter

FILLING:
1 c. sugar
1/4 c. butter or margarine
1/4 c. evaporated milk
1 1/2 c. marshmallow creme
1/4 c. creamy peanut butter
1 tsp. vanilla extract
1 1/2 c. salted peanuts, chopped

CARAMEL LAYER:
1 (14 oz.) pkg. caramels
1/4 c. whipping cream

ICING:
1 c. (6 oz.) milk chocolate chips
1/4 c. butterscotch chips
1/4 c. creamy peanut butter

First Layer: Combine in a small saucepan. Stir over low heat until melted and smooth. Spread onto the bottom of a lightly-greased 9x13-inch pan. Refrigerate until set.

Filling: Melt butter in a heavy saucepan over medium-high heat. Add sugar and milk. Bring to a boil. Boil and stir for 5 minutes. Remove from heat. Stir in marshmallow creme, peanut butter and vanilla. Add chopped peanuts. Spread over first layer. Refrigerate until set.

Caramel Layer: Combine the caramels and cream in saucepan. Stir over low heat until melted and smooth. Spread over filling. Refrigerate until set.

Icing: In another saucepan, combine chips and peanut butter; stir over low heat until melted and smooth. Pour over caramel layer.

Refrigerate for at least 1 hour. Cut into 1-inch squares. Store in refrigerator. Yield: 8 dozen.

Chris Van Beek

Fantasy Fudge

3 c. sugar
3/4 c. margarine
2/3 c. (5 1/3 oz. can) evaporated milk
2 c. (12 oz.) chocolate chips
1 (7 oz.) jar marshmallow creme
1 tsp. vanilla
1 c. nuts

Combine sugar, oleo and milk in a 2-quart glass bowl. Microwave, uncovered, on HIGH for 5 minutes, or until mixture starts to boil. Stir once. Microwave, uncovered, on HIGH for 5 minutes. Stir in chocolate chips until smooth. Blend in marshmallow creme and vanilla. Stir in nuts. Pour into a buttered 9x13-inch pan. Cool until set, and then cut.

Joyce Baker

Peanut Brittle

1 c. sugar
1 c. raw Spanish peanuts
1/2 c. white syrup
Pinch of salt

Microwave for 4 minutes on HIGH; stir. Microwave for 4 minutes, stirring frequently.
Add:
2 T. butter
1 tsp. vanilla

Stir until butter is melted. Cook 2 minutes on HIGH. Stir in 1 teaspoon baking soda and spread on a greased pizza or 9x13-inch pan.

Joyce Baker

Peanut Butter Balls

3 c. powdered sugar
9 T. oleo
Dash of salt
2 tsp. vanilla
1 1/2 c. nuts (opt.)
2 c. peanut butter

Mix and form into balls. Chill.
Melt 1 (12-ounce) package chocolate chips and 1/4 bar paraffin wax (quite thin). Dip chilled peanut butter balls into chocolate mixture. Put onto waxed paper and chill again. Yield: about 60.

Winova Van Regenmorter

Peanut Butter Balls

1 c. butter
1 lb. powdered sugar (approx. 3 1/2 c.)
2 c. peanut butter
1 tsp. vanilla
1 (12 oz.) pkg. chocolate chips
1/2 bar paraffin wax

Mix butter, powdered sugar, peanut butter and vanilla. Roll into balls and drop onto waxed paper; freeze.
Melt wax and stir in chocolate chips until all is melted. With toothpicks, dip balls into chocolate and drop back onto waxed paper. With a teaspoon, drop a bit of chocolate onto each ball to cover toothpick hole.

Jan Van Voorst

Peanut Butter Balls

1/2 c. margarine
2 c. creamy peanut butter
2 to 4 c. powdered sugar
3 c. Rice Krispies

Mix and make into balls; chill. (Be very careful when adding the powdered sugar--it can get too dry--<u>fast</u>.) Dip into chocolate dip--use a toothpick to dip.

CHOCOLATE DIP: Melt together in microwave:
2 (12 oz.) pkg. milk chocolate chips   18 sm. Hershey's bars

Melt on stove, 1/2 bar paraffin wax, in a small pan. Add to chocolate dip. You may not need all of the paraffin.
Wendy Heemstra

Peanut Butter Patties

2 c. powdered sugar
3/4 c. peanut butter
6 T. oleo

Mix and form into balls; flatten like thick half-dollars. Place on waxed paper, on cookie sheet and chill.
Melt 1 (12-ounce) package milk chocolate chips and 1/2 squares of paraffin wax over hot water. Dip patties in chocolate mixture and cool on waxed paper.
These freeze well.
Melissa De Jager

Peanut Clusters

12 oz. chocolate chips
12 oz. butterscotch chips
12 oz. Spanish peanuts

Melt chips together. Add peanuts. Drop by teaspoons onto waxed paper.
Rev. Wayne Sneller

English Toffee

1 lb. butter (do not substitute)
1 c. sugar
1/3 c. white corn syrup

Melt butter in a heavy 6-quart pan over medium heat. Add sugar and syrup. Stir constantly, until mixture reaches 320° on a candy thermometer. Batch should turn golden brown and double in size. Pour into a well-greased cookie sheet. Let cool and harden; break into pieces.
Reminder: Use heat-safe utensils--no plastic spatulas!
Michelle Bomgaars

Truffles

1/4 c. whipping cream
1/3 c. sugar
6 T. butter
1 (7 oz.) Hershey's bar, broken in pieces (chocolate cookies-n-cream, or cookies-n-mint)
1 tsp. vanilla

In a saucepan, stir together whipping cream, sugar and butter. Cook over low heat, stirring constantly, until just begins to boil. Remove from heat; add candy pieces and vanilla. Stir until chocolate is melted and is well blended. Refrigerate several hours or overnight, until hardens.

Using a melon ball scoop, form into balls. Roll in anything from nuts to chocolate sprinkles, or dip in melted chocolate chips and paraffin wax mixture. Store in refrigerator.

Michelle Plendl

Wedding Mints

3 oz. cream cheese, softened
3 T. soft margarine
3 1/2 c. powdered sugar
1/4 tsp. mint flavoring
A few drops food coloring
Sugar

Cream together cream cheese, butter, coloring and flavoring. Slowly add powdered sugar. Roll in small balls; roll in sugar and press into molds. Or flatten with a fork for less fancy mints. Lay out on waxed paper and allow to dry slightly. Store in airtight container with waxed paper between layers. Yield: about 150 mints.

Stores in freezer for several months.

Michelle Bomgaars

Casseroles & Meats

Chicken

Chicken-Broccoli Casserole

16 oz. broccoli
4 c. cooked chicken, diced
2 cans cream soup (chicken or celery)
1 1/2 soup cans milk
2 boxes Stove Top stuffing
2 to 3 c. shredded Cheddar cheese

Partially cook broccoli; put in a greased 9x13-inch pan. Put chicken on top of broccoli. Mix soup and milk; put 1/2 of this mixture on top of chicken. Make 2 boxes Stove Top stuffing according to box directions; put the stuffing mixture next. Add the rest of the soup mixture; top with the Cheddar cheese. Cover with foil. Bake at 350° for at least 1 hour. The last 15 minutes, take foil off.

Evonne Wielenga,
Colette Hofmeyer, Eileen Wichers

Chicken Casserole

1 can cream of chicken soup
1 can cream of rice soup
1 can chow mein noodles
1 sm. can Carnation milk
2 cans boned chicken
1 can peas, drained
Crushed potato chips

Mix all together. Bake in 325° oven for 45 minutes to 1 hour.

Crystal Brink

Chicken Casserole

1 chicken, cut in sm. pieces & cooked
2 c. noodles or macaroni, cooked
1/2 c. diced Velveeta cheese
4 c. broth
8 T. flour
Potato chips, to taste

Cook broth and flour until thick. Mix chicken, noodles, cheese and broth mixture in casserole dish. Sprinkle crushed potato chips on top. Bake 1 hour at 325°.

Lisa Wielenga

Chicken Poppy Seed Casserole

1 sm. can of chicken
Cooked rice
2 cans cream of chicken soup
1 sm. ctn. sour cream
1 stack Ritz crackers
1 stick melted butter
Poppy seeds

Cook rice. You will need enough to cover the bottom of a 9x13-inch pan. Mix together chicken, soup and sour cream. Spread over rice. Crush 1 stack of Ritz crackers over the top. Pour melted butter on top. Sprinkle with poppy seeds. Bake at 350° for 30 to 40 minutes.

Kim Oolman

Chicken-Vegetable Casserole

2 1/2 c. cut-up chicken
1 can cream of chicken soup
1/2 c. chicken broth
1 c. (or less) chopped celery
1 c. (or less) chopped onions
1 pkg. mixed vegetables, or peas, cooked
1 pkg. Stove Top dressing

Put first 6 ingredients in a 9x13-inch pan or large casserole. Prepare dressing according to directions. Spread over top of casserole. Cover with foil for baking. Bake 1 hour at 350°; remove foil for the last 10 minutes.

Arloa Jansma

Easy Chicken Casserole

3 c. cooked, diced chicken or turkey
2 c. raw macaroni
1 can cream of mushroom soup
1 can cream of chicken soup
1 sm. can chicken broth
1 c. milk
1 onion, diced
1 c. celery, diced
1 c. shredded Cheddar or Provolone cheese

Mix all at once. Put in a greased 9x13-inch pan. Top with cheese. Cover; refrigerate all day or overnight. Bake, uncovered, about 1 hour at 350°.

Diane Munro

Potluck Chicken Casserole

8 c. cubed, cooked chicken
2 (10 3/4 oz.) cans condensed cream of chicken soup, undiluted
1 c. (8 oz.) sour cream
1 c. butter-flavored cracker crumbs (about 25 crackers)
2 T. butter, melted
1 tsp. celery seed

Combine chicken, soup and sour cream; spread into a greased 9x13x2-inch baking dish. Combine crumbs, butter and celery seed; sprinkle over chicken mixture. Bake, uncovered, at 350° for 30 to 35 minutes, or until bubbly. Yield: 10 to 12 servings.

Carol Kleyer

Chicken Hot Dish

FIRST LAYER: Cut-up chicken

SECOND LAYER: 1 c. Minute Rice

THIRD LAYER: 1 pkg. frozen California Blend vegetables

2 cans cream of chicken soup
1 c. milk
1/2 stick oleo
1/2 c. chopped onion

Heat together; pour over above. Spread 1 cup shredded Cheddar cheese on top.

Imo Mulder

Chicken Hot Dish

1 (26 oz.) pkg. VIP hash browns, thawed
1 (24 oz.) pkg. frozen California Blend vegetables
3 c. cubed, cooked chicken
1 (10 3/4 oz.) can cream of chicken soup
1 (10 3/4 oz.) can cream of mushroom soup
1 c. chicken broth
3/4 c. French-fried onions

In a greased 9x13x2-inch baking dish, layer the potatoes, vegetables and chicken. In a bowl, combine soups and broth; pour over chicken. (Dish will be full.) Cover; bake at 375° for 1 hour. Uncover; sprinkle with French-fried onions. Bake 10 minutes longer, or until heated through.

Helen Oolman

Make-Ahead Chicken Hot Dish

2 1/3 to 3 c. diced, cooked chicken
2 c. uncooked macaroni or noodles
1 can cream of chicken soup
1 can cream of mushroom soup
1 can milk
1 3/4 c. chicken broth
1 sm. onion
1/2 tsp. salt
1 (4 oz.) pkg. Cheddar cheese
1/4 green pepper

Grease a 9x13-inch pan. Mix all ingredients; pour into pan. Cover with foil; refrigerate overnight. Uncover; cover with crushed potato chips, and bake 1 1/2 hours in 350° oven.

Brenda Herbst

Chicken à la King

1 can cream of chicken soup
3 T. flour
1/4 tsp. pepper
1 lb. boneless, skinless chicken breasts, cubed
1 celery rib, chopped
1/4 c. onion
1 (10 oz.) pkg. frozen peas, thawed
Hot cooked rice

In a slow-cooker, combine soup, flour and pepper until smooth. Stir in chicken, celery, green pepper and onion, Cover; cook on low for 7 to 8 hours. Stir in peas; cook 30 minutes longer. Serve over rice.

Amy Krogman

Chicken and Onion Rice Dish

2 T. vegetable oil
4 boneless chicken breast halves
1 c. Minute Rice
1 c. water
1 can onion soup
4 T. butter
1 (4 oz.) can mushrooms with liquid
Pepper
Paprika

Heat 2 tablespoons oil; place chicken in. Brown both sides 10 to 15 minutes. Sprinkle with pepper and paprika while browning. Remove chicken; pour off grease. Add to pan, 1 cup rice, 1 cup water and soup; mix together. Add butter. Bring to a boil; stir 1 minute on low heat. Add chicken; cover and simmer 30 minutes. Add mushrooms with liquid; stir well. Sprinkle with paprika before serving. Yield: 4 servings.

Cherie Van Donkelaar

Chicken-Rice Dinner

2 c. uncooked Minute Rice, sprinkled in a greased pan
1 chicken
1 can cream of mushroom or chicken soup
1 can cream of celery soup
1 c. or soup can of milk
1 pkg. dehydrated onion soup

Lay pieces of unbrowned chicken on top of rice. Mix soups and milk; pour over chicken and rice. Sprinkle onion soup on top. Cover tightly with a lid or foil. Bake for 2 hours in 325° to 350° oven.

Pam Jeltema,
Winova Van Regenmorter

Low-Fat Chicken and Rice

1 can low-fat cream of mushroom soup
1 can low-fat chicken noodle soup
1 soup can 1% or skim milk
1 c. instant rice
Chicken breast pieces, skinless
1 pkg. dry onion soup mix

Spray a 9x13-inch pan with cooking spray. Mix soups, milk and rice; pour into the pan. Arrange chicken breast pieces on the soup-rice mixture. Sprinkle the onion soup mix evenly over all. Cover with foil. Bake at 325° for 2 1/2 hours.

Note: I usually start with the chicken frozen. If you like more rice, increase the rice amount to 1 1/2 cups and add an extra soup can of milk.

Marilyn Kruid

Imagination is the best kite one can fly.

Chicken Crêpes

CREPES:
3 eggs, beaten
2/3 c. flour
1 c. milk

Combine until smooth; let stand for 1/2 hour. Pour 1/4 cup batter into a lightly-greased skillet. Spread around until thin; cook <u>only</u> 1 side. You can do this the night before. Put waxed paper between each one and store in the refrigerator.

FILLING:
1/4 c. green onion, sliced
1/2 tsp. salt
1/4 c. butter
3 T. flour
Dash of pepper
1 c. milk
2 1/2 c. shredded Cheddar cheese
1 1/2 c. chopped, cooked chicken

Melt butter; blend in flour, salt and pepper. Stir until smooth. Remove from heat. Gradually stir in milk to make a white sauce. Return to heat; boil and stir for 1 minute. Add the rest of ingredients. Fill each crepe with 1/4 cup of mixture. Place in a greased 9x13-inch pan. Pour remaining mixture on top. Bake at 350° until golden and bubbly, about 30 to 40 minutes. Yield: 10 crepes.
Note: May want to increase white sauce a bit.

Shellie Vander Schaaf

Chicken Loaf

6 c. bread, cubed
2 eggs, beaten
1 c. celery
1/2 c. broth
1 1/2 c. milk
2 c. chicken
1 can cream of chicken soup

Mix all ingredients together; place in a 9x13-inch pan. Spread cream of chicken soup over the top. Bake for 1 hour at 325°.

Pam Jeltema

Easy Chicken Pot Pie

3 c. cubed chicken or turkey
1 (16 oz.) can drained mixed vegetables, or 2 c. frozen mixed vegetables
1 (10 oz.) can cream of celery soup
1/4 c. chopped onion
2 T. flour
2 c. chicken broth
1/4 tsp. dried rosemary, crushed

BISCUIT TOPPING:
1 c. self-rising flour*
1/2 tsp. lemon pepper or pepper
1 c. buttermilk
1/2 c. melted oleo or butter

Combine just until moistened.
*For self-rising flour, place 1 1/2 teaspoons baking powder and 1/2 teaspoon salt in a measuring cup; add flour to equal 1 cup.
Preheat oven to 425°. In a saucepan, combine chicken, vegetables, soup, onion and flour; mix well. Add broth, rosemary and pepper. Bring to boil over medium heat, stirring occasionally. Boil 1 minute. Pour into an ungreased 2 1/2-quart shallow baking dish. Pour the biscuit topping over all; bake for 25 minutes, until golden brown. Serve with tossed salad or applesauce.

Dee Ann Cleveringa

Chicken Pie

1/3 c. margarine
1/3 c. flour
1 T. onion flakes
1 T. chicken soup base
2+ c. cooked, cut-up chicken, turkey, pheasant, or 2 cans tuna
2 pie shells
1 (16 oz.) pkg. mixed vegetables, thawed
1/2 tsp. salt
1/4 tsp. pepper
1 3/4 c. water
2/3 c. milk

Melt margarine; stir in flour, onion flakes, soup concentrate, salt and pepper. Stir until smooth. Add water and milk, stirring constantly. Heat to boil; boil 1 minute. Stir in chicken and vegetables. Pour into unbaked pie shells. Bake 45 to 60 minutes at 350°.
Note: They can be frozen for baking later.

Mary Ann Winchell

Alice Springs Chicken

4 chicken breasts, 1/2" thick, boneless & skinless
Honey mustard
6 pieces bacon, fried & crumbled
1/2 tsp. McCormick Season-All
1/2 c. sliced mushrooms
3 c. shredded Colby-Monterey Jack cheese

HONEY MUSTARD:
1/2 c. prepared salad mustard
1/4 c. honey
1/4 c. light corn syrup
1/4 c. mayonnaise

Rub chicken with Season-All; set aside to marinate at least 1 hour. Sauté chicken on medium heat in pan with just enough oil to prevent sticking. Cook on both sides until light golden brown and cooked in the middle, but not dry. Remove from pan. Put in a 9x13-inch pan. Spread chicken with honey mustard, then a layer of mushrooms, bacon, and cover with cheese. Bake in 350° oven until cheese melts.
Honey Mustard: Blend all together.

Rachael Kuiken

Baked Chicken Breast

4 chicken breasts
Corn flakes, crushed
1 stick oleo, melted
Mozzarella cheese

Melt oleo. Roll chicken breasts in melted oleo. Roll in corn flake crumbs. Bake 1 hour in 350° oven. Top with cheese; return to oven for 5 minutes, or until cheese melts.

Crystal Brink

Baked Chicken Dish

1 lg. chicken, cooked until done
1 pt. to 1 qt. broth
6 slices bread, toasted & cubed
1 can cream of chicken soup
1 med. onion, diced
1 stalk celery, diced
1/2 c. butter or oleo
5 eggs, beaten
Salt & pepper, to taste

Remove chicken from bones. Cut into small pieces (4 cups). Sauté onion and celery in oleo. Mix all ingredients; put in a 9x13-inch pan. Cover with crushed potato chips. Bake at 350° for 45 to 60 minutes.

Mary Ann Winchel,
Judy Vlietstra

Company Chicken

6 to 10 chicken breasts,
   skinned & deboned

Brown chicken breasts in Crisco; lay in a flat pan. Pour sauce over chicken.

SAUCE:
3/4 c. chopped celery
1/2 c. chopped onion
4 T. margarine
2 cans cream of chicken soup
1 can chicken broth

Pour sauce over browned chicken. Bake, covered with tin foil, for 1 hour; bake, uncovered, for 1/2 hour at 325°.
Wilma Ruisch

Paper Sack Chicken

SAUCE:
3 T. catsup
2 T. vinegar
1 T. lemon juice
2 T. Worcestershire sauce
3 T. brown sugar
4 T. water
2 T. butter
1 tsp. dry mustard
1 tsp. chili powder
1 tsp. paprika
1 tsp. salt

Heat sauce. Dust the cut-up chicken well with flour, salt and pepper. Grease the interior of a common grocery bag. Pour sauce over the chicken; put pieces in the bag. Fold and fasten the end. Lay on a cookie sheet. Bake at 350° for 1 1/2 hours. Slit sack open, fold back and serve.
Adam Blom

Parmesan Chicken

1/4 c. butter
3/4 c. butter-flavored crackers
1/2 c. grated Parmesan cheese
1 T. minced onion
1 T. parsley flakes
1/2 tsp. garlic powder
1/8 tsp. pepper
2 1/2 to 3 lb. cut-up chicken or
   boneless chicken breasts

Melt butter. Dip chicken in butter and then in crumb mixture. Place in a baking dish. Sprinkle with remaining mixture. Bake at 300° for 2 to 2 1/2 hours. Uncover last 45 minutes.
BJ De Weerd

Party Chicken

1 lg. pkg. dried beef
8 boned, skinless chicken breasts, halved
8 ham strips
2 cans mushroom soup
1 lg. ctn. sour cream
1/2 c. chopped onions

Line a 9x13-inch casserole dish or pan with the dried beef. Roll each breast half around a strip of ham. Place on top of the dried beef. Combine remaining ingredients; pour over chicken. Bake, uncovered, at 275° to 300° for 3 hours, basting occasionally.

Rachel Hubers

Easy Chicken and Pasta

1 lb. skinless, boneless chicken, cut up
1 T. vegetable oil
1 can cream of mushroom soup
2 1/4 c. water
1/2 tsp. dried basil leaves, crushed
2 c. frozen vegetables combo (broccoli, cauliflower, carrots)
2 c. uncooked corkscrew pasta
Grated Parmesan cheese

In a skillet, brown chicken in hot oil; set aside. Add soup, water, basil and vegetables. Heat to a boil. Add uncooked pasta. Cook over medium heat for 10 minutes, stirring often. The pasta cooks right in the soup. Add browned chicken. Cook 5 minutes, or until pasta is done, stirring often. Sprinkle with cheese.

Karla Hundt

One-Pan Potatoes and Chicken Dijon

4 med. potatoes, sliced 1/4" thick & microwaved 8 to 10 minutes, until tender
1 lb. boned & skinned chicken breasts, sliced 1/2" thick
2 T. vegetable oil
1/4 c. honey-Dijon BBQ sauce
1 tsp. dried tarragon

While potatoes cook, in a large skillet, toss and brown chicken in oil over high heat for 5 minutes. Add potatoes; sauté and toss until potatoes are slightly browned. Add BBQ sauce and tarragon; toss until heated through. Yield: 4 servings.

Beth Zeutenhorst

Easy Chicken Crescent Rolls

2 pkg. crescent rolls
1 can cream of chicken soup
1 can white chicken
Shredded Cheddar cheese
Milk

Combine cream of chicken soup, 3/4 soup can of milk and 1 cup shredded cheese in a saucepan. Warm on stove top until cheese is melted. Combine chicken and 1 cup shredded cheese in a small bowl; mix well. Put approximately 1 tablespoon of mixture inside crescent roll; roll. Arrange in a 9x13-inch pan. Pour soup mixture over crescent rolls. Bake at 350° for 25 minutes, or until lightly browned. Sprinkle with shredded cheese. Bake another 5 minutes, or until cheese is melted.

Chris Van Beek

Chicken Bundles

8 oz. cream cheese, softened
  (low-fat, lite okay)
5 T. margarine, melted (reserve
  1 T.)
4 c. cooked chicken, cut up
1/4 c. milk
1/2 tsp. salt
1/4 tsp. pepper
2 T. chives
2 (8 oz.) cans crescent
  refrigerated rolls
3/4 c. seasoned croutons,
  crushed
Sesame seeds (opt.)

Blend cream cheese with 4 tablespoons margarine until smooth. Add chicken, milk, salt, pepper and chives; mix well. Separate rolls into 8 rectangles (not 16 triangles); firmly press perforations to seal. Spoon 1/2 cup chicken mixture into center of dough. Pull 4 corners to top center. Twist firmly together; pinch side seam to seal. Place squares on ungreased cookie sheet. Brush with 1 tablespoon margarine. Sprinkle with croutons or seeds. Bake at 350° for 20 to 30 minutes, or until golden brown. Serve with warmed mushroom soup.
  Sauce: One can cream of mushroom soup, thinned with milk to desired consistency.
  Variation: Leftover turkey can be used.
  Note: This recipe also works as a main dish entrée, served with a green salad and fresh fruit. It is very filling! This recipe can also be halved.

Barb Oldenkamp

Chicken Crescents

1 (3 oz.) pkg. cream cheese, softened
3 T. melted margarine
2 c. cooked chicken, diced
2 T. milk
1 T. chives
1 T. pimento (opt.)
1/4 tsp. salt
1/8 tsp. pepper
1 can crescent rolls
1/2 c. bread crumbs or crushed croutons, seasoned

Blend cream cheese with 2 tablespoons melted margarine. Add chicken, milk, chives, pimento (optional), salt and pepper. Mix well. Separate crescent rolls into 4 rectangles. Firmly press perforations to seal. Spoon 1/2 cup of chicken mixture into center of each rectangle. Pull 4 corners of dough to top of center of chicken mixture. Twist slightly; seal edges. Brush top with remaining margarine. Dip in crumbs. Bake on ungreased cookie sheet (baking stone also works good) at 350° for 20 to 25 minutes, or until golden brown.
Koreen Van Horn

Chicken Crescent Wreath

2 (8 oz.) tubes refrigerated crescent rolls
1 c. (4 oz.) shredded cheese
2/3 c. cream of chicken soup
1/2 c. chopped fresh broccoli
1/4 c. water chestnuts (opt.)
1 (5 oz.) can white chicken, or 3/4 c. cubed, cooked chicken
2 T. chopped onion

Arrange crescent rolls on a 12-inch pizza pan, forming a ring, with pointed ends facing the outer edge of pan and wide ends overlapping. Combine the remaining ingredients; spoon over wide ends of rolls. Fold points over filling and tuck under wide ends. (Filling will be visible.) Bake at 375° for 20 to 25 minutes, or until golden brown. Yield: 6 to 8 servings.
Beth Zeutenhorst

Chicken Fingers

1 c. Capn' Crunch
1 c. corn flakes
1 c. flour
1 tsp. garlic powder
1 tsp. onion powder
1 tsp. pepper
1 c. milk
2 eggs
1 lb. chicken breasts, cut into strips

Blend cereals in blender until the consistency of fine crumbs. Pour into a bowl. Combine flour, onion, garlic and pepper in a bowl. Beat eggs; mix with milk in a third bowl. Dredge chicken in milk mixture, then in flour mixture and finally, in cereal crumbs. Deep fry at 325° for 3 to 4 minutes, or until cooked thoroughly.
Rachael Kuiken

Tender Chicken Nuggets

1 1/2 c. crushed corn flakes or
Rice Krispies
1/2 c. grated Parmesan cheese
1/2 tsp. salt
1/4 tsp. pepper
1/8 tsp. garlic powder

1/2 c. prepared Ranch salad
dressing
1 lb. boneless, skinless
chicken breasts, cut into 1"
cubes

In a shallow bowl, combine the first 5 ingredients. Place dressing in another bowl. Toss chicken cubes in dressing. Roll in the cornflake crumb mixture. Place in a greased 9x13x2-inch baking pan. Bake, uncovered, at 375° for 15 to 20 minutes, or until juices run clear. Serve with additional dressing for dipping, if desired.
Joan Dekker

Sweet-Sour Chicken

1 T. cornstarch
1 T. cold water
1/2 c. sugar
1/2 c. soy sauce
1/4 c. vinegar
1 clove garlic, minced

1/2 tsp. ground ginger
1/4 tsp. pepper
2 to 2 1/2 lb. chicken breasts
1 (1 lb. 4 oz.) can pineapple
chunks, drained

In small saucepan, combine cornstarch and water. Add sugar, soy sauce, vinegar, garlic, ginger and pepper. Cook, stirring constantly, over medium heat until mixture thickens and bubbles. Place chicken in a greased, shallow baking pan. Cover with sauce. Bake in 425° oven for 1 hour, turning after 1/2 hour. During last 10 minutes, add pineapple.
Donna J. Muilenburg

Teriyaki-Sesame Chicken

1/2 c. orange juice (not
sweetened)
2 T. teriyaki sauce
1/4 tsp. garlic powder
1/4 tsp. ground ginger

2 lb. chicken breasts, skinned,
deboned & split
2/3 c. dried bread crumbs
1 T. sesame seed

In a large bowl or Tupperware pan, combine juice, teriyaki sauce, garlic powder and ginger. Add chicken breasts; turn to coat with marinade. Cover bowl with plastic wrap or put lid on marinade pan and refrigerate at least 2 hours (can do overnight, turning several times). Preheat oven to 350°. Combine bread crumbs and sesame seeds. Remove chicken breasts from marinade (save) and coat both sides with crumbs. Place in a 9x13-inch pan, sprayed with Pam. Pour reserved marinade over chicken. Bake 45 minutes. Broil 3 to 5 minutes, until lightly browned. Yield: 8 to 10 half-breasts.
Marietta VanDer Weide

Cheesy Mexican Chicken

6 boneless, skinless chicken
  breast halves (about 2 lb.)
1 can cream of chicken soup
2 c. shredded Cheddar cheese
1/2 c. milk
1 pkg. taco seasoning
3 c. reg. or chili corn chips

Place chicken in a 9x13-inch baking dish. Mix soup, 1 1/2 cups cheese, milk and seasoning mix. Spoon over chicken. Top with chips; cover. Bake at 375° for 30 minutes. Remove; top with remaining 1/2 cup cheese. Bake, uncovered, 10 minutes, or until cheese is melted. Can serve with rice, but not required.

Jennifer (Wiersema) Probst

Chicken Chalupas

1 sm. can of chicken
1 can cream of chicken soup
8 oz. sour cream
2 c. mild Cheddar cheese,
  grated
6 lg. flour tortillas

Combine soup, sour cream and 1 1/2 cups of grated cheese. Set aside 1 cup of this mixture. Combine chicken with remainder of the mix; divide and put on tortillas. Roll each; place, seam-side-down, in a 9x13-inch pan. Spread remaining sauce over top of filled tortillas. Sprinkle on remaining cheese; bake at 350° for 45 minutes.

Kim Oolman

Chicken Enchiladas

1 can cream of chicken soup
1 can cream of mushroom soup
1 c. sour cream
1 can diced green chili peppers
  (opt.)
1 or 2 chicken bouillon cubes
3 to 4 lb. chicken or turkey,
  cooked & cut up
Celery, to taste
Onion, to taste
2 1/2 c. grated Cheddar cheese
1 c. grated Swiss cheese
2 doz. soft tortillas

Combine and heat soups, sour cream, chilies and chicken bouillon. Cut cooked chicken into pieces. Combine chicken, grated cheese, chopped onion and celery. Fill the 2 dozen soft shells with the chicken mixture; place into two 9x13-inch pans, sprayed with Pam. Pour sauce over; heat in oven at 350° until very hot, 30 to 40 minutes. Top with lettuce, tomatoes and sour cream when served. Yield: 10 to 12 servings.

Note: Can use 1 pan and freeze the other.

Becky Vander Stelt

Chicken Enchilada Casserole

1 can cream of mushroom soup
1 can cream of chicken soup
1 (4 oz.) can chopped green chilies
2 c. Cheddar cheese, divided
Onion, to taste
2 c. cooked chicken, or 2 lg. cans chunk chicken
3/4 c. milk
1 c. sour cream
8 flour tortillas

In a bowl, combine soups, sour cream, milk and chilies. Chop onion; add to soup mixture. Add 1 cup shredded Cheddar cheese. Heat in microwave for 4 minutes, or until hot. Chop chicken or flake canned chicken. Add to mixture. Cut up tortillas into squares; put in the bottom of a 9x13-inch pan. Add soup mixture; top with remaining cheese. Bake at 350° for 30 minutes.

Cheryl Van Wyk

Spanish Chicken

1 can Van de Kamp's Spanish rice
3 boneless, skinless chicken breasts
1 c. Cool Ranch Doritos
1 c. cheese-flavored potato chips
2 T. low-fat Cheez Whiz
Olive oil
Sour cream

Cube thawed chicken breasts. Crush the Doritos and cheese-flavored chips together in a large Ziploc bag. Place the chicken into the bag; shake until coated. In a large frying pan, heat olive oil until it sizzles; add breaded chicken. Fry until done. Also, place the rice into a saucepan; heat. When the rice is warm, add the Cheez Whiz; stir until combined. Spoon rice and Cheez Whiz mixture onto plate; place chicken on top. Garnish with sour cream.

Angela Van Voorst

Turkey Divan

2 (10 oz.) pkg. frozen broccoli
6 slices cooked turkey (pkg. of lunchmeat turkey, cut up in chunks, is real good)
6 slices American cheese
1 can cream of chicken soup
1 can French-fried onions

Microwave broccoli 6 minutes in the box. Place broccoli in bottom of a 7x12-inch baking dish. Top with turkey and cheese. Spoon soup over the mixture and cover with waxed paper. Microwave 10 to 12 minutes. Spread French-fried onions over the mixture; cook, uncovered, 2 minutes.

Colette Hofmeyer

Beef

Beef Hot Dish

2 lb. ground beef
Lipton onion soup mix
1 can mushroom soup
1 can cream of chicken soup
1 can mixed vegetables, undrained
1 can peas & carrots, undrained
1 (8 oz.) pkg. egg noodles, uncooked
1 c. Minute Rice, uncooked
16 oz. sour cream
1 tsp. celery salt

Brown ground beef in onion soup mix. Mix together with remaining ingredients in a 9x13-inch pan. Bake in 350° oven for 1 1/2 hours.

Marietta VanDer Weide

Busy Day Casserole

1 lb. ground beef
1 (15 1/2 oz.) jar spaghetti sauce
1 c. water
1 1/2 c. elbow macaroni, uncooked
1 c. Mozzarella cheese

Crumble ground beef in a 3-quart casserole; cook on HIGH in microwave for 4 to 5 minutes. Stir halfway through cooking time; drain. Mix in sauce, water and macaroni. Cook, covered, on HIGH for 12 to 14 minutes, or until macaroni is tender. Stir and rotate dish halfway through time. Sprinkle cheese on top of casserole; let stand, covered, 4 to 6 minutes before serving. Yield: 6 servings.

Elvera Van Horssen

Cheeseburger Casserole

1 lb. ground beef
1/4 c. chopped onion
1/4 c. catsup
1/8 tsp. pepper
1/2 lb. sliced cheese
1 can refrigerated biscuits
8 oz. tomato sauce

Brown ground beef with onion in a skillet; drain off fat. Add tomato sauce, catsup and pepper; heat. Alternate meat and cheese in a casserole dish. Put biscuits around the edge, on top of meat and cheese. Bake at 400° for 20 to 25 minutes.

Lorna Bylsma

Cheeseburger Pie

Unbaked pie shell
1 lb. ground beef
1/2 c. chopped onion
1/2 c. evaporated milk
1/2 c. catsup
1 tsp. Worcestershire sauce
1/3 c. bread or cracker crumbs
1 tsp. salt
1/4 tsp. pepper
1 1/2 c. grated cheese

Brown beef and onion over medium heat; drain. Stir milk, catsup, crumbs and spices into beef and onion. Spread in shell. Bake 20 minutes at 400°. Top with cheese. Bake 10 more minutes. Let stand 20 minutes before serving.
Brenda Herbst

Cheeseburger Pie

1 lb. hamburger
1 can cream of mushroom soup
Velveeta cheese
1 roll of refrigerated biscuits
Salt
Pepper
Onion
Lawry's seasoned salt
1 tsp. dill pickle juice

Preheat oven to 425°. Brown hamburger with salt, pepper, onion and Lawry's; drain off fat. Stir cream of mushroom soup and dill pickle juice into the ground beef. Put in an 8x8-inch pan. Top with cheese slices to cover the ground beef mixture. Flatten the biscuits; place over the cheese slices. Pinch the edges together. Bake for 10 to 15 minutes, until biscuits are browned.
Amy Vander Zwaag

Cheesy Potato Beef Bake

1 lb. ground beef
2 (4 oz.) cans mushrooms, drained
2 (5 1/4 oz.) pkg. au gratin potatoes
4 c. boiling water
1 1/3 c. milk
2 tsp. margarine
1 tsp. salt
1/2 tsp. seasoned salt
1/2 tsp. pepper
1 c. shredded Cheddar cheese

In a skillet over medium heat, cook beef until no longer pink; drain. Place in a 9x13-inch greased baking pan. Top with mushrooms. Combine potatoes and contents of sauce. Mix packets, water, milk, margarine, salt, seasoned salt and pepper. Pour over beef and mushrooms. Cover; bake at 400° for 30 minutes. Sprinkle with cheese. Bake, uncovered, for 5 minutes, or until cheese is melted. Let stand 10 minutes before serving. Yield: 8 servings.
Elvera Van Horssen

Crock-Pot Casserole

4 lg. potatoes, sliced
5 carrots, sliced, or 1 bag baby carrots
2 onions, chopped
1 can beans, drained
2 lb. ground beef, browned
2 cans tomato soup
1 can water

Place layers of vegetables in crock-pot in order given. Season each layer with salt and pepper. Put the ground beef on top of last layer. Mix soup with water; pour over top. Cover; set on low for 6 to 8 hours, or high 2 to 4 hours.
Kathy Dykstra

Easy Hamburger Hot Dish

1 lb. hamburger
1 c. chopped onion
1 c. chopped celery
3 c. raw potatoes, cubed
1 can vegetable soup
1 can tomato soup
1 soup can water
1 tsp. salt
1/2 tsp. pepper

Brown hamburger; drain. Add remaining ingredients. Simmer about 45 minutes.
BJ De Weerd

Emergency Steak

1 lb. ground beef
1/2 c. milk
1/4 tsp. pepper
1 T. minced onion
1 tsp. salt
1 c. crushed Wheaties

Mix together; place on a lightly-greased pan. Pat into shape of a T-bone steak, 1 inch thick. Broil.
Cindy VanDer Weide

Family Casserole

1 lb. hamburger
1 pkg. egg noodles
8 oz. shredded Cheddar cheese
2 (15 oz.) cans tomato sauce
1 can chili with beans
1 can corn, drained

Brown hamburger; drain. Cook noodles. Combine ingredients. Heat thoroughly. Serve.
Greg Haverdink Family

Farmers' Delight

1 1/2 lb. hamburger
1 sm. onion, chopped
Salt & pepper, to taste
2 c. dry egg noodles
1 can cream of celery soup
1 can cream-style corn
1/2 can water
2 c. Velveeta cheese, cubed

Brown hamburger, onion, salt and pepper. Boil noodles; drain. Combine hamburger mixture, noodles, soups, corn and water in a casserole dish. Top with cheese. Bake at 350° for 35 to 40 minutes. Bake, covered, for the first 20 minutes.

Amanda Wiersema

Farmhouse Barbecue Biscuits

1 (10 oz.) tube refrigerated
   biscuits
1 lb. ground beef
1/2 c. ketchup
3 T. brown sugar
1 T. cider vinegar
1/2 tsp. chili powder
1 c. (4 oz.) shredded Cheddar
   cheese

Flatten biscuits into 5-inch circles; press into sides of greased muffin cups. In a skillet, brown ground beef; drain. In a small bowl, mix ketchup, brown sugar, vinegar and chili powder. Add to meat; spoon into biscuits. Sprinkle cheese on top. Bake at 375° for 20 minutes.

Eileen Wichers

French-Style Green Bean Casserole

1 lb. hamburger
1 can French-style green beans
1 can tomato soup (can
   substitute cream of chicken
   soup)
Salt & pepper, to taste
2 to 4 c. cooked rice (instant or
   regular)

Cook rice as directed. Brown hamburger; season to taste. Add 1 can French-style green beans (with liquid) and 1 can tomato soup. Stir; simmer about 20 minutes. Serve over rice.

Jonna Wierda

Hamburger and Stuffing Casserole

1 1/2 lb. ground beef or pork, lightly browned & drained
1 c. sliced or chopped celery
1/4 c. chopped onion
1 1/2 c. water
7 oz. croutons, or 3 to 4 c. dry bread cubes
1 can cream of chicken soup
1 can cream of celery soup

Layer meat, then croutons or bread crumbs, in a large baking dish. In a saucepan, cook celery and onion in water until no longer crunchy. Remove from heat; combine with soups. Pour over stuffing mixture. Bake for 1 hour at 350°. Let stand a few minutes before serving. Yield: about 8 servings.

Kristi Hargens

Hamburger Casserole

1 1/2 to 2 lb. hamburger
1 can vegetables (corn, beans, etc.)
1 can cream of mushroom soup
1/2 c. milk
1 (6 oz.) pkg. Stove Top stuffing

Brown hamburger; salt and pepper to taste. Mix soup and milk; add can of vegetables. Mix in hamburger; spread in the bottom of a greased baking dish. Follow directions on box of Stove Top stuffing; put on top of the hamburger mixture. Bake in 375° oven for 45 minutes.

Different twist to hamburger casserole.

Evonne Wielenga

Hamburger Hot Dish

8 oz. frozen hash browns, thawed
1 lb. hamburger
1 med. onion, chopped
Salt & pepper
1 (10 oz.) pkg. frozen peas, thawed (can use any vegetable)
1 (10 oz.) can cream of chicken soup
1 c. milk
6 slices American cheese
1 (3 oz.) can French-fried onion rings

Butter a 9x13-inch glass pan. Cover with hash browns. Brown meat and onion; place on top of potatoes. Salt and pepper; sprinkle with peas. Mix soup and milk together; pour over all. Lastly, place cheese slices on top; cover with foil. Bake at 350° for 45 to 60 minutes. Remove foil; sprinkle French-fried onions on top. Return to oven, with heat off, for 7 to 10 minutes. Yield: 8 to 10 servings.

Vera Brouwer,
Julie Leusink

Haystack Supper

1 3/4 c. crushed saltines (about 40 crackers)
2 c. cooked rice
3 lb. ground beef
1 lg. onion, chopped
1 1/2 c. tomato juice
3/4 c. water
3 T. taco seasoning mix
Seasoned salt, salt & pepper, to taste
4 c. shredded lettuce
3 med. tomatoes, diced
1/2 c. butter or margarine
1/2 c. flour
4 c. milk
1 lb. process American cheese, cubed
3 c. (12 oz.) shredded sharp Cheddar cheese
1 (10 oz.) jar stuffed olives, drained & sliced
1 (14 1/2 oz.) pkg. tortilla chips

Divide crackers between two ungreased 9x13x2-inch baking dishes. Top with rice. Cook beef and onion until meat is no longer pink; drain. Add tomato juice, water and seasonings; simmer for 15 to 20 minutes; spoon over rice. Sprinkle with lettuce and tomatoes. In a saucepan, melt butter; stir in flour until smooth. Gradually add milk. Bring to a boil; cook and stir for 2 minutes. Reduce heat; stir in American cheese until melted. Pour over the tomatoes. Top with Cheddar cheese and olives. Serve over chips. Refrigerate any leftovers. Yield: 10 to 12 servings.   *Emily Maassen*

Hamburger-Potato Casserole

1 lb. hamburger
6 med. potatoes
1 can cream of onion soup
1 can milk
1 med. onion

Brown hamburger in electric fry pan; salt and pepper, to taste, Slice potatoes over top of meat. Slice onion over. Mix soup and milk together; pour over mixture. Simmer until done, about 45 minutes.
Quick, easy, and very tasty.   *Jan Budden*

Mom's Hamburger Helper

1 lb. ground beef or pork, browned & drained
1 lb. cooked potato slices or chunks
1 can cream of chicken, celery or mushroom soup
Seasonings, to taste

Brown meat; salt, pepper, chopped onions, etc., may be added to vary the results. Use leftover boiled potatoes or use frozen potatoes (either fry lightly, boil or microwave, covered, until soft, not mushy). Drain fat from meat, if needed. Add cream of soup and 1 soup can of liquid (water, canned broth or milk). Stir in potatoes. Heat thoroughly. Yield: 4 servings.
Faye Vander Lugt

Quick, Easy Meal

1 lb. hamburger, browned & drained
1/2 onion, chopped
1/2 green pepper, chopped
2 c. canned or fresh tomatoes
Salt & pepper, to taste
1/4 tsp. chili powder
1/8 tsp. oregano
1 sm. can pork & beans
Sprinkle of garlic salt

Heat mixture until hot and bubbling. Sprinkle with garlic salt. Serve with toast or on toast.
Note: May be doubled for more servings.

Evelyn De Vries

Rog's Favorite Casserole

1 1/2 lb. ground beef
1 lg. onion
1 can Veg-All, drained
1 can cream of mushroom soup
1 can cream of chicken soup
1 pkg. dry onion soup mix
1 (8 oz.) ctn. sour cream
8 oz. cooked noodles (I use angel pasta, cut up before mixing)

Brown hamburger and onion; drain off grease. Add the rest of the ingredients. Put in a 9x13-inch pan. Top with crushed potato chips. Bake at 300° for 30 minutes.

Linda Broek

Western Casserole

1 lb. ground beef, browned
1 can whole kernel corn or green beans
1 can tomato juice
1/2 tsp. chili powder
1 c. shredded Cheddar cheese
1 T. minced onion
Salt & pepper, to taste
1 can refrigerated biscuits

Mix all ingredients except biscuits in a large buttered casserole. Bake, uncovered, 20 minutes at 400°. Top with biscuits. Bake another 20 to 25 minutes, until biscuits are brown.

Gert Sjaarda

BBQ Meat Balls

1 to 1 1/4 lb. ground beef	1 egg
1/2 c. oatmeal	1 tsp. salt
1/2 c. milk	Onion, to taste

Mix; shape into small meat balls. Microwave 5 minutes, or bake 20 minutes at 350°. Drain well.

SAUCE:

1/2 onion, sautéed in 1 T. butter	1/4 c. brown sugar
3/4 c. catsup	2 T. vinegar
3/4 c. water	2 T. mustard
	1 tsp. salt

Sauté onion in butter. Add rest of ingredients; simmer about 5 minutes. Pour onto meat balls. Bake 45 minutes at 325°.

Vera Brouwer

Lazy Daisy Meat Balls

1 lb. ground beef	2 T. onion, grated
1 tsp. salt	1/4 c. water
1/8 tsp. pepper	1 egg, beaten
1/8 tsp. celery salt	1 (10 oz.) can cream of mushroom soup
1/2 c. dry bread or cracker crumbs	1/4 soup can water

Mix meat, egg, seasonings, bread crumbs, water and onion. Form into 15 to 20 small meat balls. Roll in flour; brown in hot shortening. Mix soup and water; pour over meat balls. Cover and simmer at least 30 minutes; or transfer to a casserole dish and bake in moderate oven for 45 minutes to an hour. The gravy is good over mashed potatoes.

Joan Dekker,
Marietta VanDer Weide

Norwegian Meat Balls

3 lb. ground beef
3 eggs
1/2 c. milk
1 c. cracker crumbs
1 chopped onion
1 tsp. salt
1 tsp. pepper
1 T. baking powder
1 T. cornstarch
1 tsp. allspice
Dash of nutmeg

Mix ingredients well. Form into small balls; <u>roll tight.</u> Brown well in oil in a frying pan. Drain fat from pan. Add 1 can cream of mushroom or cream of chicken soup, mixed with 1 soup can of water. Pour over cooked meat balls; simmer a while longer.

Dawn Beukelman

Porcupine Meat Balls

1 lb. ground beef
1/3 c. rice, uncooked
3 T. onion, chopped
1 can condensed tomato soup
1/2 c. water

Combine beef, rice and onion. Add salt and pepper to taste. Mix thoroughly. Shape into small balls. Place in pan. Combine soup and water; pour over meat balls. Cover. Bake at 350° for 30 minutes. Uncover; bake 30 minutes longer.

Wanda Hofmeyer

Meat Loaf

2 lb. ground beef
2 eggs
1 1/2 c. fine cracker crumbs
3/4 c. catsup
1 tsp. Accent
1/2 c. warm water
1 pkg. onion soup mix

Mix and put in a loaf pan. Cover with topping.

TOPPING:
1/4 c. brown sugar
1/4 c. catsup
Pinch of ground cloves

Mix well. Bake at 350° for 1 hour.

Wanda Hofmeyer

Meat Loaf

2 eggs, beaten
1/2 c. catsup
3/4 c. warm water
2 lb. ground beef
1 pkg. Lipton dry onion soup mix
1 1/2 c. soft bread crumbs

Mix all together; put in pan. Bake at 350° for 1 hour. Drain grease off just before serving. Put a layer of cheese on top. Return to oven just a few minutes.

Winova Van Regenmorter

Mom's Meat Loaf

2 eggs
3/4 c. milk
2/3 c. finely-crushed saltines
1/2 c. chopped onion
1 tsp. salt
1/2 tsp. rubbed sage
Dash of pepper
1 1/2 lb. ground beef
1 c. ketchup
1/2 c. packed brown sugar
1 tsp. Worcestershire sauce

In a large bowl, beat eggs. Add milk, saltines, onion, salt, sage and pepper. Add beef; mix well. Shape into a 4 1/2 x 8 1/2-inch loaf in an ungreased shallow baking pan. Combine remaining ingredients; spread 3/4 cup over meat loaf. Bake at 350° for 60 to 65 minutes, or until no pink remains; drain. Serve with remaining sauce. Yield: 6 to 8 servings.

Carol Kleyer

Thirty-Minute Meat Loaf

1 lb. ground beef
1 1/2 c. soda crackers, crushed
1/2 c. catsup
1 egg
1/4 c. minced onion
2 tsp. seasoned salt

Mix all ingredients; put in an 8x8-inch pan. Spread evenly. Add more catsup to top. Bake at 350° for 30 minutes.

Carolyn De Jager

Beef Enchiladas

1 1/2 lb. ground beef
1 1/2 pkg. taco seasoning
Dry onion, to taste
1 pkg. soft taco shells
1 c. sour cream
1 can cream of chicken soup
1/2 c. milk
8 oz. shredded cheese

Brown ground beef; drain. Add 1 package of taco seasoning and dry onion. Fill taco shells with meat mixture; roll them up and place in a pan. Melt the cream of chicken soup, milk, shredded cheese, sour cream and 1/2 package taco seasoning. Pour over the rolled-up shells. Bake at 350° for 15 minutes. May garnish with black olives, lettuce, shredded cheese and salsa.

Vi De Jong

Beef Enchiladas

1 can enchilada sauce
1 can tomato soup
1 can cream of mushroom soup
1 to 1 1/2 lb. ground beef
1 pkg. lg. flour tortilla shells
8 oz. shredded Cheddar cheese

Heat oven to 350°. Brown ground beef. In a separate bowl, mix enchilada sauce, tomato soup and cream of mushroom soup. Pour 1/4 of the soup mixture over the ground beef. In a 9x13-inch greased pan, lay beef mixture down the middle of the shell. Roll up; place in pan. Pour remaining soup mixture over the tortillas. Sprinkle with cheese. Bake at 350° for 20 minutes.

Jill Schouten

Sour Cream Enchiladas

1 lb. hamburger
1 can cream of chicken soup
6 oz. sour cream
1 pkg. taco seasoning
Flour tortillas
Grated cheese

Brown hamburger; drain off fat. Add half of taco seasoning. Mix soup, sour cream and rest of taco seasoning. Spoon small amount in bottom of a 9x13-inch pan to keep from sticking. Place a handful of cheese in each tortilla, then a spoonful of meat. Fold up; place in pan with the seam down. Top with soup mixture, then with more cheese. Bake at 325° for 20 minutes, or until cheese is melted.

Michelle Bomgaars

Easy Mexican Casserole

1 to 1 1/2 lb. hamburger, browned & drained
Salt, pepper & onion, to taste
1 pkg. taco seasoning, mixed with water as directed
1 to 2 c. low-fat Cheddar cheese, grated
8 oz. lite sour cream
1 pkg. crescent rolls

Put browned hamburger, that has been mixed with onion, seasonings and taco mix, into a 9x13-inch pan. Layer grated Cheddar cheese over meat. Spread sour cream over cheese layer. Open crescent roll package; take apart and layer over sour cream. Bake at 375° for 15 minutes, or until light brown. Eat with salsa and sour cream, if desired.

Evelyn De Vries

Nacho-Roni

1 lb. ground beef
8 oz. rotini or other sm. noodles
1 can fiesta nacho cheese soup
1/4 c. milk

Brown ground beef. Cook noodles according to package directions; drain. Add noodles to ground beef. Stir in soup and milk. Heat through; serve.

Michelle Bomgaars

Taco Bake

1 to 1 1/2 lb. browned hamburger
16 oz. pizza sauce
1 T. onion flakes
1 pkg. taco seasoning
8 oz. sour cream
1 pkg. Pillsbury crescent rolls
2 c. Cheddar cheese
2 c. Mozzarella cheese
Crushed Doritos

Press crescent rolls in a 9x13-inch pan. Add taco seasoning to browned hamburger, then pizza sauce, onion flakes and sour cream. Cover with cheeses. Bake at 350° for 45 minutes; top with chips. Let stand 5 minutes; serve.

Julie Leusink

Taco Casserole

1 lb. hamburger
Salt, pepper & onion, to taste
1 c. thick salsa
1 can tomato soup
1/2 c. milk

1 1/2 to 2 c. grated cheese (reserve 1/2 c.)
6 to 8 sm. or 4 lg. tortilla shells, cut in squares, 1" to 1 1/2"

Brown hamburger with salt, pepper and onion, to taste; drain. Mix all ingredients, except 1/2 cup cheese. Grease a 9x9-inch dish. Put a little sauce in the bottom of dish, then pour the rest of mixture. Bake at 400° for 30 minutes. Top with 1/2 cup cheese until melted. Serve with salsa and sour cream, if desired.

Evelyn De Vries

Taco Casserole

1 lb. browned hamburger
1 can cream of celery soup
1 can cream of chicken soup
1 can cream of mushroom soup

1 can Cheddar cheese soup
1 can taco sauce
1 can sliced green chili peppers
1 sack Doritos

Mix soups, taco sauce and peppers together. In an ungreased pan, place a thin layer of Doritos, then a thin layer of hamburger, then a thin layer of soup mixture; repeat, finishing with soup. Bake at 350° for 25 to 30 minutes. Yield: 6 servings.

Stephanie Feenstra

Taco in a Pan

1 lb. hamburger
1/2 onion, chopped
1 (8 oz.) ctn. sour cream
1 tube crescent rolls

1 (8 oz.) can tomato sauce
1 c. Cheddar cheese
1 env. taco seasoning
1 1/2 c. crushed Fritos

Brown onion and hamburger; drain. Add tomato sauce and taco seasoning. Pat crescent rolls (do not separate) in a greased 9x13-inch pan. Spread 1 cup of crushed Fritos over crust; spread hamburger mixture over chips. Top with sour cream and Cheddar cheese. Top with remaining chips. Bake at 375° for 25 to 30 minutes. After baking, top with taco sauce, lettuce, olives, tomatoes, or whatever you like.

Note: Can double recipe, using an 11x15-inch pan.

Mary Ann Winchell,
Wilma Vander Stelt

Taco Meat Filling

1 lb. ground beef
1/2 c. chopped onion
1 (8 oz.) can tomato sauce
1 tsp. chili powder

Brown beef in a skillet, stirring until crumbly. Drain excess fat. Stir in remaining ingredients. Simmer, covered, for 10 minutes. Makes filling for 8 tacos.

Eunice Koopmans

Easy-Fix Roast

1 (3 lb.) beef roast
1/4 c. oil
1 (10 3/4 oz.) can onion soup
1 (10 3/4 oz.) can cream of mushroom soup
1/2 tsp. garlic powder
Salt & pepper

Brown roast in oil, turning to brown all sides. Place meat in a slow-cooker or in a roasting pan. Pour soups over roast. Add garlic powder, salt and pepper to taste. Cook at 325° for 3 hours, or until tender. Yield: 8 servings.

Lynn Herzog

Mock Prime Rib

8 lb. rolled arm roast

Mix:
1 pkg. Good Seasons Italian dressing mix
1 pkg. Schilling au jus mix
1 can Swanson's beef broth

Put roast in crock-pot. Pour mixture over it. Do about 10 1/2 to 12 hours on low. Slice. Pour mixture over meat.

Note: I usually turn the meat over 1 time during cooking time. You can speed up the time if you cook it on high for a while.

Winova Van Regenmorter

Poor Man's Prime Rib

3 lb. boneless roast (lean)
1 pkg. dry Good Seasons Italian dressing mix
1 pkg. Schilling au jus mix
1 can beef broth

Put all into crock-pot; cook 12 hours on low.

Jan Budden

Salisbury Steak

1 lb. ground beef
1/4 c. dry bread crumbs
1 beaten egg
1 tsp. salt
1/8 tsp. pepper

1 T. minced onion
1/4 c. finely-chopped celery
1 can cream of mushroom soup
1/2 c. water

Combine ground beef, bread crumbs, egg, salt, pepper, onion and celery; shape into oval patties. Brown on both sides in a skillet. Combine soup and water; pour over meat. Cook slowly in a covered skillet for 25 minutes. Soup and meat juices will make good gravy. *Dawn Beukelman*

Swiss Steak

2 to 3 lb. round steak
1 med. sweet onion
1 pt. tomato juice

1 T. celery seed
1 c. chopped celery
Salt & pepper

With a heavy knife, pound flour into steak on both sides. Heat a little cooking oil in an electric frypan until hot (350°). Brown meat on both sides. Turn heat down to simmer. Slice onion over top. Pour tomato juice over all. Sprinkle with celery seed and chopped celery. Simmer for 1 hour, or until tender. *Jan Budden*

Swiss Steak

1 lb. round steak
1 can tomato soup

1 can water

Flour the steak; brown in a small amount of oil and sliced onions. Cover with the tomato soup and water. Cover; simmer 45 minutes. The sauce makes a good gravy. *Eunice Koopmans*

Swiss Steak

1 1/2 lb. round steak
2 T. flour
Salt & pepper, to taste
1 med. onion, sliced

1 carrot, sliced
1 stalk celery, diced
1 (15 oz.) can tomato sauce

Cut steak into serving pieces. Season flour with salt and pepper. Dredge meat in seasoned flour. Place onions in bottom of crock-pot; add meat. Top with carrots and celery; cover with tomato sauce. Cover; cook on low 8 to 10 hours, or 3 to 5 hours on high.

Elvera Van Horssen

Tender Baked Round Steak

1 1/2 lb. round steak or stewing beef
1 can cream of mushroom soup
1 can mushroom bits & pieces, drained
1/2 pkg. Lipton dry onion soup mix
1 c. 7-Up

Put all ingredients in a heavy roasting pan; cover. Bake for 2 1/2 hours at 350°. <u>Do not peek!</u>
Chris Van Beek

Beef Stew

2 lb. boneless beef shank, cut in 1" cubes
2 tsp. salt
1 T. Worcestershire sauce
1/4 tsp. pepper
2 T. fat
3 carrots
1 c. chopped onions
12 sm. potatoes, cut in 1" pieces
2 c. canned tomatoes
2 c. water
1 pkg. frozen beans

Brown meat slowly in hot fat; add salt, pepper, onion, tomatoes, water and Worcestershire sauce. Cover; simmer 1 1/2 hours. Add carrots, potatoes and vegetables. Cover; simmer 30 minutes longer, or until done.
Note: Best if made the day before.
Eunice Koopmans

Five-Hour Beef Stew

1 to 2 lb. beef stew meat, cut in sm. tidbits
1 med. onion, diced
1 c. celery, chopped
1 c. carrots, sliced
4 potatoes, peeled & cut in fourths
1 pt. tomatoes
2 T. brown sugar
1 pkg. brown gravy mix
1 tsp. salt
2 T. quick tapioca
1 c. cooked peas

Put meat and onions in a crock-pot. Add celery, carrots and potatoes. Mix in tomatoes, brown sugar and gravy mix. Add salt and tapioca. Cook for 5 hours in crock-pot on medium heat. Add 1 cup cooked peas when ready to serve.
Elvera Van Horssen

Oven Beef Stew

1 1/2 lb. stewing beef
1 can tomato soup
1 can cream of mushroom soup
1 soup can water
1 env. onion soup mix
1 T. brown sugar
Potatoes
Carrots
Peas
Green peppers

Brown stew meat in a small amount of oil; put in a 9x13-inch pan. Add soups, water, onion, soup mix and brown sugar. Stir in cut-up potatoes and carrots. Can also add green peppers and peas, if desired. Bake at 300° for 4 to 5 hours.
Chris Van Beek

Old-Fashioned Goulash

1 c. elbow macaroni
1 lb. hamburger, browned & drained
2 c. tomato juice
1 (8 oz.) can tomato sauce
1/2 tsp. salt
1/4 tsp. pepper
1/4 tsp. onion salt
1 tsp. Lawry's seasoned salt

Cook macaroni until tender; drain. Add remaining ingredients. Heat through until thickened, but don't overcook.
Note: Can be cooked in skillet, microwave or crock-pot.
Karen Bos

Pork

Bacon and Cheese Puff Pie

10 slices bacon
1 can crescent rolls
1 med. tomato, sliced
Salt & pepper
5 slices American cheese
3 eggs, separated
3/4 c. sour cream
1/2 c. flour
1/2 tsp. salt
Paprika

Place crescent rolls in pie plate. Layer bacon, tomatoes and cheese. Sprinkle with salt and pepper. Beat egg whites until stiff. In a separate bowl, mix yolks, sour cream, flour and salt; fold in egg whites until a few lumps remain. Pour over pie. Bake at 350° for 35 to 40 minutes, until knife comes out clean.
Koreen Van Horn

Ham Balls

1 lb. ground pork
1 lb. ground, fully-cooked ham
2 eggs
3/4 c. milk
2/3 c. crushed shredded wheat
 cereal

SAUCE:
1 1/2 c. brown sugar
1/3 c. vinegar
2/3 c. water
3/4 tsp. ground mustard

In a bowl, combine the pork, ham, eggs, milk and cereal; mix well. Shape into 1 1/2- to 2-inch balls; place in a greased 9x13x2-inch baking dish. In a saucepan, combine sauce ingredients; bring to a boil over medium heat. Reduce heat; simmer, uncovered, for 4 minutes. Pour over ham balls. Bake, uncovered, at 350° for 60 to 70 minutes, or until browned. Yield: 8 servings.
Carol Kleyer

Ham Loaf or Ham Balls

2 lb. ground pork
4 c. ground ham
2 c. crushed graham crackers
3 eggs
1 1/2 c. milk

SAUCE:
1 (10 3/4 oz.) can tomato soup
1/2 can water
3/4 c. brown sugar
3 T. mustard

Mix well. Form into balls or pat into loaf pan. Makes 24 balls or 1 loaf. Bake at 350° for 30 to 45 minutes. Before cooking, top with sauce.
Note: I usually serve one, and freeze the other for a quick meal later on.
Dawn De Weerd

Ham Rolls

MEAT:
2 lb. ham loaf meat
1/2 lb. ground beef
1 1/2 c. graham cracker crumbs
2 eggs
1 c. milk

SAUCE:
1 can tomato soup
1 c. brown sugar
2 T. vinegar
1 T. dry mustard

Mix all meat ingredients. Make into size of large eggs. Place in a large shallow cake pan; top with sauce. Cover with foil; bake 1 1/2 hours at 350°.
Mary Ann Winchell

Crock-Pot Scalloped Potatoes and Ham

8 to 10 med. potatoes, peeled & sliced
6 to 8 slices ham
1 diced onion
1 can cream of celery or mushroom soup
Salt & pepper, to taste
1 c. shredded Cheddar or American cheese

Put 1/2 of potatoes, ham and onion in crock-pot. Sprinkle with salt, pepper and cheese. Repeat with remaining potatoes, ham and onion. Spoon undiluted soup over all. Cook on low for 8 to 10 hours, or on high for 4 hours.

Linda Van Regenmorter

Ham, Broccoli and Potato Casserole

2 lb. Southern-style hash browns
2 c. sour cream
1/2 tsp. pepper
1 can cream of chicken soup
1/2 c. butter or oleo, melted
2 c. cubed, cooked ham
1 (10 oz.) bag broccoli cuts
1 1/2 c. shredded Cheddar cheese
1 can French-fried onions

Combine all ingredients, except onions; mix well. Place in a 9x13-inch and a 9x9-inch pan. (Too much for a 9x13-inch pan alone.) Sprinkle French-fried onions over top; bake at 350° for 45 minutes to 1 hour.

Darlene Kluis

Rice Casserole

2 1/2 c. uncooked rice
1 can of Spam
1 1/2 c. peas (add more or less, to fit your desire)

Cook 2 1/2 cups of rice in a rice cooker. When finished, scoop into a microwave bowl. Cut Spam; add peas, Mix into bowl. Cook in microwave for a total of 5 minutes, taking out and stirring every so often, until finished. Taste a pea to make sure. Yield: at least 5 servings.

LaDonna De Vries

Barbecued Spareribs

2 1/2 lb. spareribs
1 1/2 T. vinegar
2 T. brown sugar
3 T. lemon juice
3 T. Worcestershire sauce
3/4 c. catsup
3/4 c. water
1 tsp. salt
1/4 tsp. pepper
1/4 tsp. chili powder
1 lg. onion, chopped

Place ribs in a baking pan. Combine ingredients for sauce. Spread over spareribs. Bake 1 to 1 1/2 hours at 350°.

Marietta VanDer Weide

Dominican Pork Chops

1 fresh lime, squeezed
1 tsp. Mrs. Dash
1 T. vegetable oil
1/4 tsp. ground ginger
Breakfast pork chops, 1/4" thick, or 2 or 3 chops per person, or 5 per Al

In a shallow dish, combine juice of the lime, oil and seasonings; coat pork chops. Allow chops to marinate for at least 20 minutes. Preheat grill to high heat. Grill chops equal time on both sides until the edges are nice and crispy. Eat them with your fingers while singing, "Don't Worry, Be Happy!"

Alison Lenters

Grilled Marinated Pork Chops

Italian dressing
Salt & pepper, to taste
Iowa chops or butterfly chops

Spread Italian dressing on both sides of chops; put in a glass baking dish. Cover with Saran Wrap. Put in refrigerator several hours or overnight. (You can layer the chops if you have several.) Grill until done.

Evelyn De Vries

Pork Chop and Potato Bake

6 pork chops
1 can cream of celery soup
1/2 c. milk
1/2 c. sour cream
1/4 tsp. pepper
1 pkg. frozen hash browns, thawed
1 1/2 c. Cheddar cheese
1 can French-fried onions

Brown pork chops in oil. Sprinkle with seasoned salt and pepper. Set aside. Combine soup, milk, sour cream, pepper and 1/2 teaspoon seasoned salt. Stir in hash browns, 1 cup cheese and 1/2 can French-fried onions. Spoon mixture into a 9x13-inch pan. Arrange pork chops over potatoes. Bake, uncovered, at 350° for 50 minutes. Top with remaining cheese and onions. Bake, uncovered, for 5 minutes or longer. *Tammy Sheller*

Pork Chop Dinner

6 to 8 pork chops
2 c. water
2 med. carrots, sliced thin
1 pkg. frozen green beans
2 T. butter
1 pkg. Betty Crocker scalloped potatoes
1 can cream of celery soup
2/3 c. milk
1/2 T. Worcestershire sauce

Lightly salt and brown chops. Heat water to boiling in 3-quart pan. Add carrots and beans. Heat to boiling and add butter and potatoes. Mix soup, milk and Worcestershire sauce. Add soup mixture to vegetables. Then put into large glass baking dish. Top with chops. Cover with foil. Bake at 350° for 45 minutes. Uncover and bake until tender, 10 to 15 minutes. Let stand 5 minutes before serving. *Eunice Koopmans*

Pork and Noodle Casserole

2 lb. 75% to 80% lean ground pork
1 1/2 c. chopped onions
8 oz. med. noodles, cooked & drained
8 oz. sharp process American cheese, shredded
2 (10 3/4 oz) cans condensed tomato soup
1/3 c. chopped green peppers
1/4 c. chili sauce
1 1/2 c. soft bread crumbs
3 T. butter, melted

Brown pork and onions. Drain off fat. Combine with noodles, cheese, soup, 1 1/2 cups water, green pepper, chili sauce, 1 teaspoon salt and a dash of pepper. Mix. Pour into 9x13-inch baking dish or two 8x8-inch baking dishes and freeze one for later. Combine crumbs and butter. Sprinkle on top of casserole(s). Bake uncovered at 350° for 40 to 45 minutes.

Gert Sjaarda

Preferred Pork Chops

4 chops
8 med. potatoes, sliced
1 onion, sliced

1 can tomato soup
1/2 can water
Salt & pepper, to taste

Brown pork chops in frypan in a little oil. Take out of pan and put potatoes and onion in pan. Place meat on top and season. Mix soup and water. Pour over the top. Cover and simmer 1 to 1 1/2 hours at 325°.

Jan Budden

Tender Pork Roast

6 to 8 lb. pork roast, boneless
Season-All seasoning salt

4 T. liquid smoke
5 c. hot water

Coat roast well with Season All. Place in roaster pan. Combine liquid smoke and water. Carefully pour in bottom of pan. Place in 375° oven and bake with cover on for 2 hours. No peeking! Continue checking occasionally, until done. This is great for sandwiches.

Michelle Bomgaars

Seafood

Pan-Fried Walleye

Beaten egg
Potato flakes

Soda crackers
Walleye fillets

Season walleye. Then dip in egg. Roll in crushed mixture of potato flakes and soda crackers. Brown in oleo. Put in oven until done; about 20 to 30 minutes at 325°.

Wanda Kuiken

Salmon Loaf

1 lb. can salmon
1 can cream of mushroom or
   cream of celery soup
1 c. dry bread or cracker crumbs

2 eggs, slightly beaten
Onion, finely chopped
Celery, finely chopped

Debone salmon. Mix thoroughly with other ingredients. Pour into greased loaf pan. Bake for 1 hour at 375°.
Can add 1/2 cup Miracle Whip and 1 tablespoon lemon juice.

Ruth Heidebrink

Seafood-Stuffed Potatoes

4 med. baking potatoes
3/4 c. fat-free sour cream
3/4 c. shredded reduced-fat Cheddar cheese
1/4 c. melted margarine
3 T. skim milk
1/8 tsp. onion powder
1/8 tsp. pepper
8 oz. crab-flavored seafood

Pierce potatoes several times with a meat fork. Bake at 425° for 45 minutes to 1 hour, or until done. Cool to touch. Cut a thin slice from the top of the potato. Carefully scoop out the pulp, leaving the shell intact. Set shells asides. Combine potato pulp and all other ingredients except the seafood. Beat with electric mixer until smooth. Stir in seafood chunks. Spoon into shells. Sprinkle with paprika. Bake at 450° for 15 minutes, or until heated through. Low-fat and delicious.

Diane Munro

Shrimp Scampi

1/2 c. white wine
1/2 c. melted butter
1 T. garlic powder
1 lb. shrimp, peeled & deveined (Sam's Club sells this in their frozen section; just thaw before using)

Combine all in a shallow casserole dish. Bake at 350° for about 9 minutes, or until shrimp turns pink.

Michelle Bomgaars

Tuna Casserole

1/2 lb. Velveeta cheese
1 can cream of chicken or celery soup
1/2 c. milk
4 oz. noodles, cooked & drained
2 (6 1/2 oz.) cans tuna, drained
Pepper
1/2 c. coarsely-crumbled saltines
2 T. melted margarine

Heat cheese, soup and milk until cheese melts. Add cooked noodles and tuna to above mixture. Top with crumbs, mixed with melted margarine. Bake, uncovered, 20 to 30 minutes at 325°.

Mary Ann Winchell

Tuna Pie

1 1/2 c. raw potatoes
2 c. raw carrots
1/4 c. chopped onion
1/4 c. chopped parsley
1 tsp. salt
1/8 tsp. pepper
1 1/4 c. water
1 (6 1/2 oz.) can tuna
1 can cream of chicken soup

Combine in a saucepan. Add 6 1/2-ounce can of tuna. Cover; boil slowly for 15 minutes, until vegetables are tender. Stir in 1 can cream of chicken soup. Pour in a greased casserole. Top with buttered bread triangles. Bake at 350° until lightly browned, 15 minutes. Yield: 4 to 6 servings.

Dawn Beukelman

Lasagna, Pizza & Miscellaneous

Chicken Lasagna

9 lasagna noodles
3 to 4 c. diced, cooked chicken
8 oz. Mozzarella cheese
1/2 c. Parmesan cheese
1/2 c. minced onion
1/2 c. finely-chopped celery
3 T. margarine
1 (1 lb.) jar Ragu alfredo sauce, or 1 can cream of chicken soup, 1 can cream of mushroom & 1/3 c. broth or milk

Cook lasagna noodles until nearly done. Sauté onion and celery in margarine. Add chicken, and alfredo sauce or soups, to broth or milk. Put in a 9x9- or 9x11-inch pan in layers, starting with noodles, chicken and sauce mix, Mozzarella cheese and Parmesan cheese, a total of 3 layers. Bake in 350° oven for approximately 45 to 60 minutes, until lightly browned on top.

Diane Munro

Chicken Lasagna

1 (8 oz.) pkg. lasagna noodles
3 c. diced, cooked chicken
1 1/2 c. cottage cheese
1/2 c. Parmesan cheese
2 c. shredded American cheese
8 oz. Mozzarella cheese
3 T. butter
1/4 c. chopped onion
1 can cream of chicken soup
1 can cream of mushroom soup
1/3 c. broth or milk

Mix soups, broth, onion, butter and chicken. Layer in a 9x13-inch pan. First, half of the noodles, then meat mixture, and cheeses; repeat. Top with a few crushed potato chips. Bake for 45 minutes at 350°. Let stand 5 minutes before cutting.
Elaine Vander Broek

Easy Lasagna

1 lb. hamburger
1 jar Prego (onion & garlic)
3 c. Mozzarella cheese
1 lg. ctn. cottage cheese
9 or 10 lasagna noodles

Brown hamburger. Boil noodles. Add Prego to hamburger when brown. Simmer 10 minutes. Put a little meat mixture, in bottom of a 9x13-inch pan to keep noodles from sticking. Layer 3 noodles, meat sauce, 1/3 cottage cheese and 1 cup Mozzarella cheese. Add 2 more layers. Bake at 350° for 1 hour. Add salad and garlic bread for a complete meal.
Deb den Hoed

Easy Lasagna

1 lb. hamburger
1 sm. jar Prego
8 oz. Mozzarella cheese
1/3 c. Parmesan cheese
8 oz. sour cream
1 pkg. crescent rolls
1/4 c. butter

Brown hamburger; drain. Stir in Prego. Simmer until hot. Put in a 7x11-inch pan. Mix Mozzarella cheese and sour cream. Put on top of meat mixture. Melt butter; mix with Parmesan cheese. Brush on top of crescent rolls. Bake at 325° for 30 to 45 minutes, or until brown. Let stand 5 minutes before serving.
Chris Van Beek

Lasagna

1 lb. ground beef
1/2 c. chopped onion
1 (15 oz.) can tomato sauce
1 (6 oz.) can tomato paste
1/2 c. water
1 clove garlic, minced
1 tsp. oregano
1/2 tsp. pepper
1 (8 oz.) box lasagna noodles, cooked
1 (12 oz.) pkg. shredded Mozzarella cheese
1/2 lb. American cheese, thinly sliced
1/2 c. Parmesan cheese, grated

Brown beef; add onion. Cook until tender. Stir in tomato sauce, tomato paste, water, garlic and seasonings. Cover; simmer 30 minutes. In a 9x13-inch baking dish, layer noodles, meat sauce and cheeses. Repeat layers. Bake at 350° for 30 minutes.

Dawn Beukelman

Lasagna

1 lb. ground beef
1/2 c. onion, chopped
1 (1 lb.) can tomatoes
1 (6 oz.) can tomato paste
1/2 c. water
1 clove garlic, minced
1 tsp. oregano
1/2 tsp. pepper
1 (8 oz.) box lasagna noodles, cooked
2 (6 oz.) pkg. Mozzarella cheese
1/2 lb. American cheese, thinly sliced
1/2 c. Parmesan cheese, grated

Brown ground beef; add onion. Cook until tender. Stir in tomatoes, tomato paste, water, garlic and pepper. Cover; simmer 30 minutes. In a 9x13-inch baking dish, layer noodles, meat sauce, and cheeses. Repeat layers. Bake at 350° for 30 minutes.

Evonne Wiegelenga

Old-Fashioned Lasagna

Lasagna noodles
1 lb. ground beef
1 (1 lb. 10 oz.) jar spaghetti sauce
15 oz. ricotta cheese
2 c. shredded Mozzarella cheese
2 T. Parmesan cheese
1 egg
1 T. dried parsley flakes
1 T. oregano
Salt & pepper, to taste

Brown ground beef; drain. Add spaghetti sauce; mix. In a medium bowl, mix ricotta, 1 cup Mozzarella, Parmesan cheese, egg and seasonings. In a 9x13-inch pan, layer ingredients as follows: meat sauce, 3 noodles, ricotta mixture, etc. Continue until ingredients are gone. Sprinkle with Mozzarella cheese. Cover with foil. Bake 30 minutes at 350°. Remove foil; bake 15 more minutes, until hot and bubbly.

Heather Hofmeyer

Sunday Lasagna

Brown:
2 lb. ground beef
1/2 c. chopped onion

Add:
2 tsp. dried parsley
1/4 tsp. powdered garlic
1 tsp. dried sweet basil
2 (8 oz.) cans tomato sauce
1 (4 oz.) can mushrooms
2 tsp. oregano
2 tsp. salt
1/2 tsp. pepper

Simmer this mixture.
Combine:
2 c. cottage cheese
1 c. Mozzarella cheese

Using 1 package lasagna noodles, layer half of <u>uncooked</u> noodles in a well-greased 9x13-inch pan. Next, add a layer of meat mixture, then a layer of cheese mixture. Repeat layers. Pour over all, enough tomato juice (about 2 cups), so you can see the juice around the edges. Bake 2 hours at 300°.
Note: Works great to make the night before! *Marietta VanDer Weide*

Macaroni and Cheese

1 scant c. macaroni (enriched elbow)
1 T. flour
Pinch of salt
A little pepper
Butter (size of walnut)
1 c. milk
3/4 c. diced cheese
18 crackers

Boil water and salt. Add macaroni; boil until done (about 5 minutes). Drain. Cover with cold water. Let stand. Drain. Make white sauce using milk, pepper, salt and flour; bring to boil. Add macaroni and cheese. Butter mixing bowl. Roll out 18 crackers. Melt butter; mix with crackers. Put over macaroni. Bake 30 minutes at 350°. *Elnora McGilvra*

Manicotti

Manicotti shells
Brown & serve sausages
Sliced Mozzarella cheese
Shredded Mozzarella cheese
Prego pasta sauce

Boil manicotti shells until tender. (Cook carefully, they stick.) Cook brown & serve sausages; wrap in a small slice of Mozzarella cheese. Stuff into shells. Cover with Prego. Top with shredded Mozzarella cheese. Bake at 350° until cheese melts and sauce is bubbly. *Becky Vander Stelt*

Pasta Mix

8 oz. your choice of pasta, dried
1 c. canned mushrooms
1/2 onion, cubed or diced
3 c. spaghetti sauce

Sauté onion and mushrooms in a pan with vegetable oil. Add salt, pepper, garlic salt, and Italian seasonings to taste. Boil pasta 9 to 11 minutes, or until tender. Heat sauce on stove or in microwave until hot. Combine all ingredients; serve.
A low-fat dish.

Amanda Van Voorst

Spaghetti

2 lb. hamburger, browned & drained
10 oz. spaghetti noodles, cooked & drained
32 oz. Ragu spaghetti sauce

Mix these 3 items together.

1 lb. Velveeta cheese
1/4 c. butter
2 T. Parmesan cheese
1 T. flour

Mix Velveeta cheese and butter. Add Parmesan cheese and flour to cheese mixture to thicken. In a 9x13-inch pan, layer 1/2 of the meat mixture and spaghetti on the bottom of the pan. Spread 1/2 of the cheese sauce. Add remaining meat-spaghetti mixture; top with cheese sauce. Bake 45 minutes at 350°.

Dawn Beukelman

Spaghetti

6 oz. spaghetti
1/4 c. grated Parmesan cheese
2 eggs, well beaten
Spaghetti sauce
2 T. margarine
1 c. Mozzarella cheese
1 lb. sausage, browned
8 oz. drained cottage cheese

Cook spaghetti; drain. Stir margarine into hot spaghetti. Stir in Parmesan cheese and eggs. Form spaghetti into a "crust" in a 9-inch pie plate. Cook in microwave on HIGH, uncovered, for 2 minutes. Brown sausage. Stir in just enough spaghetti sauce to make a nice moist mixture. Cook, uncovered, at HIGH until sauce is bubbly, 3 to 3 1/2 minutes. Spread cottage cheese over bottom of spaghetti "crust." Fill with meat sauce. Cook on HIGH until heated through, 6 to 7 minutes. Top with Mozzarella cheese. Cook at HIGH until cheese is melted, 1 minute more. Let stand 8 to 10 minutes before serving.

Wendy Heemstra

Spaghetti Bake

1 1/2 lb. ground beef	1 1/2 tsp. oregano
1/2 c. chopped onion	1 tsp. salt
1 clove garlic, minced	1 tsp. basil
1 (28 oz.) can tomatoes	8 oz. spaghetti, broken, cooked & drained
1 (15 oz.) can tomato sauce	8 oz. shredded Mozzarella cheese
1 (4 oz.) can mushroom stems & pieces, drained	1/3 c. grated Parmesan cheese
2 tsp. sugar	

Brown ground beef with onion and minced garlic; drain off excess fat. Stir in undrained tomatoes, tomato sauce, mushroom stems and pieces, sugar, oregano, salt and basil. Bring meat mixture to boiling; boil gently, uncovered, for 20 to 25 minutes, stirring occasionally. Remove meat sauce from heat; stir in drained spaghetti. Place half of the spaghetti-meat sauce in a 9x13-inch baking dish. Sprinkle with Mozzarella cheese. Top with remaining spaghetti meat sauce; sprinkle with grated Parmesan cheese. Bake casserole at 375° for 30 minutes. Yield: 12 servings.

Emily Maassen

Spaghetti Casserole

MEAT MIXTURE:
6 oz. spaghetti
1 lb. hamburger
1 (32 oz.) jar spaghetti sauce

CHEESE MIXTURE:
3 T. oleo, melted
1 c. American or Velveeta cheese
1/4 tsp. salt
1 c. milk
1/3 c. water
2 T. flour
2 T. Parmesan cheese

Boil spaghetti until done; drain. Brown hamburger; drain. Mix spaghetti, hamburger and 32-ounce jar spaghetti sauce; set aside. Melt 3 tablespoons butter; stir in 2 tablespoons flour and 1/4 teaspoon salt. Add 1 cup milk and 1/3 cup water. Cook until thickened, stirring occasionally. Add 1 cup American or Velveeta cheese and 2 tablespoons Parmesan cheese. Stir until cheese melts. Layer in a 9x9-inch pan: 1/2 meat mixture, 1/4 cheese mixture, 1/2 meat and 3/4 cheese. Bake at 350° for 30 minutes.

Chris Van Beek

Bubble Pizza

1 1/2 lb. ground beef
1 (15 oz.) can pizza sauce
2 tubes refrigerated biscuits
1 1/2 c. shredded Mozzarella cheese
1 c. shredded Cheddar cheese

In a skillet, brown the beef; drain. Stir in pizza sauce. Quarter the biscuits; place in a greased 9x13-inch pan. Top with the beef mixture. Bake, uncovered, at 400° for 20 to 25 minutes. Sprinkle with cheese. Bake 5 to 10 minutes longer, or until cheese is melted. Let stand for 5 to 10 minutes before serving.

Sherri Altena

Bubble Pizza

2 tubes buttermilk biscuits
1 jar quick sauce
1 lb. ground beef
Onion, to taste
1 can mushrooms (opt.)
Chopped green pepper (opt.)
2 c. shredded Mozzarella cheese

Brown hamburger and onions. Cut biscuits in fourths. Put in pizza sauce; stir. Add hamburger. Add other ingredients; stir. Put into a greased 9x13-inch pan. Bake at 350° for 30 minutes. Put cheese on the last 5 minutes.

Jennifer Vander Schaaf

Chicken-Cheese Pizza

1 tsp. olive oil
3/4 lb. boneless, skinless chicken breast, cut in 1/2" pieces
1 red pepper, cut in strips
1 tsp. rosemary or oregano
1 (12 or 16 oz.) Italian bread shell or prepared pizza crust
1/4 c. prepared refrigerated pesto (I use pizza sauce)
1 1/2 c. (6 oz.) shredded cheese (Cheddar & Mozzarella)
3 T. green onion slices
1/2 c. (2 oz.) shredded Parmesan cheese

Heat oil in a large nonstick skillet over medium-high heat. Add chicken, pepper and rosemary; stir-fry about 5 minutes, or until chicken is no longer pink. Remove from heat. Place shell on a large baking sheet; spread evenly with pesto or pizza sauce. Sprinkle with 3/4 cup double cheese. Arrange chicken mixture over cheese; top with remaining double cheese, green onions and Parmesan cheese. Bake at 450° for 12 to 14 minutes. Yield: 6 servings.

Vera Brouwer

Crescent Roll Pizza

2 pkg. crescent rolls
1 lb. hamburger
1 can pizza sauce
Shredded cheese (Cheddar or Mozzarella)
Other "pizza" ingredients you like

Line a 9x13-inch pan with 1 package of crescent rolls. Brown hamburger; add pizza sauce when browned. Simmer 5 minutes. Spread this mixture over rolls. Sprinkle cheese and other pizza ingredients. Put second package of rolls on top. Bake at 350° for 30 minutes, uncovered.

Angela Van Ommeren

Crock-Pot Pizza

1 1/2 lb. hamburger
1 onion
1 (14 oz.) can pizza sauce
1 (14 oz.) can spaghetti sauce
12 oz. noodles
4 oz. Cheddar cheese
4 oz. Mozzarella cheese
1 pkg. sliced pepperoni
Mushrooms (opt.)
Green peppers (opt.)

Brown hamburger and onion; drain off grease. Add sauces; simmer. Boil noodles until tender; drain. In a crock-pot, put a layer of noodles, meat mixture, cheeses and pepperoni; repeat layers. Cook on high for 30 minutes, then low for 1 hour, until cheese melts. Can also bake in 350° oven until cheese melts.

Julie Leusink

Pizza Casserole

1 lb. ground beef or pork
Salt, to taste
3 c. tomato juice
6 to 8 oz. noodles, cooked
Pepperoni slices (opt.)
4 to 6 oz. shredded Mozzarella cheese
1/2 c. chopped onions
1/2 tsp. oregano
1/4 tsp. garlic powder
6 to 8 oz. shredded Cheddar or American cheese

Brown meat and onions; salt, if desired. Drain off fat if needed. Add tomato juice (can substitute 1-pound can tomatoes and 6-ounce can tomato paste) and seasonings. Heat through. In a 2-quart dish, layer (or stir if you like), half of noodles and meat mixture; sprinkle with Cheddar cheese. Repeat with remainder of noodles and meat. Spread Mozzarella over the top. Pepperoni slices, mushrooms and peppers can be added to suit your family's taste. Bake, uncovered, 30 minutes, until well heated and cheese melts.

Faye Vander Lugt

Pizza Casserole

12 oz. rigatoni pasta
2 lb. hamburger
1 lb. sausage
1 onion
1 (8 oz.) can mushrooms, cut up (use liquid)
1 tsp. oregano
32 oz. Mozzarella cheese
1 can tomato soup
32 oz. spaghetti sauce
1 (14 oz.) jar pizza sauce
1 c. hot water
1 pkg. pepperoni
1 tsp. garlic powder
Salt & pepper

Brown hamburger and sausage with onion; drain fat. Salt, pepper and garlic. Cook noodles; drain. In a large bowl, mix all other ingredients except 1 cup Mozzarella. Add meat to mixture. Add noodles; mix well. Bake at 350° for 45 minutes with cover. Remove cover; sprinkle remaining Mozzarella cheese on top. Bake another 15 minutes, uncovered. Yield: two 9x13-inch pans.

Betty L. VanDer Weide

Pizza Casserole

2 lb. ground beef
1 jar Ragu pizza sauce
2 pkg. crescent rolls
Pepperoni (opt.)
3 c. shredded Mozzarella cheese

Brown meat; drain well. Add pizza sauce. Place 1 package of crescent rolls in bottom of a 9x13-inch pan; press seams together. Layer the beef, pepperoni and cheese. Top with other package of rolls. Bake at 350° until golden brown, about 20 minutes.

Winova Van Regenmorter

Pizza Casserole

6 c. diced potatoes
1 lb. ground beef
1/4 c. diced onion
1 can Cheddar cheese soup & 1/2 can milk
1 can tomato sauce or pizza sauce
1/2 tsp. oregano
1/2 tsp. salt
1/2 tsp. sugar

Put potatoes into a greased 3-quart casserole dish. Brown ground beef; add onion and Cheddar cheese soup with milk. Spread meat mixture over diced potatoes. Mix together last 4 ingredients; pour over meat mixture. Bake at 350° for 1 1/2 hours. Top with lots of Mozzarella cheese. Bake until cheese is melted.

Peggy Wichers,
Colette Hofmeyer

Pizza Hamburger Casserole

2 (8 oz.) cans crescent rolls
1 1/2 lb. hamburger
1 pkg. sloppy joe mix
1 c. water
1 (12 oz.) can tomato paste
8 oz. Mozzarella cheese
8 oz. Cheddar cheese

Brown hamburger; drain. Add tomato paste, sloppy joe mix and water; simmer 5 minutes. Put 1 can of rolls in bottom of a 9x13-inch pan. Put hamburger mixture in, then cheeses. End with a package of crescent rolls. Bake at 350° for 25 minutes.

Kathy Dykstra

Pizza Hot Dish

1 lb. ground beef
2 c. noodles
1 (4 oz.) can mushrooms
1 (4 oz.) can black olives
1/2 lb. pepperoni
1 can favorite pizza sauce
2 c. shredded Mozzarella
   cheese

Brown ground beef. Cook noodles; drain. Mix in pizza sauce and pepperoni. Spread into a 1 1/2-quart (well-greased) pan. Sprinkle shredded cheese on top; bake 30 minutes at 350°. Add any ingredients your family likes.

Marietta VanDer Weide

Pizza in the Round

1 med. green bell pepper
1/2 c. onion, chopped
3/4 lb. lean ground beef
1 garlic clove, pressed
4 oz. (1 c.) Mozzarella cheese,
   shredded
1 c. pizza sauce, divided
1 tsp. Italian seasoning mix
1 tsp. salt
2 (8 oz.) pkg. refrigerated
   crescent rolls
2 T. fresh grated Parmesan
   cheese

Preheat oven to 375°. Cut off top 1/4 of pepper. Save bottom part. Chop top part of pepper to make 1/4 cup. Chop onion. Cook and stir ground beef, bell pepper, onion and garlic until done. Drain well. Shred Mozzarella. In a bowl, combine meat mixture, Mozzarella cheese, 1/4 cup pizza sauce, seasoning mix and salt. To assemble ring, unroll crescent dough. Separate into 16 triangles. Arrange triangles in a circle on a 15-inch round baking stone, with wide ends of triangle overlapping in the center and points toward the outside. Scoop meat mixture evenly onto the widest end of each triangle. Bring point of triangles up over filling and tuck under wide ends of dough at center of ring (filling will not be completely covered). Bake 20 to 25 minutes, or until deep golden brown. Sprinkle with Parmesan cheese. Heat remaining pizza sauce and fill bell pepper bottom; place in center of ring.

Cheryl Van Wyk

Pizza Loaf

1 lb. ground beef
1/2 c. minced onion
Salt & pepper, to taste
1 tsp. paprika
1/2 tsp. oregano
1/2 tsp. garlic salt
1 (8 oz.) can tomato sauce
1 loaf frozen bread dough
1 c. Cheddar cheese
3/4 c. Mozzarella cheese

Sauté beef and onion until meat is browned. Mix in spices. Add tomato sauce. Simmer 30 minutes, covered. Cool. Prepare bread dough through first rising. Punch down; roll into 12x15-inch rectangle. Place meat mixture down center of dough, using 1/3 of width. Sprinkle cheese on top of meat (Cheddar, then Mozzarella). Make cut 1 1/2 inches apart down each side of dough. Bring strips of dough over filling, crisscrossing each side. Seal overlapping strips with a drop of water. Place on a greased baking sheet; brush with melted butter. Bake at 350° for 30 to 40 minutes, until browned.

Amanda Wiersema

Pizza Pies

2 slices of bread
Butter
Pizza sauce
Meat topping (your choice)
Onions
Green peppers
Olives
Mushrooms
Any other toppings you like
Mozzarella cheese

Butter bread on outside. Place in camp cooker. Put pizza sauce, meat, vegetables, and top with cheese. Cook over campfire until golden brown on both sides.

Variation: Use pie filling instead to make a dessert. Sprinkle with sugar and cinnamon after it is cooked.

Marlene Van Beek

Quick and Easy Pizza

Day-old Farmers Bread or
　hoagie buns
Pizza sauce
Pepperoni
Mozzarella cheese
Chopped green peppers &/or
　onions (opt.)
Any other combinations desired

Split bread or buns; lay on cookie sheet. Spread pizza sauce on bread. Arrange meat over sauce. Add the combination of extras you like. Sprinkle cheese on top. Bake at 350° to 375° for 15 to 20 minutes, until cheese is melted and pizza is hot.

Evelyn De Vries

Upside-Down Pizza

1 lb. hamburger, browned & drained
1 (8 oz.) can pizza sauce
1 c. Mozzarella cheese
1/2 c. Bisquick
1/2 c. milk
1 egg
1 c. shredded Cheddar cheese

Put browned hamburger in a 9x13-inch pan. Cover with pizza sauce; sprinkle on Mozzarella cheese. Mix Bisquick, milk and egg; pour over Mozzarella cheese. Sprinkle Cheddar cheese on top. Bake at 425° for 15 minutes.
This is a fast meal. You can add olives to meat, and substitute spaghetti sauce for the pizza sauce.
Tammy Sneller

Stromboli

Bread dough
Pepperoni
Ham
Mozzarella cheese
Italian seasoning
Spaghetti sauce

Roll bread dough into a rectangular shape. Sprinkle with Italian seasoning. In a strip, layer ham, pepperoni and Mozzarella cheese, 1 1/2 inches from the edge. Roll once. Add another layer of meats and cheese. Roll into a big roll. Prick with a fork. Let rise until double. Bake at 350° for 20 minutes, with tinfoil on. Remove foil; bake for 15 to 20 minutes, until golden brown. Brush with butter. Cut into strips. Serve with warm spaghetti sauce. Enjoy.
Kari Van Klompenburg

Casserole Sauce Mix-Cream Soup Substitute

2 c. instant nonfat dry milk
3/4 c. cornstarch
1/4 c. instant chicken bouillon
2 T. dried onion flakes
1 tsp. dried thyme
1 tsp. dried basil
1/2 tsp. pepper

Combine all ingredients; mix well. Store in an airtight container. The recipe makes 3 cups or equivalent of 9 (10 1/2-ounce) cans of condensed cream soup to substitute for 1 can of soup. Combine 1/3 cup dry mix with 1 1/4 cups water in a saucepan. Cook and stir well until thickened. If desired, can add 1 tablespoon margarine.
Nutritional Information: 95 calories, compared to 330 calories in a can of condensed soup.
Chris Van Beek

Campfire Bundles

1 lg. sweet onion, sliced
1 each: lg. green, sweet red & yellow pepper, sliced
4 med. potatoes, sliced 1/2" thick
6 med. carrots, sliced 1/4" thick
1 sm. cabbage, sliced
2 med. tomatoes, chopped
1 to 1 1/2 lb. fully-cooked Polish sausage, cut into 1/2" pieces
1/2 c. butter or margarine
1 tsp. salt
1/2 tsp. pepper

Place vegetables in order listed on three pieces of double-layered heavy-duty foil (about 18x18 inches). Add sausage; dot with butter. Sprinkle with salt and pepper. Fold foil around the mixture; seal tightly. Grill, covered, over medium coals for 30 minutes. Turn and grill 15 to 30 minutes longer, or until vegetables are tender. Yield: 6 servings.

Emily Maassen

Hobo Dinners

On foil, place a hamburger patty; season with salt and pepper. Slice potatoes, onions and carrots on top. Add a couple dabs of oleo. Salt and pepper, to taste. Seal up the foil. Cook over fire or top rack of grill, turning occasionally, until cooked.

Marlene Van Beek

Meat Marinade

1 1/2 c. salad oil
3/4 c. soy sauce
1/4 c. Worcestershire sauce
2 T. dry mustard
1 tsp. black pepper
1/2 c. wine vinegar
1/3 c. ReaLemon
1 1/2 tsp. dried parsley flakes (opt.)
2 garlic cloves, crushed (opt.)

Combine in blender. Marinate steaks or chops for at least 4 hours or overnight. Grill meat.

Mary Ann Winchell

Sausage Gravy for Biscuits and Gravy

1 lb. pork sausage
1/4 c. butter or margarine
2/3 c. flour
1/2 tsp. pepper
1/2 tsp. salt
1 tsp. sage
3 c. milk

Brown sausage; drain off fat, but be sure to reserve 1/2 cup of fat to put in the pan to start making your gravy. Add the butter to this fat; melt. Take it off the heat while you add the flour and seasonings. Stir until flour is no longer seen and it is smooth. Add the milk gradually, stirring as it is added, so it stays smooth. Heat, stirring constantly, until thick. Serve over hot biscuits or toast.

Lonna Kluis

Ethnic

Balka-Brai
(Dutch)

5 c. water
4 c. cracklings
2 tsp. salt
1 tsp. allspice
1 tsp. cloves
1 tsp. pepper
1 c. cornmeal
1 c. buckwheat flour
2 c. white flour

Bring the first 6 ingredients to a rolling boil. Add cornmeal and cook for 3 minutes. Add buckwheat flour and cook for 1 to 2 minutes longer. Add white flour; add this slowly and stir over low heat with a heavy spoon. Pack in a loaf pan. When cool, cut in thin slices and fry in butter until browned. Serve with syrup. Refrigerate unused portion.

Committee

Currant Bread
(Dutch)

2 1/2 lb. flour
2 c. warm water
2 tsp. salt
1/2 stick oleo or butter
3 tsp. sugar, divided
2 pkg. dry yeast
2 c. currants
1 tsp. lemon extract

Combine yeast, 2 teaspoons sugar and 1/2 cup warm water; set aside. Use a large bowl; put flour on one side; to other side, put warm water, salt, oleo and 1 teaspoon sugar. Add yeast mixture when oleo (or butter) is melted. Mix. If dough is too stiff, add more water. Pour lemon extract over currants. Mix into flour mixture with your hands. Let rise in a bowl; punch down and put into 3 bread pans. Let rise again and bake at 350° to 370° for 20 minutes.

Note: Can substitute raisins for currants. Plump them in hot water and drain before adding to bread.

Committee

Almond Roll
(Dutch)

1 lb. butter
4 c. flour
1 c. cold water

Mix butter and flour until fine. Add cold water. Blend like pie crust. Mix and let stand in refrigerator overnight.

FILLING:
1 lb. almond paste
1 1/2 c. sugar
3 eggs, beaten
1 tsp. real lemon

Mix almond paste and sugar; add beaten eggs and lemon juice. Mix well and chill overnight.

Divide dough into 4 parts. Roll out one part to the size of a cookie sheet. Cut into 2 strips (the longest way). Use 1/8 of filling for each strip. This recipe makes 8 almond rolls. Roll up from side (16 inches). Brush with cream and sprinkle with sugar. Chill for 1 hour. Prick holes with a fork in top. Bake at 350° for almost 45 minutes, or until light brown.

Mary Ann Winchell

Dutch Butter Cookies
(Krak al Ingen)

1 lb. butter
1 lb. flour
1/2 c. water

Prepare like pie dough and place in refrigerator overnight. The next morning, roll out to size and length of a pencil. Form into a figure-8. Dip both sides in sugar and bake at 375° for about 30 minutes, until browned.

Committee

Jan Hagel Cookies
(Dutch)

1 c. oleo or butter
1 c. sugar
2 c. flour
1 egg, separated
1 tsp. cinnamon
Chopped nuts

Cream oleo, sugar and egg yolk. Sift flour and cinnamon; add to creamed mixture, a little at a time. Pat down very thin on a cookie sheet and brush with unbeaten egg white and a few drops of water. Sprinkle with nuts. Bake for 25 minutes at 350°. Cut while warm.

Committee

St. Nick Cookies
(Dutch)

1 c. brown sugar
1 c. white sugar
1 c. Spry (Crisco)
1/2 c. oleo
1/2 c. sour cream
4 c. flour

1 tsp. baking soda
1/4 tsp. cloves
1/4 tsp. nutmeg
1/4 tsp. allspice
4 tsp. cinnamon

Cream sugars and shortenings; add sour cream. Sift dry ingredients together and add to creamed mixture. Form into 2 rolls; wrap in waxed paper and refrigerate overnight (or can also freeze). Slice thin and bake in 350° oven.

Committee

St. Nicholas Cookies
(Dutch)

1 c. butter (butter only), softened
3/4 c. white sugar

3/4 c. brown sugar
1 egg

Beat together.
Add the following ingredients, in order listed:

2 c. flour
1 tsp. baking soda
1/2 tsp. salt
2 tsp. cinnamon

1 tsp. ground cloves
1 c. rolled oats
1 tsp. nutmeg

Roll into small balls, about 1 teaspoon. Place on cookie sheet; flatten with floured tumbler. Bake for 15 minutes at 350°.

Rob and Shelly Sikma

Laughter is the spice of life.

Stroopwaffles
(Dutch)

2 pkg. dry yeast	1/4 c. warm water

Dissolve yeast in water; set aside.
Cream:

2 lb. brown sugar	1 lb. lard (can use Crisco)
1 lb. butter	2 eggs

Add:

2 tsp. cinnamon	1 c. milk
1 tsp. salt	Dissolved yeast mixture

Stir in 2 cups flour. Add 4 to 4 1/2 pounds more flour (pour in 2 cups at a time. The last flour will have to be kneaded in, as the dough gets very firm. Make balls the size of a walnut. Store in a cool place overnight.

The next morning, make the filling by placing following ingredients in a crock-pot:

1 1/2 lb. brown sugar	2 c. dark Karo syrup (stroop)
1 lb. butter	

Heat 2 to 3 hours (on low) before you begin baking the waffles, stirring occasionally. Bake the waffles in a "stroopwaffle" iron. Immediately after taking out of the iron, slice each "waffle" in half. Put a little of the syrup mixture on one half, and cover with the second half. Let cool before packaging. These freeze well. Yield: about 14 dozen.

"Stroopwaffles" are like a filled cookie. They are a Dutch delicacy, and are delicious with a good cup of coffee.

Marilyn Kruid

Grandma's Oli Bollen
(Dutch)

6 c. flour	2 to 3 apples, peeled & chopped
2 c. sugar	1 pkg. yeast in 1/2 c. warm water
1 tsp. salt	4 to 6 eggs, beaten
1 tsp. baking powder	1 1/2 c. warm milk
2 to 3 c. raisins	

Mix dry ingredients. Add fruit and liquid. Mix thoroughly and let rise for 2 hours in a warm place. Drop by tablespoon into hot oil. Fry until brown on both sides. Eat warm, rolled in sugar.

These are a Christmas tradition at our family celebration.

Dawn De Weerd

Zuider Zee
(Dutch)

1 pkg. (1 doz.) rusks
1/4 c. sugar
1 tsp. cinnamon
3 T. butter
1 qt. milk
4 egg yolks

1/2 c. sugar
3 T. cornstarch
Vanilla
4 egg whites
3 tsp. sugar

Roll rusks and combine with 1/4 cup sugar, cinnamon and butter. Press into a buttered 9x13-inch pan, reserving 1/4 of the mixture for the top. Make custard by combining milk, egg yolks, 1/2 cup sugar, cornstarch and vanilla. Put over rusk mixture. Cover with beaten egg whites and sugar. Sprinkle reserved rusk crumb mixture over. Bake for 30 minutes at 300°. ***Committee***

Poffertjes

4 T. sugar
1 tsp. salt
1 c. hot water

1 c. flour
3 eggs

Mix and pour like pancakes. Serve with butter and powdered sugar.
Mary Ann Winchell

Pigs-in-the-Blanket
(Dutch)

DOUGH:
5 c. flour
1 1/2 tsp. baking powder
1 T. sugar

1 1/2 tsp. salt
3 sticks oleo
2 eggs, beaten
1 1/2 c. milk

FILLING:
3 lb. pig-in-the-blanket meat

1 egg
2 rusks

Mix flour, baking powder, sugar, salt and oleo until crumbly, like pie dough. Beat eggs. Add milk and add to the crumbly mixture. Refrigerate until cool (overnight). Roll out 1/4 of the dough at a time. Cut in strips about 3 inches wide. Cut the strips into 2-inch lengths. Place filling down the center and roll up, sealing the ends. You can freeze until ready to bake.

Baking Time from Frozen: 375° for 10 minutes, and then at 350° for 45 minutes.

Note: Line the baking pan with brown paper to soak up grease.
Committee

Huss Pot
(Dutch)

Potatoes
Carrots
1 can brown beans
Salt, to taste
Sausage or ring bologna

Pare potatoes to fill 1/2 of pan. Put as many carrots on top as potatoes. Add beans (may use pork and beans). Sprinkle with salt. Boil with sausage or ring bologna on top. When done, mash with potato masher. Cut up meat in chunks.
Note: Use just enough water so it doesn't burn.

Committee

Red Cabbage and Apples
(Dutch)

1/3 c. sugar
1 tsp. salt
1/4 c. vinegar
1 c. water
1/2 c. butter
4 qt. shredded cabbage
 (3 to 3 1/2 lb. head)
5 tart apples

In a deep saucepan, combine sugar, salt, vinegar, water and butter. Heat to boiling. Stir in shredded cabbage and tart apples, peeled and shredded. Cover and simmer for 2 to 2 1/2 hours, stirring occasionally.
Delicious!

Dorothy VanDer Weide

Dutch Salad Dressing

Dice and brown 2 slices bacon.
Mix together:
1 T. flour
1 egg
1 c. water
1/2 c. sugar
1/4 c. vinegar

Add mixture to bacon on stove and cook until thick. Cut garden lettuce fine. Add chopped onion and a diced, hard-cooked egg. Pour dressing over.

Committee

Specken-Dicken
(German Griddle Cake)

1/2 c. lard
1 c. brown sugar
2 eggs
2 T. molasses
1 tsp. salt
1 heaping tsp. baking soda
4 c. whole wheat flour
Bologna, sausage or bacon

Mix together; add enough sour milk or buttermilk to thin like other griddle cakes. Pour on frying pan and add slices of bologna, sausage or bacon. This is a New Year's Day German tradition.

Cindy VanDer Weide

German Potato Salad

4 to 5 boiled potatoes, sliced
8 slices bacon, cut in pieces
1 med. onion, diced
3 T. celery, diced
1 heaping T. diced green pepper
3 T. flour
2 c. hot water
1/2 c. brown sugar
4 T. vinegar

Place bacon, onion, celery and pepper in a large frying pan. Fry until ingredients turn light golden. Add flour and continue frying until it gets as brown as you like. Add hot water, vinegar and brown sugar. Cook slowly for about 5 minutes. Add more salt and pepper to taste. Cook in skillet for 1/2 hour and mix with potatoes. Put into casserole and bake at 300° for 30 to 45 minutes.

Joyce Baker

German Peppernuts

3/4 c. oleo
2 c. brown sugar
1 1/2 c. white sugar
2 eggs
Dash of salt
1 tsp. baking soda dissolved in
 1/2 c. cold coffee
1 tsp. anise oil
1 1/2 tsp. cinnamon
4 c. flour (or more if needed)

Mix with mixer and add 4 cups flour. Add more flour, if needed to work with. Roll out as thick as your pinky, but not with rolling pin. Wrap in waxed paper; freeze. Slice thin and bake for 10 minutes at 300°.

Joyce Baker

Kheema Chaval
(Indian--Rice with Ground Beef)

3 T. cooking oil	1 onion, finely chopped
2 T. finely-grated fresh ginger	1 tsp. cayenne pepper
2 cloves fresh garlic, finely chopped	2 to 3 diced cloves
1/2 tsp. turmeric	3 to 4 tiny pieces cinnamon stick
1 tsp. black pepper	1 tsp. cumin powder
1 tsp. coriander powder	1 lb. ground beef
2 c. rice	4 c. water
1 T. butter	Salt, to taste

Heat oil in a pan. Drop the onion in the hot oil and fry for a few minutes. Add ginger and garlic. Fry for a few more minutes. Cook the ground beef in a separate pan. Drain fat and rinse with hot water. Add the meat to the ginger and garlic mixture. Stir well. Add all of the spices and cook over a low fire for 15 minutes. Cook the rice separately with the 4 cups water, butter and salt. Once the rice is cooked, mix the ground beef mixture to the rice. Toss until the two are mixed.

Variation: To make Kheema Sabzi Chaval (Rice with Ground Beef and Vegetables), add the following vegetables to the onion mixture just before you add the meat:

1/2 c. frozen peas	1/4 c. julienne-sliced carrots
1 chopped sweet red or green pepper	

Marilyn Kruid

Kheera Ka Rayta
(Indian--Yogurt with Cucumbers)

2 med. size cucumbers, washed	Salt, to taste
2 c. plain yogurt	Black pepper

Grate or dice the cucumbers. Add the cucumbers and salt to yogurt. Sprinkle with black pepper. If desired, garnish with finely-chopped coriander leaves.

Marilyn Kruid

Watermelon with Yogurt
(Indian)

4 lb. watermelon
5 T. plain yogurt
5 T. sugar

Cut watermelon in chunks; remove all seeds. Place watermelon pieces in a blender. Add yogurt and sugar. Blend for 2 minutes. Refrigerate. Serve in chilled glasses.

Marilyn Kruid

Fettuccine Alfredo
(Italian)

1 pt. heavy whipping cream
1 stick butter or margarine, cut up
3 oz. cream cheese, cubed
3/4 c. Parmesan cheese (fresh works best)
1 tsp. garlic powder
Cooked fettuccine or other noodles

Combine cream, butter and cream cheese in a saucepan. Simmer until melted and smooth, stirring occasionally. Add Parmesan and garlic powder. Simmer for 20 to 30 minutes on low. Serve over cooked noodles. Can add grilled chicken breast for something different.

Michelle Bomgaars

Pepperoni Stromboli
(Italian)

2 (1 lb.) loaves frozen bread dough, thawed
1/2 c. pizza sauce or spaghetti sauce
1/2 tsp. dried oregano
4 oz. (or more) sliced pepperoni
2 c. (8 oz.) Mozzarella cheese
1/3 c. grated Parmesan cheese

Punch dough down on lightly floured surface. Roll each loaf into 20x8-inch rectangle. Place 1 rectangle on a greased baking sheet. Spread sauce in an 18x4-inch strip down the center. Sprinkle with oregano, pepperoni and Mozzarella cheese. Fold sides of dough over filling. Set aside. Cut the remaining rectangle into 3 strips and loosely braid them. Pinch ends to seal. Place braid on top of the cheese and dough. Pinch dough to seal. Sprinkle with Parmesan cheese. Bake at 350° for 30 minutes, or until golden brown. Yield: 8 to 10 servings.

Mike Klemme

Chicken Enchiladas
(Mexican)

3 c. cooked, cubed chicken
1 c. salsa
1 (4 oz.) can chopped green chilies
10 (8") flour tortillas
2 1/2 c. whipping cream (heavy cream)
3 c. (8 oz.) grated Monterey Jack cheese

Combine chicken, salsa, green chilies and 1 cup of cheese. Fill each tortilla with a portion of chicken mixture. Roll up and place, seam-side down, in a greased 9x13-inch pan. Pour cream over top. Sprinkle evenly with remaining cheese. Bake at 350° for 40 minutes, or until golden brown and most of the cream is absorbed.

Shellie Vander Schaaf

Quesadillas

1/3 c. pitted ripe olives, chopped
1 c. shredded Cheddar & Monterey Jack cheese blend
1/3 c. salsa
1/4 c. loosely-packed cilantro, snipped
3 T. green onions, sliced
8 (7") flour tortillas
Vegetable oil

Preheat oven to 425°. Combine olives, cheese and salsa. Add cilantro and onions. Place 4 tortillas on a cookie sheet or baking stone. Divide cheese mixture evenly among tortillas. Spread over tortillas. Top each tortilla with second tortilla. Press firmly. Spray tops with vegetable oil. Bake for 8 to 10 minutes, or until tops are lightly browned. Cool, cut, and serve. (Should get 6 wedges out of each quesadilla.)

Raegen Blom

Work is love made visible.

Swedish Meatballs

1/2 lb. ground beef	3 T. onion, chopped
1/2 lb. ground pork	1 T. butter
1/2 c. dry bread crumbs	1 1/2 tsp. salt
1 1/2 c. milk	1/4 tsp. white pepper
1 egg	2 to 3 T. butter (to fry in)
GRAVY:	3/4 c. cream
1 T. flour	Salt & pepper, to taste

Melt butter in skillet. Sauté onion until golden brown. Soak bread crumbs in milk. Add meat, egg, onion, salt and pepper. Mix thoroughly, until smooth. Shape into balls. Fry in butter until evenly browned, shaking pan continuously to make balls round. Remove meat from pan and put into a bowl. Put a small amount of water in pan each time meatballs are removed, and shake around, thereby saving pan juices, so obtained when meatballs are fried.

Gravy: Mix flour and cream; put into pan juice, stirring constantly. Simmer for 10 minutes. Add more milk or cream if gravy is too thick.

Shellie Vander Schaaf

Asian Chicken Pasta

8 oz. angel hair pasta	1/4 tsp. salt & pepper
1 1/2 T. lite soy sauce	1 T. sesame seeds
1 T. vinegar (rice wine)	1 T. peanut oil
2 tsp. sesame oil	1 (15 oz.) can baby corn, drained & rinsed
3 cloves garlic, minced (3 tsp. divided)	1 red or green pepper, diced
1 lb. boneless, skinless chicken breasts, cut into thin strips	2 carrots, chopped
	3 scallions, cut into 1/2" pieces

Cook pasta according to package.

Meanwhile, combine soy sauce, vinegar, sesame oil and 1 teaspoon garlic. Sprinkle both sides of chicken with salt and pepper. In a dry skillet over medium heat, cook sesame seeds until golden brown, about 2 minutes. Remove from pan; set aside. In the same skillet, heat peanut oil over medium heat. Add remaining garlic. Cook, stirring, until golden, about 1 minute. Add chicken. Cook, stirring occasionally, until no longer pink, about 6 minutes. Remove from heat; keep warm. Drain pasta. In a large serving bowl, combine corn, pepper, carrots and scallions with pasta, chicken and soy sauce mixture. Sprinkle with reserved sesame seeds.

Audrey Vander Stelt

Notes & Recipes

Desserts & Pies

Desserts

Apple Crisp

For a 9x13-inch Pan: Spray glass pan with cooking spray. Layer in the pan, 6 cups of sliced apples.
Mix until crumbly:

1 c. flour
1 c. brown sugar
1 c. white sugar
1 c. oatmeal
1 stick oleo

Sprinkle over apples. Microwave on HIGH for 15 minutes. Rotate pan 1/2-way through the cooking time.

For 9-Inch Pie Pan: Use 4 cups apples.
Mix until crumbly:

1/2 c. flour
1/2 c. brown sugar
1/3 c. white sugar
1/2 c. oatmeal
1/2 stick oleo

Sprinkle over apples. Microwave on HIGH for 12 to 15 minutes. Rotate pan 1/2-way through cooking time.

Marilyn Kruid

Extra-Special Apple Crisp

6 c. sliced apples
1 1/2 c. sugar
1 1/2 c. water
3 1/2 T. cornstarch
3 tsp. cinnamon
1 1/2 c. flour
1 1/4 c. oatmeal
1 1/2 c. brown sugar
3/4 c. melted butter

Spread apples in a 9x13-inch pan. Cook sugar, water and cornstarch until clear and thickened. Pour over apples; sprinkle with cinnamon. Mix until crumbly: flour, oatmeal, sugar and butter. Sprinkle over apples. Bake at 350° for 45 to 55 minutes.

Betty L. VanDer Wiede

Apple Crunch

4 lg. apples
Cinnamon
1 c. sugar

1 c. flour
1/2 c. butter

Cut apples and spread in a buttered 9x9-inch pan with cinnamon. Cream sugar, flour and butter. Spread over apples and bake in 350° oven until golden brown, 1 hour.

Marietta VanDer Wiede

Banana Dessert

CRUST:
1 1/2 c. flour   3/4 c. butter

Combine and bake at 350° for 15 minutes. Cool.

FILLING:
8 oz. cream cheese   1 c. Cool Whip
                          1 c. powdered sugar

Combine and put on top of cooled crust. Slice bananas over cheese mixture. Beat until thick, 2 (3-ounce) packages banana instant pudding and 3 cups milk. Pour over sliced bananas. Top with Cool Whip.

Cindy VanDer Wiede

Banana Cream Brownie Squares

3/4 c. dry-roasted peanuts, chopped, divided
1 (9"x13"-pan-size) pkg. brownie mix
3 med. bananas
1 1/4 c. cold milk

1 (8 oz.) ctn. whipping cream
1 pkg. vanilla instant pudding
9 strawberries
1 oz. semi-sweet chocolate, grated or chopped

Preheat oven to 350°. Make brownie mix. Chop and add peanuts to brownie mix. Cool. Slice 2 bananas. Place in a single layer over brownie. Whisk pudding mix into milk. Beat until it begins to thicken. Fold in 2 1/2 cups whipped topping. Spread mixture over bananas. Refrigerate for 30 minutes. Sprinkle with peanuts. Garnish with dollops of whipped cream. Place sliced strawberries and bananas in center of whipped cream. Grate chocolate over top. Cut into squares.

Note: Can drizzle chocolate sauce for substitute.

Naomi Van Regenmorter

Blueberry Delight

2 c. crushed graham crackers
1/2 c. margarine
1 c. sugar
2 eggs

8 oz. cream cheese
1/2 tsp. vanilla
1 can blueberry pie mix
Cool Whip

Blend crackers, butter and 1/2 cup sugar. Press into a 9x12-inch pan. Mix eggs, cream cheese, the remaining 1/2 cup sugar, and vanilla. Pour over crust. Bake at 350° for 15 minutes. (It will set as it cools.) When totally cool, pour pie mix over, and chill. Spread Cool Whip on top.

Kari Dykstra

Old-Fashioned Bread Pudding

4 c. bread cubes
1/2 c. white sugar
1/4 tsp. salt
1 tsp. cinnamon

1/2 c. raisins, soaked in a little water until plump
2 eggs
2 c. milk

Spread bread cubes in an 8- or 9-inch glass pie plate. Sprinkle with sugar, salt, cinnamon and raisins. Add beaten eggs to milk and pour over other ingredients. Microwave on MEDIUM for about 5 minutes. Rotate dish, then bake another 5 minutes. Center sets as it cools.

Ruth Heidebrink

Brownie Delight

1 (9"x13"-pan-size) pkg. brownie mix
1 (8 oz.) & 1 (3 oz.) pkg. softened cream cheese
2 c. powdered sugar

1 (16 oz.) ctn. Cool Whip
2 c. cold milk
1 sm. pkg. instant chocolate pudding
1/2 c. chopped pecans

Prepare and bake brownies according to package, using a greased 9x13-inch pan. Cool completely. In a mixing bowl, beat cream cheese and sugar for 2 minutes. Fold in 2 cups Cool Whip. Spread over brownies. In another bowl, combine the milk and pudding mix; beat until smooth. Refrigerate for 5 minutes. Spread over cream cheese layer. Spread with remaining Cool Whip; sprinkle with pecans. Refrigerate until serving. Yield: 12 to 15 servings.

Arla Korver

Buster Bar Dessert

1 pkg. Oreo cookies, crushed
1/2 c. oleo, melted
1/2 gal. vanilla ice cream
1 jar hot fudge sauce
1 (8 oz.) ctn. Cool Whip
Salted peanuts

Mix oleo and Oreos. Press all but 1 cup into a 9x13-inch pan. Spread ice cream on next and freeze. Pour hot fudge sauce over the ice cream, and then a layer of salted peanuts. Spread Cool Whip and sprinkle the reserved Oreos on top.

Koreen Van Horn

Buster Bar Dessert

2 "rows" Oreos
1/2 c. melted oleo
1/2 gal. ice cream
1 1/2 c. chopped peanuts
2 c. powdered sugar
1 c. evaporated milk
2/3 c. chocolate chips
1/2 c. oleo
1 tsp. vanilla

Crush Oreos. Add 1/2 cup melted oleo. Press into a 9x13-inch pan. Chill. Spread ice cream over crust. Sprinkle with peanuts. Freeze. Mix the remaining ingredients. Cook for 8 to 10 minutes. Cool. Spread over peanuts and freeze.

Judy Vlietstra

Butterfinger Bar Dessert

CRUST:
2 c. graham cracker crumbs
1 c. melted margarine
1 c. soda cracker crumbs

Press into a 9x13-inch pan.

FILLING:
1 sm. box chocolate instant pudding
1 sm. box butterscotch or vanilla pudding
2 c. milk
1 qt. softened ice cream

TOPPING:
1 (16 oz.) ctn. Cool Whip
3 Butterfinger candy bars, crushed

Spread Cool Whip over filling. Sprinkle crushed Butterfinger bars over top.

Carolyn De Jager

Butterfinger Dessert

2 c. crushed graham crackers
1 c. crushed Club crackers
1/2 c. margarine
2 pkg. instant vanilla pudding
2 c. milk
1 qt. ice cream
1 lg. ctn. Cool Whip
Butterfinger candy bars

Mix cracker crumbs with margarine and press into a 9x13-inch pan. Mix instant pudding with milk. Add vanilla ice cream. Spread mixture on crumbs and let set 1 hour. Spread with Cool Whip and top with crushed Butterfinger bars. Refrigerate.

Wanda Kuiken

Butterfinger Delight

1 angel food cake
6 Butterfinger candy bars
1/4 c. oleo
2 c. powdered sugar
2 tsp. vanilla
4 egg yolks
1 qt. Cool Whip
1/2 c. nuts (opt.)

Cream butter, sugar, vanilla and eggs. Fold in Cool Whip. Tear up angel food cake and put 1/2 into a 9x13-inch pan. Spread 1/2 of creamed mixture over it, then 1/2 of crushed candy bars and nuts. Repeat layers. Chill.

*Evelyn De Vries,
Laura Haverdink, Wanda Kuiken*

Buttery Cinnamon Skillet Apples

1/3 c. butter or oleo
1/2 to 3/4 c. sugar
2 T. cornstarch
1 1/2 c. water
1/4 to 1/2 tsp. cinnamon
4 med. cooking apples, cored, unpeeled, cut in half

In a skillet, melt butter over medium heat (3 to 4 minutes) Stir in sugar and cornstarch; mix well. Add remaining ingredients. Cover; cook over medium heat, spooning sauce over apples occasionally, until apples are fork-tender and sauce is thickened (12 to 15 minutes). To serve, place 2 apple halves in individual dessert dish; spoon 1/2 cup sauce over each of 2 apple halves. Yield: 4 servings, 2 cups sauce.

Alice Vander Broek

Holiday Cheese Tarts

1 (8 oz.) pkg. cream cheese, softened
1 (14 oz.) can sweetened condensed milk
1/3 c. lemon juice
1 tsp. vanilla
2 (4 oz.) pkg. single-serve Keebler ready-crusts

In mixer, beat cream cheese until fluffy. Gradually beat in condensed milk until smooth. Stir in lemon juice and vanilla. Spoon into crusts. Chill 2 hours, or until set. Just before serving, top with cherry pie filling--or you can use assorted fruits, such as strawberries, blueberries, orange segments and pineapple.
Betty Jasper,
Jan Budden

Cherry Angel Food Trifle

1 angel food cake
2 boxes instant vanilla pudding
1 (16 oz.) ctn. Cool Whip
1 can cherry pie filling
1 (3 oz.) pkg. raspberry Jello
1 lg. can crushed pineapple, undrained
1 T. cornstarch
3/4 c. sugar
1 tsp. red food coloring
1 c. chopped pecans (opt.)

Combine pineapple, cornstarch, sugar and food coloring. Heat until thick, in microwave. Add Jello (no water). Cool. (Add pecans, optional.) Prepare vanilla pudding according to package directions. Add 1 teaspoon vanilla and 1/2 teaspoon almond flavoring to pudding mixture. In a glass bowl, layer cake (torn in pieces), pudding, cherry mixture, and Cool Whip. Repeat layers, ending with Cool Whip. Sprinkle more pecans on top. Yield: 30 servings.
Winova Van Regenmorter

Cherry Crunch

40 graham crackers, rolled fine
3 1/4 c. sugar
1 tsp. cinnamon
1 1/2 sticks butter or oleo
1 qt. sour cherries (not bing)
5 T. cornstarch
5 egg whites, stiffly beaten

Melt butter. Mix in cracker crumbs, 3/4 cup sugar and cinnamon. Pat 3/4 of mixture in the bottom and on sides of a 9x12-inch buttered pan.

Mix cornstarch and 1 1/2 cups sugar together. Add cherries in saucepan. Cook until thickened and clear, stirring constantly. Pour over crust mixture in pan.

Beat egg whites; add 1 cup sugar. Spread this mixture over cherries. Cover with remaining crumb mixture. Bake for 35 minutes at 275°.
Wanda Kuiken

Cherry-Rhubarb Cobbler

FILLING:
- 1 (21 oz.) can cherry pie filling
- 3 c. chopped rhubarb
- 1 c. sugar
- 4 T. butter or margarine

CRUST:
- 1/2 c. shortening
- 1 c. sugar
- 1 egg
- 1 c. flour
- 1 tsp. baking powder
- 1/2 c. milk

Filling: Spread fruit in a 9x13-inch pan. Sprinkle with sugar; dot with butter.
Crust: Cream shortening and sugar in a mixing bowl. Add egg and beat well. Combine flour and baking powder; add alternately with milk to creamed mixture. Pour over fruit. Bake at 350° for 50 to 60 minutes. Yield: about 12 servings.

Vera Brouwer

Cherry Yogurt Parfaits

- 1 (21 oz.) can cherry pie filling, divided
- 2 (8 oz.) ctn. vanilla yogurt, divided
- 1 c. graham cracker crumbs (about 16 sq.), divided

Combine 1 cup pie filling and 1 carton of yogurt; place about 2 tablespoons of each in 6 parfait glasses. Top each with 1 to 2 tablespoons of the graham cracker crumbs, about 2 tablespoons pie filling and about 2 tablespoons yogurt. Divide the remaining cracker crumbs and pie filling-yogurt mixture between parfait glasses. Chill. Yield: 6 servings.

Emily Maassen

Chocolate Candy Bar Dessert

- 2 c. Oreo cookie crumbs
- 1/4 c. melted oleo
- 8 oz. softened cream cheese
- 1/4 c. sugar
- 12 oz. Cool Whip
- 6 Heath bars, chopped (reserve 1/4 c. for top)
- 3 c. cold milk
- 2 sm. pkg. instant chocolate pudding

Mix cookie crumbs and melted oleo; press firmly onto bottom of a 9x13-inch pan. Refrigerate 10 minutes.

Beat cream cheese and sugar in a medium bowl until smooth. Gently stir in 1/2 of the Cool Whip. Spread evenly over crust. Sprinkle chopped candy bars over cream cheese layer.

Pour milk into a large bowl. Add pudding mixes; beat with wire whisk for 1 minute. Pour over chopped candy bar layer. Let stand 5 minutes, or until thickened. Spread the remaining Cool Whip over pudding layer. Refrigerate 2 hours, or until set. Garnish with additional chopped candy bars. Cut in squares. Store in refrigerator.

Brenda Oolman

Chocolate Dessert

1 c. flour
1 c. + 2 T. sugar
1/2 c. butter
1/2 c. chopped nuts
1 (8 oz.) pkg. cream cheese
1 c. Cool Whip
2 pkg. instant chocolate pudding
4 c. milk

Mix flour, 2 tablespoons sugar, butter and nuts together. Pat into a 9x13-inch pan and bake for 15 minutes at 375°. Mix cream cheese and 1 cup sugar; add Cool Whip. Spread over cooled crust. Beat pudding with milk. Spread carefully over first layer and refrigerate. When firm, ice with whipped topping. Keep refrigerated.

Lisa Wielenga

Chocolate Chip Sensation

1 (16 oz.) pkg. chocolate chip cookie dough
1 (8 oz.) pkg. cream cheese
1/3 c. sugar
1 pt. half & half
1 sm. pkg. instant chocolate pudding
1/4 c. chopped nuts (opt.)

Preheat oven to 375°. Roll cookie dough out. (Best if baked on stoneware.) Bake for 12 to 15 minutes. Cool. Combine cream cheese and sugar. Spread on cool cookie. Mix half & half; let set until firm. Spread pudding over cream cheese layer. Cut and serve.

Carolyn De Jager

Chocolate Cake Dessert

1 white or yellow cake mix without pudding
1 (6 oz.) pkg. instant chocolate pudding
2 eggs
2 c. water

TOPPING:
1/4 c. oleo
1 c. powdered sugar
2 egg yolks
1 (8 oz.) ctn. Cool Whip

Mix cake mix, pudding, 2 eggs and water together. Put into a 9x13-inch greased pan. Bake at 350° for 30 minutes. Cool completely. Mix together oleo, powdered sugar and egg yolks. Add Cool Whip. Spread on cooled cake. Sprinkle with Skor or Heath pieces. Keep refrigerated.

Jill Schouten

Chocolate Pudding Cake

2 c. cold water
1/4 c. cocoa
1 c. brown sugar
1 layer mini marshmallows

Prepare a devils food cake mix as directed on the package and pour over above ingredients. Bake for 45 minutes at 350°. Serve warm, with a scoop of ice cream. Put some of the chocolate sauce from the pan on top of the ice cream.

Helen Oolman

German Chocolate Cake

1 German chocolate cake (baked in a 9"x13" pan)
8 oz. cream cheese
1 1/3 c. milk
1 (5 1/2 oz.) pkg. instant pudding (vanilla)
8 oz. Cool Whip
2 or 3 crushed Butterfinger candy bars

Bake cake in a 9x13-inch pan; let cool. Mix cream cheese, milk and pudding. Pour on cake. Add the Cool Whip on top of filling. Put the crushed Butterfingers on top. Put dessert into refrigerator.

Jeanne Van Roekel

Chocolate Cream Dessert

3 c. crushed vanilla wafers
2/3 c. butter or margarine, melted
1/4 c. sugar
1/2 tsp. cinnamon

FILLING:
1 (7 oz.) milk chocolate candy bar, plain or with almonds, broken into pieces
1 (10 oz.) pkg. lg. marshmallows
1 c. milk
2 c. whipping cream, whipped
1/2 tsp. vanilla
Sliced almonds, toasted (opt.)

In a bowl, combine wafer crumbs, butter, sugar and cinnamon; mix well. Set aside 1/3 cup for topping. Press remaining crumb mixture into a greased 9x13-inch pan; refrigerate until firm. In a saucepan, heat the candy bar, marshmallows and milk over medium-low heat until chocolate and marshmallows are melted, stirring often. Remove from heat; cool to room temperature. Fold in whipped cream and vanilla; pour over crust. Sprinkle with reserved crumb mixture and almonds. Chill for 3 to 4 hours.

Jonna Wierda

Delicious Chocolate Pudding

4 T. cornstarch
2 level T. cocoa
4 T. sugar
1/2 c. milk
Pinch of salt

2 1/2 c. milk
2 T. butter
1/2 c. brown syrup (Karo)
1/2 tsp. vanilla

Put water in the bottom of a double boiler and let it get hot while you mix the first 5 ingredients. Add milk and stir until thick. Add butter, syrup and vanilla. Pour into dishes.

Sharla De Jager

Chocolate Chip Cheesecake

1 c. graham cracker crumbs
3 T. sugar
3 T. margarine, melted
3 (8 oz.) pkg. cream cheese

3/4 c. sugar
3 eggs
1 c. mini chocolate chips
1 tsp. vanilla

Combine crumbs, sugar and margarine; press onto bottom of a 9-inch springform pan. Combine cream cheese and sugar, mixing at medium speed on electric mixer until well blended. Add eggs, one at a time, mixing well after each addition. Blend in chocolate chips and vanilla; pour over crust. Bake at 450° for 10 minutes. Reduce oven temperature to 250°; continue baking 55 minutes, or until done. Loosen cake from rim of pan; cool before removing rim of pan. Chill.

Barb Oldenkamp

Miniature Cheesecakes

3 (8 oz.) pkg. cream cheese, softened
1 c. sugar
6 eggs
1 1/2 tsp. vanilla

1 box vanilla wafers
16 oz. sour cream
1 1/2 tsp. vanilla
1/2 c. sugar

Combine cream cheese and sugar. Add eggs, one at a time, beating well after each. Add vanilla. Place one vanilla wafer in the bottom of each paper-cup-lined muffin tin. Fill cups 3/4-full. Bake for 15 minutes at 300°. Combine sour cream, vanilla and sugar. At the end of 15 minutes, add a spoonful of filling. Return to oven for 15 minutes. Cool and serve. Refrigerate leftovers.

Michelle Bomgaars

No-Bake Chocolate Cheesecake

1/2 c. semi-sweet chocolate chips
1 (8 oz.) pkg. cream cheese, softened
1 (3 oz.) pkg. cream cheese, softened
1/2 c. sugar
1/4 c. butter or margarine, softened
2 c. frozen nondairy whipped topping, thawed
1 (8") packaged graham cracker crumb crust

Microwave Directions: In a small microwave-safe bowl, place chocolate chips. Microwave on HIGH for 1 to 1 1/2 minutes, or until chips are melted and mixture is smooth when stirred. Set aside to cool.

In a large mixer bowl, beat cream cheese, sugar and butter until smooth. On low speed, blend in melted chocolate. Fold in whipped topping until blended. Spoon into crust. Cover and chill until firm. Garnish as desired.

Dawn Beukelman

No-Crust Cheese Pie

2 (8 oz.) pkg. cream cheese
2/3 c. sugar
3 eggs
1/2 tsp. almond extract

Butter (glass) pie plate and pour above mixture into it. Bake at 325° for 45 minutes. Cool for 20 minutes.
Mix:

2 c. sour cream
3 T. sugar
1 tsp. vanilla

Pour over cream cheese layer. Bake another 10 minutes.

Carmen (Winchell) Woeltge

Oreo Cheesecake

2 c. crushed Oreos
4 T. melted butter
4 (8 oz.) pkg. cream cheese
4 eggs
2 T. flour
3 egg yolks
1 1/4 c. sugar
2 c. sour cream
1/4 c. sugar

Mix Oreos and butter; press into a 9-inch springform pan. Beat cream cheese, eggs, flour, egg yolks and sugar together. (You can not overbeat.) Pour mixture onto crust. Bake at 425° for 15 minutes. Bake at 225° for 50 minutes, or until cake is firm. Take out and refrigerate. Serve with sour cream and sugar mixture on top.

Denise Vander Stelt

White Chocolate Cheesecake

1 (8 oz.) pkg. Philadelphia Brand cream cheese
2 (4-serving-size) pkg. Jello white chocolate-flavored instant pudding & pie filling
2 c. cold milk, divided
1 (8 oz.) ctn. Cool Whip whipped topping, thawed
1 (6 oz.) prepared graham cracker crumb crust

Beat cream cheese and 1/2 cup of milk in a large bowl with wire whisk until smooth. Add the remaining 1 1/2 cups milk and pudding mixes. Beat with wire whisk for 1 minute. Stir in whipped topping until smooth and well blended. Spoon into crust. Refrigerate for 4 hours, or until set. (Garnish with white chocolate curls made with Baker's chocolate, optional.) Refrigerate leftover pie. Yield: 8 servings.

Bobbie Zeutenhorst

Fruit Pizza

1 c. margarine or butter
2/3 c. powdered sugar
2 c. flour
1 (8 oz.) pkg. cream cheese
1/2 c. sugar
1 tsp. vanilla

1 tsp. lemon juice
1 c. pineapple juice or other fruit juice
2 T. cornstarch
3/4 c. sugar

DESIRED FRUIT: About 3 c. total: apples, bananas, halved strawberries, seedless grapes, blueberries, sliced pineapple, oranges, kiwi, peaches

Step 1: In a large mixing bowl, beat margarine until softened. Beat in the powdered sugar. Slowly beat in the flour until well combined.
Step 2: Spread or pat the dough into a 12-inch pizza pan. Bake in a 325° oven for 20 to 25 minutes, or until edges are lightly browned. Cool.
Step 3: Beat together cream cheese (softened), 1/2 cup sugar, vanilla and lemon juice until creamy; spread over cooled crust.
Step 4: In a small saucepan, combine juice, cornstarch and the remaining 3/4 cup sugar. Cook and stir over medium heat until thickened and bubbly. Cook and stir 1 minute more. Cool slightly.
Step 5: Top pizza with desired fruit. Spoon glaze over fruit. Refrigerate until well chilled. Yield: 12 to 16 servings.

Emily Maassen

Fruit Pizza

Set out 8 ounces cream cheese. Make crust.

CRUST:
3/4 c. powdered sugar
1 c. cold butter or oleo
1 3/4 c. flour

Mix and pat into a 14-inch pizza pan. Bake for 15 minutes in a 300° oven. Set aside. Make glaze.

GLAZE:
3 T. cornstarch
1 1/2 c. fruit juice (any kind, Hi-C Echo cooler works well)
3/4 c. sugar
1 1/2 T. lemon juice

Heat until thick. Then cool.
After crust is cool, spread the following mixture over it:
8 oz. cream cheese
1/2 c. sugar
1 tsp. vanilla

Spread on top of cooled crust. Place fruit on top of crust in a circle, such as: strawberries, peaches, kiwi, bananas, or any combination. Put glaze over all. Yield: 8 to 10 servings.

Joan Punt

Fruit Pizza

CRUST:
1 pkg. Pillsbury crescent dinner rolls

FILLING:
1 (3 oz.) pkg. cream cheese, softened
1/3 c. sugar
1 tsp. vanilla
1 c. Cool Whip

Crust: Spread on jellyroll pan and bake according to directions on package. Let cool.
Filling: Beat cream cheese, sugar and vanilla in a bowl, on low speed, until smooth. Add Cool Whip. Spread over cooled crust. Arrange fruits on top (strawberries, grapes, mandarin oranges, bananas, apples, pears--whatever fruits you want), and refrigerate until serving.

Jodie Sneller

Fruit Pizza

1 c. sugar
1 egg
1 tsp. baking soda
1 tsp. vanilla

1 c. butter
2 1/2 c. flour
1/4 tsp. salt
1/2 c. nuts

Cream sugar and butter; add eggs, flour and the rest of the ingredients. Press into a pizza pan. Bake at 350° until done, 10 to 15 minutes.

8 oz. softened cream cheese
1/2 c. powdered sugar

1 c. Cool Whip

Mix and spread on cooled crust. Top with fresh fruits (strawberries, mandarin oranges, melons, grapes, pineapple).

2 c. liquid from pineapple, or oranges, or pineapple juice

1/4 c. cornstarch
1/2 c. sugar

Mix and bring to a boil. Stir until thick and clear. Cool and spoon over fruit.

Cindy VanDer Weide

Are you working hard or hardly working.

Fruit Pizza

CRUST:
1/2 c. margarine
1 c. sugar
1 egg

Blend and add:
1/2 tsp. salt
1 tsp. baking powder
2 c. flour
1/2 tsp. vanilla

Mix like pie crust. Press into a 12x18-inch jellyroll pan. Bake at 350° for 10 minutes.

CHEESE LAYER:
8 oz. cream cheese
1/2 c. sugar
1 tsp. vanilla

Mix until creamy. Spread over crust.

FRUIT LAYER:
1 lg. can mandarin oranges
1 can chunk pineapple
1 can fruit cocktail
2 bananas

Drain until dry and place on cheese mixture. Fresh fruits can also be used and arranged in rows (strawberries, grapes, etc.).

SAUCE:
1 c. orange juice
1/4 c. lemon juice
3/4 c. water
3 T. cornstarch (which has been mixed wit the sugar)
1 c. sugar
Dash of salt

Boil for 1 minute. Cool completely and drizzle sauce over fruit.
Note: Everything must be cool before the pizza is put together.

Evonne Wielenga

A true friend will not let you stand alone.

Fruit Cobbler
(Rhubarb Peach or Cherry)

4 c. cut-up rhubarb pieces, or 4 to 5 c. sliced peaches, or 4 c. pitted cherries
3/4 c. sugar

1 tsp. baking powder
1 c. flour
3 T. butter or margarine, melted
1/2 c. milk

TOPPING:
1 c. sugar (3/4 c. if peaches)

1 T. cornstarch
1 c. boiling water

Place fruit in a 9x13-inch pan. Mix the next 5 ingredients, and then drop globs over the fruit mixture. Mix the starch and sugar together; sprinkle over the whole pan of fruit. Pour the boiling water over the whole dessert and bake for 1 hour at 350°. It will have a golden color on top, and the mixture thickens as it cools.

Lonna Kluis,
from Geraldine Renes

Fruit Cobbler

1 can favorite pie filling

DROP SHORTCAKE DOUGH:
1 c. Bisquick

1 T. sugar
1/2 c. cream

Put your favorite pie filling in a pie plate. To make shortcake dough, mix Bisquick, sugar and cream together. Drop 6 mounds of dough onto pie filling. Bake at 350° for 30 minutes.

Karen Bos

Lazy Day Cobbler

1 c. sugar
1 c. flour
1 c. milk
2 tsp. baking powder
Pinch of salt

1 can peach or cherry or apple pie filling
1/2 tsp. cinnamon
1 stick oleo

Mix sugar, flour, milk, baking powder and salt. Pour into a 9x9-inch greased pan. Spoon pie filling over top, being careful not to mix. Sprinkle cinnamon over. Melt oleo and pour on top. Bake at 400° for 30 minutes.

Jan Budden

Cream Puff Dessert

CRUST:
1 c. water
1/2 c. butter
1 c. flour
4 eggs

FILLING:
2 sm. pkg. instant vanilla pudding
3 c. milk
8 oz. soft cream cheese

Crust: Heat the water and butter to boiling. Add flour, all at once, until it forms a ball. Remove from heat. Cool. Add one egg at a time; beat well. Spread in a 9x13-inch pan. Bake for 30 minutes at 400°--no longer.

Filling: Mix pudding mixture and put onto cooled crust. Spread a layer of Cool Whip on top of this, and drizzle chocolate syrup on top of the whipped cream.

Hattie Dykstra,
submitted by Helen

Cream Puff Dessert

CRUST:
1 c. water
4 eggs
1/2 c. oleo
1 c. flour

Cook water, oleo and flour until thick. Add eggs, one at a time, stirring after each addition. Spread in a 9x13-inch ungreased pan. Bake at 400° for 30 minutes. Let cool.

FILLING:
2 pkg. instant vanilla pudding
3 1/2 c. milk
1 (8 oz.) pkg. cream cheese

Mix pudding, cream cheese and milk. Pour over puff crust. Let set.

TOPPING:
1 (8 oz.) ctn. Cool Whip
Chocolate syrup

Spread Cool Whip over pudding. Drizzle with chocolate syrup. Refrigerate.

Barb Oldenkamp

Puff Pastry

PART 1:
1 c. water
1/2 c. butter

1 c. flour
1 tsp. almond flavoring
3 eggs

PART 2:
1 c. flour

1/2 c. butter
2 T. cold water

Part 1: Boil the water with butter until dissolved. Add the 1 cup flour, stirring quickly until it forms a ball. Add almond flavoring. Add eggs, one at a time, beating well with electric mixer or wooden spoon after each egg. When well beaten, set aside.
Part 2: Blend the flour and butter as you would for pie crust. Add the cold water. Mix well. Divide this dough into 2 parts, making balls, then rolling into long pencil-sized strips. Place on ungreased baking sheet and gently press and push until you have formed 2 bases, about 3 inches wide and 12 inches long. Spread the first mixture onto the bases, bringing it close to the edges. Bake at 350° for 45 minutes to 1 hour, or until edges turn light brown. Pastry will fall in the center. Frost with powdered sugar frosting Can top with nuts or almonds, if desired.
Note: Do not cover closely when you store them, because it softens if you do so.

Linda Broek

Custard Pudding

1/2 c. sugar
1 T. cornstarch
Dash of salt

1 1/2 c. milk
3 egg yolks, beaten
1 tsp. vanilla

In a saucepan, combine sugar, salt and cornstarch. Gradually add milk. Cook and stir over medium heat until mixture comes to a boil. Cook and stir 2 minutes longer. Add a few spoonfuls of mixture to egg yolks to temper (so they won't curdle when you add them). Stir in egg yolks and cook until thickened. Remove from heat and add vanilla. Refrigerate or serve warm.

Michelle Borngaars

♥ Sugarless Dessert
(Diabetic)

1 lg. or 2 sm. boxes sugar-free Jello
1 (12 oz.) box sugar-free cook-type vanilla pudding
5 c. water
Fruit
Cool Whip

In a saucepan, put in 5 cups water, Jello and pudding. Cook over medium heat until mixture starts to boil. Boil 1 minute and remove from stove. Add fruit. The mixture will be runny. When cool, set in refrigerator overnight. If you use strawberries, use strawberry Jello; peach Jello, use fresh peaches or 1 can sugar-free fruit cocktail, bananas, cantaloupe, or other fruit. Top with Cool Whip.
Joyce Baker

"Easy" Frozen Dessert

Line bottom of a 9x13-inch pan with ice cream sandwiches. Squeeze 1 (12.5 oz.) jar of caramel sauce over top of ice cream sandwiches. Put 1 carton of Cool Whip over that. Put crushed-up candy bars over top (Snickers, Butterfinger, Heath), or crushed Oreo cookies. Freeze.
Darlene Kluis

Frosty Freeze Dessert

1 (8 oz.) pkg. cream cheese,
1 (7 oz.) jar marshmallow creme
2 c. raspberry, orange or lime sherbet
2 to 3 c. whipped topping
1 (9" or 10") graham cracker crust

In a mixing bowl, beat cream cheese and marshmallow creme until smooth. Stir in sherbet. Fold in the whipped topping and pour into crust. Freeze until firm. Remove from freezer 10 minutes before serving. May be frozen up to 2 months.
Note: It can be made in a 9x9-inch pan with a graham cracker crust.
Joan Dekker

Rich Homemade Ice Cream

6 eggs, beaten
2 c. sugar
2 tsp. vanilla
1/2 tsp. salt
1 pkg. instant vanilla pudding
1 (8 oz.) ctn. Cool Whip
1 pt. half & half
1 c. cream

Mix. Put into ice cream freezer container and fill with milk to 3/4-full. Have enough ice cubes and rock salt until mixture is frozen.
Kathy Dykstra

Homemade Ice Cream Mix

5 eggs
2 c. sugar
1/2 c. corn syrup (white)
2 T. vanilla
1 qt. Coffee Rich

Beat eggs until foamy. Add sugar slowly. Mix in corn syrup, vanilla and Coffee Rich. Fill with milk to 3/4-full.

Karla Hundt

Homemade Ice Cream

2 c. half & half
2 c. whipping cream, unwhipped
1 (14 oz.) can sweetened condensed milk
2 T. vanilla

In a large bowl, combine ingredients; mix well. Pour into ice cream freezer container. Freeze according to manufacturer's instruction. Freeze leftovers.

Kari Van Klompenburg

Hot Fudge Sauce

1 (6 oz.) pkg. chocolate chips
2 T. butter
1 (14 oz.) can sweetened condensed milk
2 T. water
1 tsp. vanilla

Melt all ingredients over medium heat, stirring constantly, until thickened. Serve warm, over ice cream.

David Dykstra

Caramel Ice Cream Dessert

1/2 gal. butterbrickle ice cream
1 pt. caramel sauce (or butterscotch-caramel)

CRUMB MIXTURE:
1/2 c. brown sugar
1/2 c. oatmeal
2 sticks oleo, melted
1 c. chopped pecans
1 c. flour

Mix crumb mixture all together. Bake for 12 minutes at 350°. Put 1/2 of crumbs in a greased 9x13-inch pan, then 1/2 of ice cream, 3/4 of caramel, rest of ice cream. Sprinkle rest of crumbs. Drizzle rest of caramel. Freeze.

Darlene Kluis

Ice Cream Crispies

2 1/2 c. Rice Krispies
1/2 c. melted butter or oleo
1 c. shredded coconut
1 c. brown sugar, packed
1/2 gal. ice cream

Set out ice cream to soften. Mix all ingredients, except ice cream. Spread 1/2 of mixture in a 9x13-inch pan. Put softened ice cream over mixture, then top with the rest of the mixture. Freeze.

Linda Broek

Ice Cream Dessert

1/4 c. melted oleo
1 c. flaked coconut
1/4 c. brown sugar
1 1/2 c. Rice Krispies
1/2 gal. vanilla ice cream
1 can cherry pie filling (or flavor you desire)

Melt oleo in a small pan. Add coconut and brown, stirring constantly. Add brown sugar and Rice Krispies. Stir to blend. Spread 3/4 of mixture in the bottom of a 9x13-inch pan. Spread softened ice cream over this. Sprinkle remaining Rice Krispie mixture on top. Freeze. Spread pie filling over just before serving.

Note: I've used fresh or frozen raspberries mixed with sugar, also.

Evelyn De Vries

Orange Sherbet Dessert

1 1/2 c. Ritz crackers, crushed
4 T. sugar
7 T. melted oleo
1/4 gal. vanilla ice cream
1/2 gal. orange sherbet
4 T. lemon juice
1 c. sugar
6 T. oleo
2 eggs, beaten

Mix cracker crumbs, sugar and oleo; press in a 9x13-inch pan. Mix ice cream and sherbet. Top with cooked topping (juice, sugar, oleo and eggs); cook until thick. Cool topping and put over ice cream.

Marie Maassen

Butter Pecan Malted Dessert

27 Oreo cookies
1 stick oleo

TOPPING:
1 1/2 c. powdered sugar
3 eggs

1/2 gal. butter pecan ice cream

1/2 c. instant chocolate malted milk
1 1/2 sticks oleo
2 tsp. vanilla

Crush the Oreos and melt the 1 stick oleo; mix together and pat into a 9x13-inch or slightly bigger pan. Chill. Cover with the slightly-softened butter pecan ice cream. Freeze.

Topping: Beat together the powdered sugar, eggs, malted chocolate, oleo and vanilla. Continue beating until light and fluffy. Put this topping over the ice cream.

Freezes and keeps well.

Evonne Wielenga

Lemon Dessert

CRUST:
1 c. flour

1 c. powdered sugar
1 (8 oz.) pkg. cream cheese
2 c. mini marshmallows

1/2 c. oleo
1/2 c. nuts

1 (8 oz.) ctn. Cool Whip
3 c. milk
3 pkg. instant lemon pudding

Crust: Mix like pie crust and put into a 9x13-inch pan. Bake for 10 minutes at 350°. Cool.

Beat powdered sugar and cream cheese until creamy; fold in 1 cup Cool Whip. Sprinkle marshmallows over crust and cover with sugar and cheese mixture.

Beat milk and pudding mix for 3 to 5 minutes. Spread over top layer, and cover with Cool Whip. Sprinkle with nuts. Chill.

The longer it stands, the better it gets.

Arloa Jansma

Lime Chiffon Dessert

1 1/2 c. crushed graham crackers 1/2 c. butter or margarine, melted
1/3 c. sugar

FILLING:
1 (3 oz.) pkg. lime Jello 1 c. sugar
1 c. boiling water 1 tsp. vanilla
1 (8 oz.) & 1 (3 oz.) pkg. cream 1 (16 oz.) ctn. Cool Whip, thawed
  cheese

Combine the first 3 ingredients; set aside 2 tablespoons for topping. Press the remaining crumbs onto the bottom of an ungreased 9x13-inch baking dish. Set aside.
In a bowl, beat cream cheese and sugar. Add vanilla; mix well. Dissolve Jello in boiling water; cool. When Jello is cool, add to cream cheese mixture and fold in Cool Whip. Spoon over crust. Sprinkle with reserved crumbs. Cover and refrigerate for 3 hours.

Lori Van Gorp

Fluffy Mint Dessert

1 (1 lb.) pkg. (40) cream-filled 2 (12 oz.) ctn. frozen whipped
  chocolate sandwich cookies,   topping, thawed
  crushed 2 c. pastel mini marshmallows
1/2 c. margarine, melted 1 1/3 c. (5 1/2 oz.) sm. pastel mints

Reserve 1/4 cup of crushed cookies for garnish. Combine the remaining cookies with butter; press into an ungreased 9x13x2-inch baking dish. Fold together whipped topping, marshmallows and mints; pour over crust. Garnish with reserved cookies. Cover and refrigerate for 1 to 2 days before serving. Yield: 18 servings.

Elvera Van Horssen

Peach Dessert

1 lg. can sliced peaches, with 1 butter pecan cake mix
  juice 1 stick oleo, melted

Pour sliced peaches with juice into a 9x13-inch pan. Sprinkle dry cake mix on top, and drizzle with melted oleo. Bake for 30 minutes in a 350° oven. Serve with butter brickle ice cream and enjoy.

Kristi VanDer Weide

Elegant Peach Delight

1 box yellow cake mix
3/4 c. oleo, softened
1 lg. can peaches, drained
1 pt. sour cream
3 egg yolks
Cinnamon

Combine cake mix and oleo. Press into an 8x12-inch pan. Add cut-up peaches. Beat sour cream and yolks. Pour over peaches, spreading to sides of pan. Sprinkle with cinnamon. Bake at 350° for 20 to 30 minutes.

Vicki Schrock

Peaches and Cream Dessert

1 (6 oz.) pkg. orange Jello
2 c. boiling water
6 oz. cream cheese
1/2 c. chopped pecans
12 oz. Cool Whip
1 (6 oz.) pkg. peach Jello
2 c. boiling water

Dissolve orange Jello and water in a bowl; cool until Jello slightly sets. Mix cream cheese, Cool Whip and pecans. Fold into Jello mixture and put into a 9x13-inch pan. Chill. Dissolve peach Jello in water. Cool until syrupy. Add 1 can peach pie filling or fresh-sliced peaches. Pour over first mixture. Chill.

Elvera Van Horssen

Peach Melba

2 (3 oz.) pkg. strawberry Jello
2 c. boiling water
1/2 c. cold water
2 c. vanilla ice cream
2 c. sliced fresh peaches

Dissolve Jello in hot water. Add cold water. Stir in ice cream until it's smooth. Add peaches. Pour into a 9x9-inch square pan and chill.
Note: Can add Cool Whip on top, if desired.

Marilyn Kruid

Cornflake Pudding

3 eggs
1/2 c. sugar
1/2 tsp. vanilla
1/2 c. dates
3 c. milk
1/4 tsp. salt
1 T. butter
2 c. corn flakes

Mix in order given. Put into baking dish. Bake for 55 minutes in a 350° oven--no longer.

Elnora McGilvra

Pumpkin Cream Dessert

24 single graham crackers, crushed
1/3 c. sugar
1/2 c. melted oleo
2 eggs
1 (8 oz.) pkg. cream cheese, softened
1 (16 oz.) can pumpkin
3 egg yolks
1/2 c. sugar
1/2 c. milk
1/2 tsp. salt
1/2 tsp. cinnamon
1/4 c. cold water
1 env. unflavored gelatin
3 egg whites
1/4 c. sugar

Mix graham cracker crumbs, 1/3 cup sugar and margarine; pat into a buttered 9x13-inch pan. Beat together 2 eggs, 3/4 cup sugar and cream cheese until light and fluffy. Pour over crust and bake for 20 minutes at 350°. In a heavy saucepan, beat together pumpkin, egg yolks, 1/2 cup sugar, milk, salt and cinnamon. Cook until thick (about 5 minutes). In a small pan, sprinkle gelatin on water and stir over low heat, just until dissolved. Stir into pumpkin mixture and cool. Beat egg whites into sugar until stiff and glossy. Fold into pumpkin mixture and pour over crust. Refrigerate several hours before serving. Top with whipped cream. Yield: 15 servings.

Marietta VanDer Weide

Great Pumpkin Dessert

1 (15 oz.) can pumpkin
1 (12 oz.) can evaporated milk
3 eggs
1 c. sugar
4 tsp. pumpkin pie spice
1 pkg. yellow cake mix
3/4 c. margarine, melted
1 1/2 c. chopped walnuts

In a mixing bowl, combine the first 5 ingredients. Transfer to a greased 9x13-inch pan. Sprinkle with dry cake mix and drizzle butter over top. Sprinkle walnuts over that. Bake at 350° for 1 hour, or until a knife inserted in the center comes out clean. Serve with ice cream or whipped cream.

Sherri Altena

Pumpkin Pie Dessert

2 c. pumpkin
1 c. white sugar
2 eggs
1 T. butter, melted
1 tsp. ginger
1/4 tsp. cinnamon
Pinch of salt
1 T. burnt sugar flavoring
1/2 c. dark Karo syrup
2 c. milk

Mix together and put into a 10-inch pie plate. Bake at 425° for 15 minutes, then at 350° for 50 minutes.

Sharla De Jager

Punch Bowl Cake

1 chocolate cake, baked, then broken in pieces
3 sm. pkg. instant chocolate pudding
4 1/2 c. milk
3 (8 oz.) ctn. Cool Whip
1 pkg. Heath Bits

Mix milk and pudding mix. Layer by thirds: cake, pudding mixture, Cool Whip and Heath Bits, ending with Cool Whip and Heath Bits.
Note: Cherry pie filling and white or yellow cake can also be used.

Mary Ann Winchell,
Diane Munro

Quick Refreshing Dessert

"Boletje" Dutch crisp-baked rusks
Fresh or frozen fruit (strawberries, peaches or raspberries)
Ice cream

Important to use Original Dutch rusks--they stay good on pantry shelf for a long time in Ziploc bag.
Place rusk in sauce dish. Spoon a little fruit on rusk, and ice cream on top. Put fruit over ice cream.
Note: If you have frozen fruit in the freezer, this can be made on very short notice.

Evelyn De Vries

Easy Rhubarb Dessert

4 c. rhubarb, cut up
1 c. sugar
1 box white cake mix
1 (3 oz.) box strawberry Jello
1 c. water
1/3 c. butter, melted

Place ingredients in a 9x13-inch glass baking dish in order given. The cake mix and Jello go on dry; water and butter on top. Bake for 45 to 60 minutes at 350°.

Vicki Schrock

Rhubarb Crisp

6 c. rhubarb, cut in sm. pieces
4 eggs
3 c. sugar

4 T. flour
Cinnamon

TOPPING:
1 c. butter

1 c. brown sugar
2 c. flour

Put rhubarb in the bottom of a greased 9x13-inch pan. Mix the eggs, sugar and flour. Pour over rhubarb and mix throughout. Sprinkle with cinnamon.
Topping: Mix butter, brown sugar and flour. Sprinkle this mixture on top. Bake in oven at 350° for about an hour.

Heather Hofmeyer

Pastor Wayne's Favorite Rhubarb Crisp

1 c. sugar
2 beaten eggs

2 T. flour

Add this to 2 cups cut rhubarb and let stand.

CRUMB TOP:
3/4 c. brown sugar
1 c. flour

1/2 c. soft butter or oleo
1/4 c. oatmeal

Put into an 8x10- or 9x9-inch pan and bake in a 350° oven until browned, approximately 45 minutes.

Emily Maassen

Rhubarb Crumble Dessert

3 c. flour
1/2 tsp. cinnamon
1 c. sugar
3/4 c. butter or oleo

6 c. diced rhubarb
1 1/2 tsp. lemon juice
1/4 tsp. salt
1 1/2 to 2 c. sugar

Sift together flour, cinnamon and sugar. Cut in butter or oleo until crumbly. Spread 1/2 of mixture evenly on the bottom of a 9x13-inch pan and press down. Combine rhubarb, lemon juice, salt and sugar. Spread evenly over first mixture. Spread remaining crumbly mixture over top. Bake at 375° for 45 to 50 minutes. Serve plain or with ice cream.

Marlene Van Beek

Rhubarb Dessert

CRUST:
1 c. flour
1/2 c. butter
2 T. powdered sugar

FILLING:
1 1/4 c. sugar
3 egg yolks, beaten
2 1/4 c. rhubarb
1/3 c. milk
2 T. flour

TOPPING:
3 egg whites
1/2 c. sugar
1/2 tsp. vanilla

Crust: Mix ingredients and place in a 9x12-inch pan. Bake at 350° until slightly browned. While crust is baking, prepare filling.
Filling: Cook filling ingredients until thick. Put on crust.
Topping: Beat 3 egg whites until stiff. Add 1/2 cup sugar and 1/2 teaspoon vanilla. Spread on filling and brown.

Margaret Cleveringa

Rhubarb Shortcake

4 c. rhubarb
3/4 c. sugar
3 T. oleo
1 c. flour
1 tsp. baking powder
1/4 tsp. salt
1/2 c. milk
1 c. sugar
1 T. cornstarch
1/4 tsp. salt
1 c. boiling water (add a couple drops of red food coloring)

Put cut-up rhubarb in an 8x8-inch greased baking dish. Cream sugar and oleo. Mix flour, baking powder and salt. Add flour mixture and milk alternately to creamed mixture. Spread over rhubarb. Combine the 1 cup sugar, cornstarch and salt; sprinkle over the top. Pour the boiling water over all in the pan. Bake in 350° oven for 1 hour.

Ruth De Koter

Rhubarb Shortcake

Put 2 cups diced rhubarb in a greased 8- or 9-inch pan. Sprinkle with 1 tablespoon red Jello.

Cream:
3/4 c. sugar				3 T. oleo

Sift together:
1 c. flour				1/4 tsp. salt
1 tsp. baking powder

Add dry ingredients to creamed mixture with 1/2 cup milk. Beat well and pour over rhubarb.

Mix:
1 c. sugar				1/4 tsp. cinnamon
1 T. cornstarch

Sprinkle over batter. Pour 1 cup boiling water over all. Bake at 350° for 35 to 40 minutes.
Note: Double this recipe for a 9x13-inch pan. Baking time is approximately the same.

Lylis Van Donkelaar

Rhubarb Torte

GRAHAM CRACKER CRUST:		2 T. sugar
1 c. graham cracker crumbs		4 T. melted butter

Reserve 2 tablespoons for top of dessert. Pat the rest of mixture into a 9x9-inch pan and bake at 350° for 10 minutes. Cool.

1 c. sugar				A few drops red food coloring
3 T. cornstarch				8 oz. Cool Whip
4 c. rhubarb, chopped			1 1/2 c. mini marshmallows
1/2 c. water				1 sm. pkg. instant vanilla pudding

Combine sugar and cornstarch; stir in rhubarb and water. Cook and stir until thickened. Reduce heat and cook for 2 to 3 minutes. Add food coloring. Spread over cooled graham cracker crust. Cool.
Mix Cool Whip and marshmallows; spread on cooled rhubarb mixture. Prepare pudding according to directions on box; spread over Cool Whip mixture. Sprinkle with reserved graham cracker crumbs. Chill.

Pam Sandbulte

Strawberry Cheesecake Pie

2 c. sliced fresh strawberries
1/4 c. chopped almonds, toasted
1 T. sugar
1 (9") graham cracker crust
1 (8 oz.) pkg. cream cheese
2 c. cold milk, divided
1 (3.4 oz.) pkg. vanilla instant pudding

In a bowl, combine the strawberries, almonds and sugar. Pour into crust. In a mixing bowl, beat cream cheese until smooth. Gradually add 1/2 cup milk. Add pudding mix and remaining milk. Beat for 1 minute, or until blended; pour over strawberries. Cover and refrigerate for 2 hours, or until set.

Lori Van Gorp

Yummy Strawberry Delight
(Low-Fat, too!)

1 angel food cake
3 baskets strawberries
1 box nonfat vanilla pudding
1 1/2 c. skim milk
1 tsp. vanilla
1 c. light sour cream
1 (8 oz.) ctn light whipped topping

Cut cake in cubes; wash and slice strawberries. Mix the pudding, milk and vanilla with beater for 2 minutes on low. Fold in the sour cream and whipped topping. Layer cake, pudding mix, strawberries, cake, pudding mix, strawberries, in a 9x13-inch glass pan.

Stacy Maassen

♥ Strawberry Dessert
(Diabetic)

1 baked angel food cake
2 (4-serving-size) pkg. sugar-free strawberry Jello
1 (8 oz.) ctn. Cool Whip
1 c. hot water
1 c. cold water
1 (8 oz.) pkg. frozen, unsweetened strawberries, thawed

Cut cake into cubes; set aside. Make Jello using hot water; stir to dissolve. Add cold water and strawberries. Stir well. Cool until it begins to jel. Whip with 1/2 of the Cool Whip. Gently fold in cubed cake. Pour into a 9x13-inch cake pan and chill. Top with remaining Cool Whip.

Elsie De Jager

♥ Strawberry Dessert
(Diabetic)

1 (3 oz.) pkg. vanilla (sugar-free) cooked pudding
1 (3 oz.) pkg. sugar-free Jello
2 1/4 c. water
4 c. strawberries (fresh)

Mix the first 3 ingredients and cook until it boils. Pour cooked syrup over the 4 cups of strawberries that you have put in the bottom of a pie pan, and cool in the refrigerator.

Henrietta De Jager

Strawberry Dessert

1/2 c. angel food cake

Crumble on the bottom of 9x9-inch pan (1-inch cubes).

1 pt. vanilla ice cream
1 pkg. instant vanilla pudding
1/2 c. milk

Blend and refrigerate until set. Put on top of cake.

1 pkg. strawberry Jello
1 1/2 c. hot water
1 bag frozen strawberries

Let set awhile, then pour over the top.

Sadie Van Peursem

Strawberry Dessert

BOTTOM LAYER:
1/4 c. brown sugar
1 c. flour
1/2 c. oleo
1 c. chopped nuts

SECOND LAYER:
1 (10 oz.) pkg. frozen strawberries
2 egg whites, unbeaten
1 c. sugar
1 pt. Cool Whip

Bottom Layer: Mix like a pie crust and put into a 9x13-inch pan (lightly greased). Bake at at 350° for 20 to 30 minutes, until browned. Cool and crumble what was just baked. Respread in bottom of pan, saving 1/3 for top of dessert later.

Second Layer: Beat ingredients on high speed for 15 minutes. Stir in Cool Whip with this strawberry mixture. Spread over crumbs in bottom of pan. Sprinkle with remaining crumbs.

Freeze. (Dessert will remain soft and easy to cut, although frozen.)

Linda Van Regenmorter,
Judy Vlietstra

Strawberry-Pretzel Dessert

3 c. coarsely-crushed pretzels
5 tsp. sugar
2 sticks oleo, melted

Mix pretzels, sugar and oleo. Pat into a 9x13-inch pan. Bake at 350° for 10 minutes. Cool.

1 ctn. Cool Whip
1 (8 oz.) pkg. cream cheese
1 c. sugar

Mix cream cheese and sugar. Add to whipped topping. Pour over cooled pretzel crust. Cool.

2 pkg. strawberry Jello
2 c. boiling water
2 (10 oz.) pkg. frozen strawberries, thawed

Mix Jello and hot water. Add thawed strawberries. Mixture should thicken as strawberries thaw. When thickened, pour over cheese layer. Refrigerate.

Wanda Hofmeyer

Strawberry-Rhubarb Angel Squares

2 c. chopped rhubarb
2 c. water
1 (6 oz.) pkg. strawberry Jello
1 (10 oz.) pkg. frozen strawberries
1 (8 oz.) ctn. Cool Whip
1 lg. angel food cake, cut into 1" cubes

In a medium saucepan, combine rhubarb and water. Cook until soft. Stir in gelatin. Add strawberries, Mix well. Refrigerate until mixture begins to thicken. Stir in Cool Whip. In a 9x13-inch pan, layer 1/2 of the cake cubes. Spoon on 1/2 of the rhubarb mixture. Repeat layers. Refrigerate at least 3 hours, or overnight. Cut into squares. Yield: 15 servings.

Elvera Van Horssen

Strawberry Shortcut

1 c. mini marshmallows
2 (10 oz.) pkg. frozen strawberries
1 pkg. strawberry Jello
2 1/4 c. flour
1 1/2 c. sugar
1/2 c. butter
3 tsp. baking powder
1/2 tsp. salt
1 c. milk
1 tsp. vanilla
3 eggs

Preheat oven to 350°. Grease a 9x13-inch pan and sprinkle marshmallows on bottom. Combine strawberries (not drained) and Jello; set aside. Combine sugar and butter; beat. Add milk, eggs and vanilla. In another bowl, combine flour, baking powder and salt. Beat 3 minutes on medium. Pour over marshmallows. Spoon strawberry mixture on top. Bake for 45 to 50 minutes.

Amy Krogman

Frosty Strawberry Squares

1 c. flour, sifted
1/2 c. brown sugar
1/2 c. walnuts
1/2 c. margarine
2 egg whies
2/3 c. sugar
1 (10 oz.) pkg. frozen strawberries, partially thawed, or about 1 1/4 c.
2 T. lemon juice
1 c. whipping cream

Mix the flour, brown sugar, walnuts and margarine to make a crumb mixture. Bake for 20 minutes at 350°, stirring occasionally. Sprinkle 2/3 of crumbs in a 9x13-inch pan.

Combine in a large bowl, egg whites, 2/3 cup sugar, strawberries and lemon juice. Beat at high speed for 10 minutes. Fold in whipped cream. Spread over crumbs. Top with the remaining crumbs. Freeze for 6 hours or overnight.

Freezes well for a couple of weeks.
A favorite from Aunt Gert Ver Mulm.

Joan Dekker

Pies

♥ Sugarless Apple Pie
(Diabetic)

Pastry for 1 double-crust pie
6 med. Red Delicious apples, peeled & sliced
1 (6 oz.) can frozen apple juice (without sugar), thawed
1 1/2 T. cornstarch
1/3 c. water
1 tsp. cinnamon
3 T. margarine

Place apples and undiluted juice into a large pan. Bring to a boil; reduce heat and simmer, covered, for about 5 minutes. Dissolve cornstarch in 1/3 cup water. Gently stir cornstarch into apple mixture. Bring to a boil; reduce heat and simmer, covered, for 10 to 15 minutes, or until apples begin to soften. Stir in cinnamon. Fill pastry shell with apples and cover with top crust. Bake at 350° for 45 minutes. Baste with melted margarine after baking.

Henrietta De Jager

♥ Sugarless Apple Pie
(Diabetic)

4 c. sliced apples
1 (6 oz.) can frozen apple juice
6 oz. water
2 T. cornstarch
1 tsp. apple pie spice
5 to 10 pkt. sugar substitute (opt.), depending on tartness of apples
1 unbaked pie crust

Mix cornstarch, apple pie spice, apple juice concentrate and water. Cook, stirring occasionally, until it begins to thicken and is clear. Stir in apples; microwave just until sauce begins to bubble. Pour into unbaked pie crust; add sugar substitute, if using. Top with crust. Bake for 1 hour at 350°, or until nicely browned.

Mary Ann Winchell

Paper Bag Apple Pie

1 unbaked 8" pie crust
4 lg. apples
1/2 c. sugar
2 T. flour

1/2 tsp. nutmeg
1/2 c. sugar
1/2 c. flour
1/2 c. butter

Prepare 1 unbaked 8-inch pie crust. Peel and slice apples; place in a bowl. Sprinkle 1/2 cup sugar, flour and nutmeg. Mix well and place in crust. Combine 1/2 cup sugar, 1/2 cup flour and butter. Blend with pastry blender until it looks like cornmeal. Spread evenly over pie. Slide pie into a large grocery paper bag. Fold ends and staple. Bake at 375° for 1 hour. <u>Do not open oven while baking</u>!

Suzanne Haverdink

Blueberry-Rhubarb Pie

2 1/2 c. frozen blueberries, thawed
2 c. frozen rhubarb, thawed

1 c. sugar
2 1/2 T. cornstarch

PASTRY:
2 c. flour
2/3 c. lard

1 tsp. salt
6 T. cold water

Mix together and pour into a 9-inch unbaked pie shell. Place top crust on. Bake for 15 minutes at 425°. Reduce to 375° and bake for about 25 minutes, until golden and bubbly.

Pastry: Cut lard into flour and salt until coarse. Add water, 1 tablespoon at a time. Yield: 2 (9-inch) crusts.

Wanda Kuiken

Humor is the good-natured side of truth.

Butterscotch Pie

FILLING:
1 c. brown sugar
1 1/2 c. milk
3 egg yolks
1 T. butter
2 T. flour
1 tsp. vanilla

Mix egg yolks in 1/2 cup of milk. Add the rest of ingredients. Cook over medium heat until thick, like pudding. (Filling can be made in the microwave, also.)

GRAHAM CRACKER CRUST:
18 graham cracker squares, crushed
1/2 c. brown sugar
1/2 c. melted butter or oleo

Mix; press into bottom of pie plate. Save a little to sprinkle over top of meringue.
Meringue: Beat 3 egg whites. Slowly add 1 tablespoon sugar for each egg white and continue to beat with mixer until stiff peaks form. Spread over filling and sprinkle with 1 or 2 tablespoons of graham cracker crust. Bake meringue 10 minutes at 375°.
Sharon Plendl

Cappuccino Pie

1 pkg. vanilla instant pudding
1 1/2 c. milk
2 tsp. instant coffee crystals
1 (8 oz.) ctn. Cool Whip
1 (8") chocolate cookie pie crust

Combine milk, pudding and coffee crystals. Fold in whipped topping. Pour into crust. Chill at least 6 hours to set.
Michelle Bomgaars

Caramel Chocolate Pie

1 c. crushed Oreos
1/4 c. butter, melted
30 caramels
2 T. butter
2 T. water
1/2 c. chopped pecans
2 (3 oz.) pkg. cream cheese
1/3 c. powdered sugar
4 oz. Baker's chocolate
3 T. hot water
1 tsp. vanilla
2 c. whipping cream
2 T. powdered sugar

Mix Oreos and butter; press into pie plate. Melt caramels, butter and water. Pour into pie crust. Sprinkle with pecans. Chill until set, about 1 hour. Beat cream cheese and powdered sugar until smooth. Spread over caramel. Chill. Melt chocolate and water. Cool to room temperature. Stir in vanilla. Beat whipping cream and powdered sugar until stiff peaks form. Reserve 1 1/2 cups. Fold in chocolate. Spread over cream cheese layer. Top with reserved whipped cream. Refrigerate at least 1 hour, until firm.
Michelle Bomgaars

♥ Chocolate-Banana Creme Pie
(Diabetic)

1 graham cracker crust
2 sliced bananas
1 (4-serving-size) pkg. sugar-free instant chocolate pudding
1 1/2 c. milk
1 (8 oz.) ctn. Cool Whip

Whip pudding and milk until thick; slice bananas into crust. Pour pudding mixture over bananas. Top with Cool Whip.

Note: Diabetic recipes aren't just for diabetics. They are very tasteful and good for anyone watching their sugar intake and weight.

Nate De Jager

Chocolate Silk Pie

1/2 c. softened (not melted) butter
3/4 c. sugar
2 oz. semi-sweet Baker's chocolate
1 tsp. vanilla
2 eggs
1 (8") graham cracker crust or chocolate crust
Whipped topping

Cream butter and sugar. Add melted chocolate and vanilla. Mix well. Add 1 egg and beat 5 minutes. Add other egg and beat 5 minutes more. Pour into crust and chill overnight to set.

Can top with a layer of whipped topping, or just garnish with it. May also double and pour into a 9x13-inch pan.

Michelle Bomgaars

Cocoa Mocha Pie

6 (2.05 oz.) Milky Way candy bars
1/4 c. milk
2 to 3 tsp. instant coffee granules
1 qt. vanilla ice cream
1 graham cracker crust

Finely chop 4 candy bars; put into bowl. Add milk and coffee; heat and stir in microwave until melted and smooth. Place ice cream in a bowl; fold in mocha mixture. Spoon into crust and freeze. Remove from freezer 15 minutes before serving. Garnish with remaining candy bars, cut up.

Cindy VanDer Weide

Coconut Custard Pie

2 c. milk
1 c. sugar
4 eggs
1/2 c. flour
6 T. margarine
1 tsp. vanilla
1/2 tsp. salt
1 c. coconut

In a blender (or food processor), combine milk, sugar, eggs, flour, butter, salt and vanilla. Cover and blend for 10 seconds. Scrape sides. Blend for another 10 seconds. Add coconut; blend for 2 seconds. Pour into a greased 10-inch pie plate. Bake at 350° for about 50 to 55 minutes, until knife comes out clean. Serve warm or cold.

Dawn De Weerd

Impossible Coconut Custard Pie

4 eggs
1 1/2 tsp. vanilla
2 c. milk
1/2 c. flour
1 c. sugar
6 T. oleo, melted
1 c. coconut

Place all ingredients in a blender and mix well. Grease and flour a large, deep pie plate. Pour mixture in, and bake at 350° for an hour, or until filling is set. It makes its own crust on top. Serve with whipped cream.
Very easy to make!

Rose Dykstra

Velvety Custard Pie

4 slightly-beaten eggs
1/2 c. sugar
1/4 tsp. salt
1 tsp. vanilla
2 1/4 c. milk, scalded
1 (9") unbaked pie shell

Thoroughly mix eggs, sugar, salt and vanilla in a mixing bowl. Slowly stir in the hot milk. Pour at once into unbaked pie shell. Sprinkle a little nutmeg over the top. Bake at 475° for 5 minutes. Reduce heat to 425° and bake another 10 minutes, or until firm. Cool on rack.

Elvera Van Horssen

Lemon Meringue Pie

1 1/2 c. sugar
1/3 c. cornstarch
1 1/2 c. boiling water
3 egg yolks
1 T. oleo
1/2 c. real lemon juice

Mix dry ingredients. Slowly add water and cook until thick, about 5 minutes. Stir a little hot mix into egg yolks which have been slightly beaten. Put all back into hot mixture and cook 2 minutes more. Remove from heat; add oleo and lemon juice. Pour into baked pie shell.

Jan Budden

Impossible Lemon Pie

1 med. lemon, cut & diced into pieces that fit into blender
1 1/3 c. sugar
4 eggs
3/4 stick soft butter
1 (9") deep-dish, unbaked pie crust
Cool Whip, whipped cream or meringue, for topping

Place the first 4 ingredients in a blender and blend until smooth. Pour purée into pie crust. Bake at 350° for 40 minutes. Cool and add desired topping.

Lorna Bylsma

Sour Cream Lemon Pie

1 c. sour cream
3 egg yolks
1 (3 oz.) pkg. regular vanilla pudding
1 1/4 c. milk
1/3 c. frozen lemonade concentrate
1 T. cornstarch
2 T. cold water
1/2 c. boiling water
3 egg whites
6 T. sugar
Pinch of salt
1 tsp. vanilla
1 baked pie crust

Combine sour cream and egg yolks, slightly beaten, in saucepan. Stir in regular vanilla pudding mix, milk and lemonade. Cook and stir until thick. Spoon into baked crust.
Meringue: Combine cornstarch, cold water and boiling water. Cook until clear and thick. Cool completely. Beat egg whites until frothy. Add sugar, salt and vanilla. Beat until peaks form. Add cornstarch mixture last. Brown in a 325° oven for 10 or 15 minutes.

Wanda Kuiken

Peanut Butter Pie

1 graham cracker crust
1 jar thick fudge topping
1 c. peanut butter
1 can sweetened condensed milk
8 oz. Cool Whip

Line crust with fudge (reserve about 1/2 cup for later). Beat together peanut butter and condensed milk. Add Cool Whip. Pour over top of the fudge. Put in the freezer. Top each piece with a dot of fudge and a piece of a peanut butter cup.

Shellie Vander Schaaf

Peanut Butter Pie

CRUST:
1 1/4 c. Oreo crumbs
1/4 c. sugar
1/4 c. melted margarine

FILLING:
1 (8 oz.) pkg. cream cheese
1 c. creamy peanut butter
1 c. sugar
1 T. softened butter or margarine
1 tsp. vanilla extract
1 c. heavy cream, whipped
Grated chocolate, or Oreo crumbs

Crust: Combine the ingredients and press into a 9-inch pie plate.
Filling: In a mixing bowl, beat cream cheese, peanut butter, sugar, butter and vanilla until smooth. Fold in whipped cream. Gently spoon into crust. Garnish with chocolate or cookie crumbs, if desired. Refrigerate. Yield: 8 to 10 servings.
Note: This recipe can be doubled and put into a 9x13-inch pan.

Evonne Wielenga

Peanut Butter Cream Pie

1 baked 9" pastry shell or
  graham cracker crust
3/4 c. powdered sugar
1/2 c. creamy peanut butter
1 sm. box vanilla instant pudding
1 (8 oz.) ctn. Cool Whip

Mix powdered sugar and peanut butter until crumbs form. Cover bottom of pie crust with crumbs; reserving 3 tablespoons for the top.
Prepare the pudding mix as directed. Spoon pudding into prepared crust. Spoon and spread Cool Whip over pudding. Top with remaining crumb mixture. Refrigerate for 4 hours before serving. Store in refrigerator.

Terry Hofmeyer

♥ Piña Colada Pie
(Diabetic)

1 graham cracker pie crust
1 (8 oz.) pkg. cream cheese
1 (10 oz.) can crushed pineapple, undrained
1 (4-serving-size) instant sugar-free vanilla pudding
1 (8 oz.) ctn. Cool Whip
1/2 c. toasted coconut

Whip cream cheese, pineapple and pudding together. Pour into crust. Top with Cool Whip and toasted coconut.

Note: To toast coconut, place in a shallow pan on a stove burner and stir constantly, until browned.

Marlene De Jager

♥ Paradise Pumpkin Pie
(Diabetic)

1 (4-serving-size) pkg. sugar-free butterscotch pudding
1 1/2 c. cold skim milk
1 T. pumpkin pie spice
1 c. canned pumpkin
1 (8 oz.) ctn. Cool Whip
Chopped pecans
1 graham cracker pie crust

Beat together pudding, milk, spices and pumpkin until thick. Pour into crust. Top with Cool Whip and sprinkle with chopped pecans.

Marlene De Jager

Impossible Pumpkin Pie

1/2 c. Bisquick
2 T. melted oleo
2 eggs
1 c. white or brown sugar
1 (16 oz.) can pumpkin
1 (13 oz.) can evaporated milk
1 tsp. cinnamon
1/2 tsp. ginger
1/4 tsp. cloves
1/4 tsp. allspice, or 2 tsp. pumpkin spice
2 tsp. vanilla

Mix all together, beating well. Pour into a well-oiled, 10-inch Pyrex pie plate. Bake for 1 to 1 1/2 hours at 325°. Serve with whipped cream.
People love this crustless pie.

Rose Dykstra

Pumpkin Pecan Pie

3 eggs
1 c. sugar
1 tsp. vanilla
1/4 tsp. salt
1 c. pumpkin
1/2 c. dark Karo syrup
1/2 tsp. cinnamon
1 c. chopped pecans

Mix and pour into unbaked pie shell. Bake at 375° for 40 minutes. Serve plain or with whipped cream.

Marietta VanDer Weide

Weight Watchers Pumpkin Pie

1 c. pumpkin
2 pkg. sugar-free vanilla pudding
1 tsp. pumpkin spice
1 1/2 c. milk

Mix well and fold in 2 cups Cool Whip. Put into baked pie crust.

Joyce Baker

Microwave Raisin Creme Pie

1 c. raisins
2 T. water
2 c. milk
1/4 c. cornstarch
1/2 c. sugar
1/2 tsp. salt
3 egg yolks
2 T. butter
1/2 tsp. vanilla

MERINGUE:
3 egg whites
1/4 tsp. cream of tartar
6 tsp. sugar
1 tsp. vanilla

Microwave raisins and water for 45 seconds; drain and cool. Put milk in a glass bowl and scald for 2 1/2 minutes in microwave oven. Blend together sugar, cornstarch and salt. Remove milk from microwave and add sugar mixture with a wire whip. Return to oven and cook for 2 1/2 to 3 1/2 minutes. Stir every minute. Beat egg yolks and add to pudding; return to oven for 30 seconds. Beat well. Add butter and vanilla. Add cooled raisins. Pour into baked pie shell. Top with meringue. Bake for 15 minutes at 350°.

Meringue: Whip egg whites and cream of tartar until fluffy. Add sugar gradually, until dissolved. Add vanilla.

Elvera Van Horssen

Rhubarb Pie

1 unbaked pie shell
2 heaping c. diced rhubarb
2 egg yolks, beaten
1 c. cream

1 c. white sugar
1/4 tsp. salt
3 T. cornstarch

Bake in 350° oven for 40 to 45 minutes. Top with meringue.

MERINGUE:
3 egg whites   1/4 tsp. salt

Beat whites and salt until foamy. Add 6 tablespoons sugar, 1 tablespoon at a time. Beat until stiff and glossy. Add 1/2 teaspoon vanilla. Spread over pie. Bake in 350° oven for 12 to 15 minutes, or until lightly browned.

Wanda Hofmeyer

Rhubarb Cream Pie

2 c. diced rhubarb
1 tsp. vanilla
1 c. sugar

1 c. cream
2 heaping T. flour

Mix rhubarb, sugar and cream. Add vanilla. Put into unbaked pie crust and cover with top crust. Bake for 1 hour at 350°.

Crystal Brink

Rhubarb Cream Pie

1 1/2 c. sugar
3 T. flour
1/2 tsp. nutmeg
Pinch of salt

1 T. butter
2 eggs, beaten
3 to 3 1/2 c. rhubarb, cut

Cut rhubarb in 1/2-inch pieces. Put into pastry-lined 9-inch pie pan. Mix dry ingredients. Add eggs and beat until smooth. Pour mixture over rhubarb. Cover with top crust and top with dots of butter. Bake in 450° oven for 10 minutes, then reduce temperature to 350° for 30 minutes.

Hint: Put many slits in top crust and sprinkle a little sugar on crust.

Wanda Kuiken

Rhubarb Custard Pie

3 egg yolks
1 1/2 c. sugar
3 T. flour
2 1/2 to 3 c. diced rhubarb

3 egg whites
1/4 tsp. cream of tartar
6 T. powdered sugar

Beat egg yolks well; add sugar and flour. Mix well. Put cut rhubarb into this mixture and let it form juice while preparing crust. Place into crust and bake at 425° for 10 minutes. Reduce to 350° for 30 minutes.
Meringue: Use 3 egg whites and beat until foamy. Add cream of tartar. Slowly add powdered sugar, one tablespoon at a time, beating approximately 3 minutes. Top the pie while it is hot. Seal edges well. Bake at 350° for about 20 minutes.

Betty Jasper,
Jan Budden

Rhubarb Rumble

3 c. chopped rhubarb
1 sm. pkg. strawberry Jello
1 1/2 c. cold milk

1 sm. pkg. instant vanilla pudding
1 graham cracker pie crust

Microwave rhubarb for 6 to 8 minutes, stirring every 2 minutes, until soft. Stir in Jello. Cool completely. Combine milk and pudding. Fold into rhubarb. Spoon into crust. Cover and chill until set.

Michelle Bomgaars

Fresh Strawberry Pie

CRUST:
1 c. flour

FILLING:
4 oz. cream cheese
1 c. sugar
1 c. water

2 T. sugar
1 stick oleo

3 T. cornstarch
2 T. white corn syrup
1 pkg. strawberry Jello
1 qt. fresh strawberries

Crust: Mix ingredients together and press into a 9-inch pie dish. Bake at 350° for 10 to 12 minutes. Cool. Spread the 4 ounces of cream cheese over the cooled crust.
Filling: Cook sugar, water, cornstarch and corn syrup until thick. Stir in Jello. Cool to room temperature. Stir in washed, cut-up strawberries. Pour into crust. Refrigerate 2 hours before serving. Top with Cool Whip.

Marilyn Kruid

Fresh Strawberry Pie

2 to 3 c. wafer crumbs, or graham cracker crumbs
1 1/2 pt. strawberries
1 1/2 c. sugar
3 T. cornstarch
1/2 c. butter
1 1/2 c. water
3 T. strawberry Jello

Crush wafers or graham crackers and mix with butter. Pat in pie tin and bake for 10 minutes at 350°. Boil water and sugar. Add cornstarch and cook until mixture is clear. Remove from stove and add Jello. Cool and add strawberries. Refrigerate. Top with Cool Whip at serving time, if desired.

Vicki Schrock

Grandma's Strawberry Pie

CRUST:
1 1/3 c. flour
1 tsp. salt

1/2 c. oil
2 T. sugar
2 T. milk

FILLING:
2 T. cornstarch

1 c. sugar
1 c. water

Crust: Mix in pie plate, and then press crust against the bottom and sides. Bake for 12 minutes at 425°.
Filling: Cook until thick and add 1 small box strawberry Jello. When the Jello is dissolved, pour over 2 pints cleaned strawberries. Refrigerate until set.

Amy Aberson

Strawberry Pie

1 1/4 c. apple juice
1/2 c. sugar
3 T. cornstarch
1 pkg. strawberry Jello
Strawberries
Graham cracker crust

Heat juice, sugar and cornstarch over medium heat, stirring constantly, until thickened. Remove from heat and add Jello. Stir until completely dissolved. Cut strawberries and put into crust--fill quite full. Pour gelatin mixture over strawberries. Refrigerate 2 hours. Garnish with Cool Whip. Yield: 8 servings.

BJ De Weerd

Strawberry Pie

1 1/2 c. water
1 c. sugar
3 T. cornstarch
1 (3 oz.) pkg. Jello
1 qt. strawberries
1 graham cracker pie shell

Boil water, sugar and cornstarch until clear. Add the Jello. Stir and set aside to cool. Pour over cleaned berries and pour into pie shell.

Sharon Schelling

Sweetheart Pie

GRAHAM CRACKER CRUST:
16 graham crackers, crushed
1/3 c. sugar
1/3 c. butter, melted

Mix together. Reserve 1/3 cup for top of pie.

1 sm. pkg. strawberry Jello
1 3/4 c. hot water
1 (10 oz.) pkg. frozen strawberries, almost thawed
1/2 c. whipped cream

Dissolve Jello in hot water; add the strawberries. Refrigerate until partially set. Fold in whipped cream. Pour into graham cracker crust. Sprinkle remaining crumbs on top. Chill at least 2 hours, or overnight.

Crystal Brink

♥ Creamy Yogurt Pie
(Diabetic)

8 oz. fat-free artificially-sweetened strawberry yogurt
1 c. light whipped topping
2 c. sliced strawberries
1 store-boughten graham cracker crust

In a medium bowl, combine yogurt and whipped topping. Fold in most of the strawberries. Spoon mixture into crust and garnish with remaining strawberries. Chill or freeze (if you freeze, remove from freezer 30 minutes before serving).

Gert Sjaarda

Toll House Pie

2 eggs
1/2 c. flour
1/2 c. sugar
1/2 c. brown sugar
1 c. melted butter
6 oz. chocolate chips
1 (9") unbaked pie shell

Beat eggs until foamy. Add flour and sugar; beat until well blended. Blend in melted butter; stir in chocolate chips. Pour into pie shell. Bake at 325° for 1 hour.

Cindy VanDer Weide

"Good and Easy" Meringue

6 egg whites
1/2 tsp. cream of tartar
12 T. powdered sugar

Beat egg whites. When they start to froth, add cream of tartar. Beat until soft peaks form, and sprinkle in powdered sugar slowly. Beat until stiff peaks form. Spoon over pie and bake at 325° for 20 minutes.

Jan Budden

Flaky Pie Crust

2 c. flour
1 c. Crisco
1 tsp. salt
1 egg
1 T. vinegar
3 T. water

Cut Crisco into flour and salt with a pastry blender. Mix egg, water and vinegar. Add to flour mixture and stir with a fork. Yield: 1 double crust.
Note: Can get one double and one single crust, if rolled thinly.

Michelle Plendl

Notes & Recipes

Salads, Dressings & Vegetables

Salads & Dressings

Chicken Salad

2/3 c. olive or vegetable oil
1/4 c. lime or lemon juice
1/4 c. parsley, minced
1/2 tsp. ground cumin
1/2 tsp. salt
1/4 tsp. crushed red pepper flakes
4 c. torn leaf lettuce
2 c. cubed chicken
1 pt. cherry tomatoes (opt.)
1/4 c. slivered almonds (opt.)
1/4 c. green onions, sliced (opt.)

Put first 6 ingredients in a pint jar and shake. Refrigerate until ready to serve. At serving time, toss lettuce, chicken and tomatoes together. Pour dressing over; toss again, and serve.

Variations: You may also substitute small pieces of cauliflower for tomatoes. Can also add a few chow mein noodles just before serving.

Marilyn Kruid

Tropical Chicken Salad

2 c. cubed cooked chicken
1 c. chopped celery
1 c. mayonnaise
1/2 to 1 tsp. curry powder
1 (20 oz.) can chunk pineapple, drained
2 lg. firm bananas, sliced
1 (10 oz.) can mandarin oranges, drained
1/2 c. flaked coconut
3/4 c. salted peanuts, chopped coarsely

Place chicken and celery in large bowl. Combine mayonnaise and curry powder. Add to chicken mixture and mix well. Cover and chill 30 minutes, or more. Before serving add pineapple, bananas, oranges and coconut. Toss gently and sprinkle with nuts.

Joyce Baker

Seafood Salad

1 pkg. imitation crabmeat, cut in half
1 sm. onion, chopped fine
1/2 lb. green pepper, chopped fine
1/2 pkg. shell macaroni, cooked, rinsed in cold water & drained
3 stalks celery, chopped fine
4 hard-boiled eggs, chopped

Place above ingredients into large bowl and mix well. In small bowl, mix well the following:

1 1/2 c. salad dressing
1 T. mustard
1 tsp. powdered garlic
1 tsp. sugar or Equal
1/2 c. 2% milk

Pour this mixture over ingredients in large bowl. Mix well and chill for at least 2 to 3 hours. Yield: 10 to 12 servings.

Joyce Baker

Cookie Salad

1 c. buttermilk
1 pkg. instant vanilla pudding
1 (8 oz.) ctn. Cool Whip
1 can mandarin oranges, drained
1 can crushed pineapple, drained
1/2 pkg. fudge-striped cookies

Mix buttermilk and pudding. Stir in Cool Whip, oranges and pineapple. When ready to serve, add 1/2 package crushed fudge-striped cookies.

Kim Oolman

Crazy Grape Salad

1 pt. cultured sour cream
1 c. powdered sugar
2 tsp. vanilla
Red & green grapes
Apples
1 jar caramel ice cream topping

Mix sour cream, powdered sugar and vanilla; pour over fruits and mix well. Before serving, drizzle caramel ice cream topping over.

Crystal Brink

Creamy Fruit Salad

3 oz. cream cheese
1/2 c. sour cream
1/2 c. mayonnaise
1/2 c. brown sugar
1 (20 oz.) can pineapple chunks, drained
1 sm. can mandarin oranges, drained
4 apples, diced
2 c. red grapes
2 c. green grapes

Cream together first 4 ingredients and pour over fruit and mix. Will keep for several days.

Pam Sandbulte

Easy Cherry Salad

1 can cherry pie filling
1 can sweetened condensed milk
1 (9 oz.) can crushed pineapple, drained
1/2 tsp. almond flavoring
1/4 c. lemon juice

Mix all together. Add 1 (8-ounce) carton Cool Whip. Blend together. Chill. Serve. May also be frozen and sliced (optional).

Winova Van Regenmorter

Easy Fruit Salad

1 (20 oz.) can pineapple chunks, drained (reserve 2 T.)
1 (17 oz.) can apricot halves, drained
1 (16 oz.) can pitted red tart cherries, drained
1 (11 oz.) can mandarin orange segments, drained
1 c. mini marshmallows
Fruit Salad Dressing (recipe below)

FRUIT SALAD DRESSING:
1 c. whipping (heavy) cream
2 T. reserved pineapple juice
Dash of salt

Mix pineapple, apricots, cherries, orange segments and marshmallows. Toss with Fruit Salad Dressing. Cover and refrigerate at least 12 hours.

Fruit Salad Dressing: Beat whipping cream in chilled bowl on high speed until soft peaks form. Stir in remaining ingredients.

Denise Dekker

Easy Fruit Salad

1 (15 oz.) can mandarin oranges, drained (juice reserved)
1 (20 oz.) can pineapple tidbits, drained (juice reserved)
1 (15 oz.) can fruit cocktail, drained (juice reserved)
2 (3 oz.) boxes tapioca pudding
1/4 c. orange juice
Water
1 banana, sliced

Drain canned fruits, reserving juices in a measuring cup. Mix mandarin oranges, pineapple and fruit cocktail in medium bowl. To the reserved juices, add orange juice and enough water to make 3 cups liquid. Cook pudding, using 3 cups liquid, according to package directions. Let cool and pour over fruit. Refrigerate overnight and add banana slices just before serving.

Alice Vander Broek

Easy Fruit Salad

1 can mandarin oranges
1 can pineapple tidbits
1 can fruit cocktail
1 c. mini marshmallows
1 cut-up banana
1 can lemon pie filling

Drain each can of fruit and put in bowl. Stir together with lemon pie filling.

Angela Van Ommeren

Frozen Fruit Cups

3 c. water
3 c. sugar
6 oz. frozen orange juice
2 lg. or 3 sm. boxes strawberries
6 bananas, finely chopped
2 1/2 c. fruit cocktail
1 lg. can crushed pineapple
1 jar maraschino cherries
1/3 c. ReaLemon

Boil water and sugar; add orange juice and cool. Mix chopped bananas with lemon juice; add rest of fruits. Put into individual servings; freeze. Thaw slightly before serving.

Mary Ann Winchell

Fruit Soup

1 pkg. tapioca pudding mix
2 c. orange juice (Sunny Delight works best)
16 oz. frozen strawberries
1 can mandarin oranges
1 can diced peaches
2 to 3 bananas, sliced

Cook tapioca according to directions, using orange juice in place of milk. Chill. Add fruit. Chill again, until ready to serve.

Michelle Bomgaars

Hot Fruit Dish

Crumble 6 coconut macaroon cookies into a buttered 9x13-inch glass pan.
Drain:

1 (No. 2) can peaches	1 (No. 2) can pineapple
1 (No. 2) can pears	1 jar maraschino cherries
1 (No. 2) can apricots	

Place fruit on top of crushed cookie mixture. Crush 6 more cookies on top of fruit.
Mix:

1/4 c. oleo   1/4 c. brown sugar

Crumble over crushed macaroon cookies. Top with 1/2 cup slivered almonds. Bake at 350° for 1 hour.

Winova Van Regenmorter

Hot Fruit Salad

1 can applesauce	1 can apricots
1 can mandarin oranges	1 can pineapple chunks
1 can peach slices	1 can cherry pie filling

Drain fruit. Place in bowl in order given: applesauce, oranges, peach slices, apricots, pineapple chunks and pie filling. Top with 1/2 cup brown sugar and 1 teaspoon cinnamon. Bake at 325° for 1 hour.

Betty L. VanDer Weide

Mystery Salad

1 can pineapple chunks	1 c. mini marshmallows
1 can mandarin oranges	1 (3 3/4 oz.) box lemon instant
2 bananas, sliced	pudding

Drain fruits, reserving liquids. Mix fruits with banana slices and marshmallows in a bowl. In another bowl, mix reserved liquids from fruits with instant pudding mix. Pour over fruit. Chill or serve immediately.

Elvera Van Horssen

Peaches and Cream Delight

2 c. milk
1 (3 oz.) box vanilla instant
 pudding
1 sm. ctn. sour cream
1 (20 oz.) can pineapple tidbits
1 can mandarin oranges
1 (29 oz.) can peaches

Combine pudding and milk thoroughly; add sour cream. Drain cans of fruit and add to pudding mixture. Chill.
Elvera Van Horssen

Piña Colada Salad

8 oz. crushed pineapple,
 drained
12 oz. whipped topping
1/2 c. milk
3 oz. coconut instant pudding
 (dry)
Crushed Oreo or Hydrox cookies

Stir together all ingredients, except cookies, and chill. Before serving, add crushed cookies.
Edith Kuiken

Pretzel Salad

1 stick oleo or butter, melted
1 c. crushed pretzels
1/3 c. sugar

Mix and bake at 400° for 6 minutes, or until light brown. Cool and break apart.

20 oz. crushed pineapple,
 drained
8 oz. softened cream cheese
1/2 c. sugar
8 or 12 oz. Cool Whip

Mix cream cheese and sugar; add pineapple. Slowly add Cool Whip, a little at a time. Add pretzel mixture and serve.
Vera Brouwer

Snicker Salad

1 pkg. French vanilla instant
 pudding
1 c. milk
3 apples
3 Snickers candy bars
1 (8 oz.) ctn. whipped topping

Combine pudding and milk; stir well. Add whipped topping. Cut Snickers into small pieces; add to first mixture. Cut apples into small pieces. Dip in lemon juice; add and stir well.
Kathy Smits

Snicker Salad

1 (3 oz.) box banana cream pudding
1 (3 oz.) box vanilla pudding
2 c. milk
2 (8 oz.) ctn. Cool Whip
5 lg. Snickers
2 to 3 apples

Combine puddings, milk and Cool Whip; mix thoroughly. Cut Snickers and apples into small pieces. Mix all together.

Heather Hofmeyer

Snicker Salad

1 (12 oz.) ctn. Cool Whip
1 pkg. instant vanilla pudding
3 to 4 Granny Smith apples
6 Snickers candy bars

Make pudding with 1 3/4 cups milk instead of 2 cups. Let set. Fold in Cool Whip. Add apples, cut up. Cut up Snickers bars; add. Enjoy!

Amy Vander Zwaag

Snicker Salad

1 (4-serving-size) pkg. instant vanilla pudding
1 c. milk

Mix well, then add 1 (8-ounce) carton whipped topping. Core and chop 1 to 2 apples (depending on size). Stir well and refrigerate until serving time. Just before serving, stir in 2 chopped-up Snickers candy bars (they cut best if refrigerated first).
Variation: Can add miniature marshmallows and sliced bananas.

Kristi Hargens

Watergate Salad

1 (8 oz.) ctn. Cool Whip
1 sm. box instant pistachio pudding
1 (1 lb.) can crushed pineapple & juice
1 c. mini marshmallows
1/2 c. chopped walnuts

Fold dry pudding mix into whipped topping. Add pineapple, juice, marshmallows and nuts. Refrigerate.

Jamie Beukelman

Blender Salad

2 (3 oz.) pkg. lime Jello
2 c. boiling water
8 oz. cream cheese
1 (No. 303) can pears (undrained)

Dissolve Jello in boiling water; cool slightly. Put in blender, add pears and cream cheese; blend well. Refrigerate until mixture begins to jell. Fold in Cool Whip. Put in 8x10-inch or larger pan.
Variation: Can use orange or peach Jello with mandarin oranges or peaches, along with other ingredients.

Mary Ann Winchell

Broken Window Glass Salad

1 (3 oz.) pkg. orange Jello
1 (3 oz.) pkg. cherry Jello
1 (3 oz.) pkg. lime Jello
3 c. boiling water
2 c. cold water
1 c. pineapple juice
1/4 c. sugar
1 (3 oz.) pkg. lemon Jello
2 env. Dream Whip

Prepare 3 flavors of gelatin separately, using 1 cup boiling water and 1/2 cup cold water for each. Pour each flavor into an 8-inch square pan. Chill until firm, or overnight. Then mix pineapple juice and sugar. Heat until sugar is dissolved. Remove from heat. Dissolve lemon gelatin in hot juice, then add 1/2 cup cold water. Chill until slightly thickened. Cut firm gelatins into 1/2-inch cubes. Then prepare dessert topping mix according to directions on package, blend with lemon gelatin. Fold in gelatin cubes. Pour into pan. Chill at least 5 hours, or overnight.

Dawn Beukelman

Cherry Coke Salad

1 can bing cherries
1 (4 oz.) can crushed pineapple
1 (6 oz.) pkg. cherry gelatin
2 (6 1/2 oz.) cans cola

Drain juice from fruit (reserve juice). Add enough water for 2 cups. Heat juice to boiling; add gelatin, stir until dissolved. Cool, add cola and fruit. Pour into 1 1/2-quart bowl or mold. Chill until set. Serve with Cool Whip.

Joyce Baker

♥ Diabetic Jello Salad

1 box sugar-free Jello (any flavor)
1 pkg. cream cheese
1 ctn. whipped topping

Make Jello according to package. Just before it starts to gel, add whipped topping and cream cheese; blend together. Chill.

Marci Jager

Holiday White Salad

1 env. unflavored gelatin
1/4 c. cold water
2/3 c. sugar
1 c. boiling water
2 c. sour cream
1 tsp. vanilla
8 oz. whipped topping
1 can fruit pie filling

Mix and dissolve unflavored gelatin and cold water. Mix sugar and boiling water and add to gelatin mixture. Blend in sour cream, vanilla and whipped topping. Put in slightly-oiled large ring mold. Chill. Unmold and fill center with pie filling. (Cherry is very good in winter, and peach in spring.)

Denise Dekker

Mimosa Mold

1 1/2 c. boiling water
1 (8-serving-size) pkg. or 2 (4-serving) pkg. Jello Brand sparkling white grape flavor gelatin dessert
2 c. cold seltzer or club soda
1 (11 oz.) can mandarin orange segments, drained
1 c. sliced strawberries

Stir boiling water into gelatin in large bowl, at least 2 minutes, until completely dissolved. Stir in cold seltzer. Refrigerate 1 1/2 hours, or until thickened. Stir in oranges and strawberries. Pour into 6-cup mold. Refrigerate 4 hours, or until firm. Unmold. Store leftover gelatin mold in refrigerator. Yield: 12 servings.

Barb Oldenkamp

Easy Orange Salad

2 (3 oz.) pkg. orange Jello
2 c. hot water
1 pt. orange sherbet
1 (11 oz.) can mandarin oranges (juice & all)

Dissolve Jello in hot water. Stir in orange sherbet until melted. Add mandarin oranges. Put into an 8x8-inch pan. Refrigerate.

Darlene Wichers

Orange Salad

1 sm. pkg. orange Jello
1 sm. pkg. vanilla pudding (not instant)
2 c. water
1 (8 oz.) ctn. Cool Whip
2 cans mandarin oranges, drained

Mix Jello, pudding and water together. Boil for 1 to 2 minutes. Cool well. When cool, beat in Cool Whip and mandarin oranges. Mix with mixer. Chill.
Dawn Beukelman

Orange Salad

2 pkg. orange Jello
1 c. boiling water
1 1/4 c. cold water
1 (6 oz.) can frozen orange juice
1 (11 oz.) can mandarin oranges
2 sliced bananas
1 c. pineapple

Combine first 4 ingredients. Let stand until thickened. Then add the mandarin oranges, bananas and pineapple. Put in 9x13-inch pan and let set. Top with Cool Whip.
Melissa De Jager

Orange Salad
(Diabetic)

1 (3 oz.) pkg. sugar-free orange Jello
1 pkg. sugar-free instant vanilla pudding
2 c. water
1 (8 oz.) ctn. lite Cool Whip
1 sm. can crushed pineapple, drained

Cook Jello, pudding and water. Stir until smooth, about 5 minutes. Cool. Fold in Cool Whip and pineapple. Refrigerate. May use fruit cocktail, drained, or any fruit.
Gert Sjaarda

Orange Salad Supreme

1 pkg. tapioca pudding mix
1 (3 oz.) pkg. orange Jello
1 pkg. vanilla pudding
2 c. hot water
2 c. whipped topping
1 to 2 cans mandarin oranges, well drained

Combine puddings, orange Jello and mix with hot water. Cook in a double boiler or over very low heat until thick, stirring carefully. Cool. Fold in whipped topping and drained oranges. Chill until set.
Variation: Pineapple chunks are also good.
Marietta VanDer Weide,
Elvera Van Horssen

Orange-Pineapple Salad

2 pkg. tapioca pudding
1 (3 oz.) pkg. orange Jello
1 lg. can crushed pineapple
2 cans mandarin oranges

Drain juice from pineapple and oranges. Add water to make 3 cups. Bring to a boil and pour over pudding and Jello. Stir well, until dissolved. Let this sit out on the counter overnight. In the morning, add pineapple and oranges; fold in 8 ounces Cool Whip. Refrigerate.

Arloa Jansma

Golden Glow Salad

1 pkg. orange Jello
1 pkg. lemon Jello
2 c. hot water
1 1/2 c. cold water
1 lg. can crushed pineapple
2 bananas
Mini marshmallows

TOPPING:
1 c. pineapple juice
1/2 c. sugar
2 T. flour
1 egg
1 c. whipped cream

Dissolve Jello in hot water. Add cold water, pineapple, bananas and marshmallows. Put into 9x13-inch pan. Refrigerate until set.

Topping: Use liquid from crushed pineapple and add enough water to make 1 cup. Heat egg and juice. Mix flour and sugar together. Add to juice and egg. Cook until thick. Cool, add whipped cream and pour over salad.

Darlene Kluis

Pimento Salad

1 pkg. lemon Jello
1 med. can crushed pineapple
1 sm. jar pimento
1 (8 oz.) pkg. cream cheese
1/2 c. nuts, chopped
1/2 c. celery, chopped
1/2 pt. whipping cream

Drain liquid from pineapple and bring to a boil and dissolve Jello. Let it stand until syrupy. Add rest of the ingredients, adding whipped cream last.

Mary Stallbaum

Peaches 'N Cream Salad

1 (3 oz.) pkg. lemon Jello
3/4 c. boiling water
1 c. orange juice
1 env. whipped topping,
 or 1 sm. ctn. Cool Whip

1 (3 oz.) pkg. cream cheese,
 softened & beaten until smooth
1/4 c. chopped pecans (opt.)

PEACH LAYER:
1 (3 oz.) pkg. lemon gelatin

1 c. boiling water
1 (21 oz.) can peach pie filling

In a bowl, dissolve gelatin in water; add orange juice. Refrigerate until partially set. Prepare topping mix (or use Cool Whip) and fold whipped topping in with cream cheese and pecans, if desired. Fold in gelatin mixture.
Peach Layer: Dissolve gelatin in water; stir in pie filling. Chill until partially set, and carefully pour over creamy mixture.

Lois Klein

Quick 'N Easy Salad

2 sm. pkg. Jello (any flavor--
 we like lime best)
1 (16 to 24 oz.) ctn. cottage
 cheese

1 lg. can crushed pineapple,
 drained
1 ctn. Cool Whip
Mini marshmallows (opt.)

Mix all ingredients together (use the Jello dry). You may add other fruits as desired. Chill before serving.

Vera Brouwer

Raspberry Cottage Cheese Salad

1 sm. ctn. cottage cheese
1 sm. ctn. Cool Whip
1 can crushed pineapple,
 drained

1 can mandarin oranges,
 drained
1 c. pecan pieces
1 sm. box frozen raspberries
1 sm. box raspberry Jello

Thaw raspberries; drain well. Mix dry Jello in Cool Whip. Fold in remaining ingredients; mix well. Chill at least 3 hours.

Wilma Ruisch

Spring Garden Salad

4 c. diced rhubarb
2 c. (or less) sugar
1/2 c. water
6 oz. strawberry Jello
Dash of salt

2 c. sliced strawberries
1 c. whipping cream, or 8 oz. Cool Whip
1 c. mini marshmallows

Cook rhubarb, sugar and water until rhubarb is tender. Remove from heat, add Jello and salt; let cool. When cool, add Cool Whip and marshmallows. Can be put on a graham cracker crust for a dessert. *Julie Leusink*

Betty's Pink Lady Salad

1 (6 oz.) pkg. strawberry Jello
2 c. boiling water
1 pt. vanilla ice cream

Bananas
Strawberries

Dissolve Jello in boiling water. Add ice cream and stir until smooth. Add sliced bananas. Fresh strawberries are nice for color. Refrigerate. Sets up almost immediately. *Lorna Bylsma*

Strawberry Fluff

1 (3 oz.) pkg. strawberry Jello (dry)
1 (3 oz.) box instant vanilla pudding
1 (9 oz.) can crushed pineapple with juice

3 c. mini marshmallows
1 (8 oz.) ctn. Cool Whip
1 (10 oz.) pkg. frozen strawberries, drained

Mix all ingredients together. *Carolyn De Jager*

♥ Strawberry Jello Salad
(Diabetic)

2 (4-serving-size) pkg. sugar-free strawberry Jello
1 c. hot water
1 c. cold water

1 (1 lb.) pkg. unsweetened frozen strawberries
1 (8 oz.) ctn. Cool Whip

Dissolve Jello in 1 cup hot water. Put in blender with 1 cup cold water and frozen strawberries; blend well. Pour into a 9x13-inch pan. When Jello is set, put Cool Whip on top.
Hint: Fresh strawberries may be used in place of frozen.
Marlene De Jager

Strawberry Salad

1 (8 oz.) ctn. Cool Whip
1 (3 oz.) pkg. dry strawberry Jello
1 ctn. strawberry yogurt
Sliced strawberries
Banana, sliced (opt.)

Mix together Cool Whip and yogurt. Sprinkle dry Jello over this mixture; mix well. Add as many strawberries as desired (about 1 pint). A sliced banana is good too, if desired.

Joan Dekker

Strawberry Salad

1 (8 oz.) pkg. cream cheese
3/4 c. sugar
1 (10 oz.) box frozen strawberries
8 oz. Cool Whip
2 bananas

Beat cream cheese and sugar together with mixer. Add Cool Whip and mix together. Stir in strawberries (juice and all), and cut-up bananas. Refrigerate overnight.

Karen Leusink

Strawberry Salad

3 (3 oz.) pkg. strawberry Jello
4 1/2 c. boiling water
3 sm. pkg. frozen strawberries
1 sm. pkg. cream cheese
1 (8 oz.) ctn. Cool Whip
2 T. sugar
1 1/2 c. mini marshmallows

Mix together boiling water and Jello. Dissolve frozen strawberries in Jello and cool. Mix Cool Whip, cream cheese and sugar. Fold in marshmallows. Fold cream mixture into the cooled Jello mixture. Pour into a 9x13-inch pan and set.

Sharon Schelling

Strawberry Salad

2 pkg. vanilla pudding (cook-type)
1 pkg. strawberry Jello
3 c. milk

Cook until thick. Cool. Add 1 (8-ounce) carton Cool Whip. Mix. Add fresh strawberries and bananas (as many as you like).

Winova Van Regenmorter

Strawberry-Cranberry Salad

2 pkg. strawberry Jello
2 c. hot water
1 can whole cranberry sauce
1 (10 oz.) pkg. frozen strawberries (undrained)
1 sm. can crushed pineapple
Nutmeats

Add hot water to Jello. Stir until dissolved. Add frozen strawberries, cranberries and pineapple. Put into 9x13-inch pan, and when set, cut nutmeats over the top.
Edith Kuiken

Finger Jello

3 (3 oz.) pkg. gelatin (any flavor)
3 c. boiling water
4 pkg. unflavored gelatin
1 c. cold water

Dissolve flavored gelatin in boiling water. Dissolve unflavored gelatin in cold water. Mix 2 gelatins together. Pour into 9x13-inch pan sprayed with vegetable spray. Chill until set. Cut into squares or use cookie cutters.
Judy Vlietstra

Classic Macaroni Salad

1 c. Hellmann's real mayonnaise
2 T. vinegar
1 T. prepared mustard
1 tsp. sugar
1 tsp. salt
1/4 tsp. pepper
8 oz. elbow macaroni, cooked & drained
1 c. sliced celery
1 c. chopped red or green pepper
1/4 c. chopped onion

Combine first 6 ingredients. Stir in remaining ingredients. Cover; chill. Yield: 5 cups.
Edith Van Roekel

Macaroni Salad and Dressing

16 oz. macaroni
3 med. carrots, shredded
3 stalks of celery, diced
3 green onions, diced

1/4 green pepper, diced
1/4 red pepper, diced
Any other raw vegetables

DRESSING:
1 pt. mayonnaise
1/2 c. sugar

3/4 c. red wine vinegar
1 c. condensed milk

Cook macaroni. Drain in colander and cool under cold running water. Add shredded carrots, diced celery, cut-up green onions and optional green and red pepper, or any other raw vegetables.

B. Duane De Jager

Macaroni Salad

1 (12 oz.) pkg. macaroni
1/4 c. green pepper
2 c. shredded carrots

1 c. chopped ham
3 stalks celery

DRESSING:
1 can sweetened condensed milk
1 c. sugar

3/4 c. vinegar
1/4 tsp. pepper
2 c. mayonnaise
1/2 tsp. salt

Prepare dressing first. Then cook macaroni according to package; cool and combine with other ingredients. Add dressing and chill several hours before serving.

Teresa Jasper

Macaroni Salad

5 c. shell macaroni
1 c. diced celery
1 diced onion

2 diced carrots
1 diced green pepper

DRESSING:
1/2 c. vinegar
3/4 c. sugar

1/2 c. condensed milk
1 c. mayonnaise

Cook macaroni and rinse with cold water. Add celery, onion, carrots and green pepper. In separate bowl, combine sugar, vinegar, milk and mayonnaise. Toss with salad. Chill.

Pam Jeltema

Macaroni Salad

1 lb. curly rotini macaroni, cooked, rinsed & cooled
1 green pepper, diced
1 med. chopped onion
4 grated carrots

DRESSING:
1 can sweetened condensed milk
1/2 c. vinegar
1/2 c. sugar
1 1/2 c. mayonnaise
1/2 tsp. salt
1/4 tsp. pepper

Stir dressing ingredients together. Combine with cooked, rinsed, cooled macaroni and prepared vegetables. Chill at least 4 hours in refrigerator. Keeps well in the refrigerator.

Note: I use fat-free sweetened condensed milk and fat-free mayonnaise.

Marilyn Kruid

Macaroni Salad

1 pkg. macaroni & cheese dinner
1 chopped fresh tomato
10 oz. frozen peas, thawed (not cooked)
3/4 c. salad dressing
1/4 c. French dressing
1/2 c. celery, diced
1/2 tsp. salt
1/2 c. chopped onion
5 hard-cooked eggs, chopped

Prepare macaroni and cheese dinner according to directions. Let cool. Add remaining ingredients; mix well. Refrigerate.

Chris Van Beek

Macaroni Salad

1 (7 oz.) pkg. macaroni (2 c.)
2 T. salad oil
2 T. vinegar
1 T. minced onion
1/2 tsp. seasoned salt
1/4 tsp. seasoned pepper
1 c. diced Cheddar cheese
1 (12 oz.) can Spam or 10 oz. chicken
1/3 c. Miracle Whip

Cook macaroni according to package directions. Drain; do not chill. While still hot, drizzle with oil and vinegar. Add onion, seasonings and cheese; toss well. Gently mix in Spam or chicken and remaining ingredients. Chill thoroughly.

Jonna Wierda

Pasta Salad

1 head broccoli
1 red onion, chopped
1 lb. bacon, cooked & crumbled

DRESSING:
2 c. Miracle Whip
1/2 c. sugar

2 c. Cheddar cheese
1 sm. pkg. rotini macaroni,
  cooked & drained

1 can sweetened condensed
  milk
1/3 c. vinegar

Cook macaroni and cool; then mix with the remaining ingredients. After the dressing is put on the salad, refrigerate for several hours, or overnight, so the flavors can mix.
Variation: You may also use peas instead of the broccoli.

Helen Oolman

Rigatoni Salad

1 lb. rigatoni noodles
2 med. cucumbers
2 tomatoes
1 green pepper
1 1/2 c. vinegar

2 tsp. table mustard
1 tsp. pepper
1 tsp. salt
1 tsp. garlic salt
1 1/2 c. sugar

Cook noodles and cool. Chop vegetables. Boil vinegar, pepper, salts, sugar and mustard for 1 minute. Cool and mix together.

Linda (Baker) Boone

Spaghetti Salad

12 to 14 oz. spaghetti, broken
  in 4 pieces & cooked
  according to directions

Strain spaghetti after rinsing in cold water.
  Add:
Chopped onion
Black olives, sliced

Cucumber, diced fine
Green pepper

DRESSING:

8 oz. Zesty Italian dressing

Add cherry tomatoes or diced tomatoes right before serving.

Eunice Koopmans

♥ Three-Bean Salad
(Diabetic)

1 can red kidney beans
1 can wax beans

1 can cut green beans
1 med. onion, chopped

DRESSING: Mix well.
1/2 c. vinegar
1/2 c. oil

Enough sugar substitute to
equal 1/2 c. sugar

Drain all the beans. Add onion. Pour on dressing. Stir several times while chilling. Add salt and pepper to taste.

Ronald De Jager

Broccoli Salad

1 bunch broccoli
1/2 c. raisins

1/2 lb. bacon
1/2 c. sunflower seeds

DRESSING:
1 c. mayonnaise
2 T. vinegar

1/4 c. sugar
1 sm. onion

Evonne Wielenga

Cabbage Salad

2 T. toasted sesame seeds
1/2 c. toasted slivered almonds
2 c. cooked, cubed chicken
1 head cabbage, shredded

1 pkg. chicken-flavored
   Ramen noodles
2 chopped green onions

DRESSING:
Seasoning pkt. from Ramen
   noodles
1/2 c. oil

3 T. vinegar
1 T. sugar
1 tsp. salt
1/2 tsp. pepper

Mix cabbage, chicken and onions together. Mix dressing together and pour over cabbage. In 350° oven, toast sesame seeds and almonds for 5 minutes. Let salad refrigerate overnight. When ready to serve, mix Ramen noodles, sesame seeds and almonds in salad.

Jill Schouten

Cabbage Salad

1 head shredded cabbage

1 bunch green onions

DRESSING:
3/4 c. oil
2 T. sugar

2 T. vinegar
1 tsp. salt
1/2 tsp. pepper

Mix together. Just before serving, add 2 packages Ramen noodles and 6 to 8 ounces slivered almonds (toasted at 350° until brown, about 15 minutes).

Evonne Wielenga

Cathy's Cabbage Crunch Salad

SALAD:
2 T. sesame seeds
1/2 c. slivered almonds
4 green onions, chopped

1 (16 oz.) pkg. shredded cabbage
1 pkg. Ramen noodles (chicken flavor--uncooked)

DRESSING:
2 tsp. sugar
1/2 c. oil
3 T. vinegar (white wine or balsamic)

1/2 tsp. salt
1/2 tsp. pepper
1 T. sesame seed oil
Chicken flavor from Ramen noodle pkg.

Break up noodles before opening package. In a skillet, lightly brown sesame seeds and almonds. Combine cabbage, sesame seeds, almonds, onion and broken noodles. Do <u>not</u> cook noodles. Combine all dressing ingredients in a jar and mix well. Pour over salad and serve.

Diane Munro

The right angle to approach any problem is the TRY angle.

Chicken and Cabbage Crunch Salad

2 chicken breasts
1 (1 lb.) bag coleslaw mix
1 (1 lb.) bag broccoli slaw
4 T. sesame seeds

1 c. slivered almonds
4 green onions
2 (3 oz.) pkg. Ramen noodles

DRESSING:
4 T. sugar
6 T. vinegar

2 tsp. Mrs. Dash
2 flavor pkt. Ramen noodles
3/4 c. vegetable oil

Lightly season and cook (grill) chicken breasts until fully cooked. When completely cool, chop into small pieces. In microwave-safe dish, toast almonds and sesame seeds, stirring frequently. Thinly slice green onions. Crush Ramen noodles into small pieces. Combine dressing ingredients in a shaker. Just before serving, in large bowl, combine salad mixes, diced chicken, Ramen noodles, toasted nuts and dressing.

Note: This makes a large salad--you can keep the components separately and combine just the amount you want to eat at that time. Keeps well before dressing is added.

Marlys Lenters

Crispy Salad

1 bag shredded cabbage
1 pkg. chicken Ramen noodles
   (crunch up--save
   seasonings)
1/2 c. shaved almonds
1/2 c. sunflower seeds

1/4 c. apple cider vinegar
3/4 c. salad oil
Dash of pepper
Seasoning pkt. from noodles
4 T. sugar

Put noodles, cabbage and sunflower seeds in a large bowl. In another bowl, put apple cider vinegar, salad oil, pepper, seasoning packet from noodles, and sugar. Mix well, and put on cabbage and mix together.

Jeanne Van Roekel

Oriental Coleslaw

1 pkg. coleslaw mix
4 green onions, chopped
1/2 c. slivered almonds, toasted
3 T. sunflower seeds
1 pkg. chicken-flavored Ramen noodles

DRESSING:
1/2 c. oil
2 T. sugar
2 T. vinegar
1 tsp. salt
Seasoning pkt. from Ramen noodles

Mix first 4 ingredients. Add crushed noodles just before serving. Combine dressing ingredients, shake up and put on just before serving.

Darlene Kluis

Oriental Coleslaw

1 pkg. coleslaw
1 pkg. broccoli slaw
1 pkg. Ramen noodles (chicken)
1/2 c. sliced almonds
1/2 c. sesame seeds
1/2 c. canola oil
1/2 c. white vinegar
1/2 c. sugar

Combine oil, vinegar and sugar with flavor packet; set aside. Mix coleslaw and broccoli slaw in large bowl; add dressing. Before serving, add almonds, sesame seeds and broken (uncooked) noodles.
Variation: Great if you add cut-up grilled chicken breasts.

Marietta VanDer Weide

Cashew-Lettuce Salad

1 head lettuce
1 c. grated Swiss cheese
1 c. cashew nuts

DRESSING:
3/4 c. sugar
1 c. oil
1/3 c. vinegar
1 tsp. prepared mustard
1 tsp. to 1 T. grated onion
1 tsp. poppy seeds
1/2 tsp. salt

Cut up lettuce. Add cheese and nuts. Beat dressing ingredients together. Pour over salad just before serving.

Evelyn De Vries,
Winova Van Regenmorter

Cashew Salad

1 head lettuce
1 bunch green leaf lettuce
1 c. Swiss cheese
1 c. cashews

DRESSING:
3/4 c. sugar
1 c. oil
1/3 c. vinegar
1 T. mustard
1 T. minced onion
1 T. poppy seeds
1/2 T. salt

Mix dressing well in blender. Toss all ingredients and add dressing just before serving.
Note: Dressing can also be mixed in a Tupperware shaker, but will have a tendency to separate.

Julie Leusink

Deb's Lettuce Salad

2 heads lettuce
2 c. Colby or Monterey Jack cheese
2 c. cashews

DRESSING:
3/4 c. sugar
1 c. oil
1/3 c. vinegar
1 tsp. mustard
1 tsp. onion
1 tsp. poppy seeds
1/2 tsp. salt

Tear lettuce into small pieces. Crush cashews, add cheese. Mix dressing ingredients and pour over lettuce just before serving.

Eileen Wichers

Cathy's Spinach Salad

2 T. soy sauce
2 tsp. white sugar
2 T. peanut oil
1/4 c. sesame seeds
1 lb. spinach

In a small pan, combine soy sauce, sugar and oil. Cook over low heat, stirring until sugar is dissolved. Cool. Toast sesame seeds in a pan. Mix into dressing. Pour over spinach; toss and serve.

Diane Munro

Country Salad Bowl

5 lg. tomatoes, sliced
2 cucumbers, sliced
1 green pepper, cut into rings
1 lg. sweet onion, cut into rings
Salt & pepper
1/4 c. French dressing

Slice tomatoes. Peel cucumbers and score with tines of fork; slice. Slice green pepper and onion rings. Arrange all ingredients in a bowl alternately; cover tightly and refrigerate. When ready to serve, sprinkle with salt and pepper and drizzle with French dressing.

Eunice Koopmans

Garden Delight

1 c. cut-up carrots
1 c. sliced cucumbers
2 tomatoes
1 c. celery
1 green pepper
2 c. broccoli
2 c. cauliflower
1 btl. Italian dressing
1 bag rotini noodles

Cut up all the vegetables. Mix in big bowl. Pour in Italian dressing and mix well. Put in refrigerator. Boil and cook rotini noodles (don't overcook). Cool and add to vegetables, mixing well. Stays good for days.

Sandy Holtrop

Mandarin Lettuce Salad

1/2 c. sliced almonds
3 T. sugar
1/2 head iceberg lettuce
1/2 head romaine lettuce
1 c. celery, chopped
Green onions, chopped
1 can mandarin oranges, drained

In a small pan over medium heat, cook almonds and sugar, stirring constantly, until coated. Cool.

Make dressing by mixing 1 teaspoon salt, dash of pepper, 1/4 cup vegetable oil, 1 tablespoon chopped parsley, 2 tablespoons sugar, 2 tablespoons vinegar and dash of Tabasco sauce; mix and chill. Combine lettuce, romaine, celery and onion. Chill. Just before serving, add dressing and oranges. Toss and serve.

Diane Munro

Onion-Cucumber Salad

1 scant c. Miracle Whip salad dressing
1 pkg. lime Jello
3/4 c. boiling water
2 T. lemon juice
1 sm. ctn. small-curd cottage cheese
1 grated cucumber
1 sm. onion, grated

Dissolve Jello in hot water. Add salad dressing, stirring until blended. Add remaining ingredients and pour into a mold. Refrigerate until set.

Imo Mulder

Pea Salad

2 c. peas, drained
3/4 c. sweet pickles, diced
1 c. diced celery
1 c. diced American cheese
1 T. grated onion

DRESSING:
1/4 c. mayonnaise
2 tsp. pickle juice
1/4 tsp. salt
Dash of pepper

Mix all together. Chill and serve.

Wanda Hofmeyer

Pea Salad

3 (16 oz.) cans peas, drained
1 lb. cubed Velveeta cheese
1 chopped onion
3 hard-boiled eggs
Salt & pepper, to taste

Mix these ingredients together, along with Miracle Whip.

Arla Korver

Pea Salad

2 c. drained peas
1/2 c. chopped celery
1/4 tsp. pepper
1 c. cubed cheese
2 sliced hard-boiled eggs
1/2 tsp. salt
1/2 c. mayonnaise
1 T. sugar

Mix and chill before serving.

Wilma Vander Stelt

Chop! Chop!

1 lg. head cauliflower
4 lg. heads broccoli
1 red onion

SAUCE:
3 T. vinegar

1 c. Cheddar cheese
1/2 lb. bacon
Sunflower seeds

1/4 to 1/3 c. sugar
1 c. mayonnaise

Chop all ingredients and toss together.

BJ De Weerd

Vegetable Salad

1 head broccoli, separated
1 head cauliflower, separated
1 lb. fried, crumbled bacon
8 oz. shredded Mozzarella cheese

1/2 c. chopped onion
2 c. Miracle Whip
1/4 c. sugar
2 T. vinegar
1/4 c. Parmesan cheese

Mix all together. Chill and serve.

Vi De Jong

Vegetable Salad

6 c. broccoli flowerets
6 c. cauliflower flowerets
1 lg. red onion, chopped

DRESSING:
1/4 c. vinegar
1 env. Hidden Valley Ranch dressing mix

2 c. cherry tomatoes, sliced
1 (6 oz.) can pitted ripe black olives, drained & sliced (opt.)

2/3 c. vegetable oil
Croutons (opt.)

In large bowl, toss together broccoli, cauliflower, chopped onion, sliced tomatoes and olives.
Dressing: In a jar with lid, shake well, the vinegar, Hidden Valley dressing and oil. Pour over salad and toss.
Refrigerate for at least 3 hours. Toss well before serving. Serve with croutons on the side.

Cherie Van Donkelaar

Dilly Potato Salad

2 lb. red potatoes
1 c. nonfat yogurt
3 T. fat-free mayonnaise
1/4 c. thinly-sliced green onions
1 tsp. Dijon mustard
1 tsp. dill weed
1/2 tsp. curry powder
1/8 tsp. pepper

Place potatoes in a large saucepan and cover with water; cover and bring to a boil. Cook until tender, about 25 to 30 minutes; drain. In a large bowl, combine the remaining ingredients. Thinly slice potatoes; add to the yogurt mixture and toss gently until coated. Refrigerate until serving time. Yield: 8 servings.

Angela Van Voorst

Hot Creamed Potato Salad

2 T. shortening
2 T. flour
1 c. milk
1 1/2 tsp. salt
A little pepper

Make a white sauce of the above ingredients, then add:
4 c. diced, boiled potatoes
2 med. onions, diced fine
1 c. celery, chopped
2 hard-boiled eggs
1/3 c. salad dressing

Cook and serve hot.

Sharla De Jager

Potato Salad

10 lb. russet potatoes (salted well)
2 doz. boiled eggs
Onion

DRESSING:
2 qt. Miracle Whip
2 to 3 tsp. celery seed
4 tsp. prepared mustard
Sugar, to taste (approx. 1 c.)

Yield: 50 servings.

Jo Kuiken

Potato Salad

6 hard-boiled eggs
6 whole boiled potatoes
1 med. onion
1 stalk celery
1 or 2 carrots
3 or 4 radishes

In a large bowl, mix above ingredients. Let stand while preparing the dressing.

DRESSING:
1/2 c. water
1 T. flour
1 egg
4 T. vinegar
1/2 tsp. salt
1/2 c. sugar
1 c. mayonnaise
1 tsp. mustard

Bring all ingredients, except mayonnaise and mustard, to boil, stirring constantly. When mixture is mixed and smooth, add 1 cup mayonnaise. Reduce heat and stir until all is completely mixed. When mixture is cool, stir in 1 teaspoon mustard. Mix well into potato mixture. Refrigerate, covered, 1 day before serving.. Yield: 10 servings.

Joan Punt

Potato Salad Light

5 med. potatoes
2 eggs
Onion, to taste
Salt, to taste

DRESSING:
3/4 c. Miracle Whip Light
1 T. prepared mustard
3 tsp. powdered sweetener
1 T. sweet pickle relish

Cook potatoes in boiling water until done. Drain, cool and peel. Cut into pieces. Hard-boil eggs. Cool, peel and cut into pieces. Mix dressing ingredients and then mix with potatoes and eggs. Cool.

Jonna Wierda

L'Trio Dressing

1 c. salad oil
1 c. sugar
1/3 c. catsup
1/3 c. vinegar
1 tsp. salt
1 tsp. celery seed
1 T. onion

Beat until thick. I like to do in the blender. It will look creamy at first, but will clear as it stands in refrigerator.

Wilma Vander Stelt

Mom Van Roekel's Salad Dressing

1/2 c. vinegar (white)
2 T. water
1/2 heaping c. white sugar
1 T. prepared mustard
1 rounded T. flour
1 egg
1 T. margarine

Boil sugar, water and vinegar until clear. In another bowl, mix egg and mustard, add flour gradually. Mix a few tablespoons of hot mixture into flour-egg mixture. Mix this into the hot mixture. Boil until thick. Add margarine, heat until smooth. Good for potato salad.
When using, I add some mayonnaise when making it, and I often double it.

Joyce Groen

Potato Salad Dressing

3 eggs, beaten
1/2 tsp. dry mustard
3/4 c. pickle juice (from home-canned pickles)
1/2 c. sugar

Boil until thick in a double boiler. Very good for potato salad. Mix half of boiled dressing and equal amount of mayonnaise and thin with a little milk for potato salad.

Darlene Kluis

Vegetables

Cheesy Potatoes

1 (26 oz.) pkg. shredded frozen hash browns
1 c. diced onion
1/3 lb. Velveeta cheese
1 can cream of chicken soup
1 c. sour cream
1 c. Cheez Whiz
1 stick margarine
Crushed corn flakes

Mix all ingredients together, except margarine and corn flakes, and place in baking dish. Melt margarine and pour over mixture, then cover with crushed corn flakes. Bake at 350° for 1 hour. Yield: 8 to 10 servings.

Elvera Van Horssen

Cottage Potatoes

5 lb. potatoes
1 lg. onion
1 green pepper
1/2 lb. American cheese, cubed
1 sm. can pimento
Chopped parsley
1 1/4 c. milk
1 c. butter, melted
1 c. corn flakes, crushed

Cook unpeeled potatoes until nearly done. Peel and slice into a large buttered baking dish. Add onion, green pepper, cheese, pimento and parsley. Cover with milk and butter. Top with crushed corn flakes. Bake at 350° for 1 hour. Yield: 12 servings.

Evonne Wielenga

Company Potatoes

6 med. potatoes
1/2 c. butter
1/2 c. flour
1 tsp. salt
1 T. minced onion
2 c. milk
1/2 to 1 c. Cheddar cheese, shredded
Crushed corn flakes

Peel potatoes and shred coarsely. Steam until tender (or cooked unpeeled; cooled, peeled and shredded). For sauce, melt butter in saucepan or microwave bowl, stir in flour. Add salt, onion, milk and cheese. Slowly heat (or microwave, stirring often) until slightly thickened. Put potatoes in large casserole and pour sauce over potatoes, mix slightly. Cover with crushed corn flakes. Bake, uncovered, at 350° for 30 minutes.
Note: May be assembled the day before--lengthen baking time.

Donna J. Muilenburg

Crunchy Potatoes

1 lb. frozen hash browns
1/2 c. oleo
2 c. shredded Cheddar cheese
1 tsp. salt
1 can cream of chicken soup
8 oz. sour cream
1/8 tsp. pepper

Mix together and place in well-greased 9x13-inch pan.

TOPPING:
1/4 c. oleo
1 c. cornflake crumbs

Bake 50 minutes at 350°.

Marietta VanDer Weide,
Connie Anderson

Grandma's Hash Brown Bake

1/2 c. butter
1 bag hash browns
1 can cream soup
16 oz. sour cream
2 c. Cheddar cheese, shredded
1/2 c. onion
2 c. corn flakes
1/4 c. butter

Melt 1/2 cup butter. Stir in soup and sour cream. Add onions. Add cheese. Stir in hash browns. Place in 9x13-inch greased pan. Sprinkle corn flakes on top. Pour melted 1/4 cup butter over cereal. Bake at 350° for 45 minutes.

Hash Brown Casserole

1 (24 oz.) pkg. frozen hash browns
2 c. sour cream
1 (10 1/2 oz.) can cream of chicken soup
1 1/2 sticks margarine, melted
1 tsp. salt
1 T. minced onion
2 c. shredded Cheddar cheese
2 c. coarsely-crushed corn flakes

Combine sour cream, soup, 1 stick oleo, salt, onion and cheese. Blend in potatoes and put in a shallow 2-quart casserole, or 9x13-inch pan. Pour rest of margarine into corn flakes and sprinkle buttered corn flakes on top. Bake, uncovered, for 50 minutes at 350°.

Lisa Wielenga

Crock-Pot Potatoes

1 pkg. frozen, cubed hash brown potatoes
1 c. (8 oz.) cubed or shredded American cheese
2 c. (16 oz.) ctn. sour cream
1 (10 3/4 oz.) can cream of celery soup
1 (10 3/4 oz.) can cream of chicken soup
1 lb. bacon
1 lg. onion, chopped
1/4 c. butter or margarine, melted
1/4 tsp. pepper

Place potatoes in an ungreased 5-quart slow-cooker. In a bowl, combine remaining ingredients. Pour over potatoes and mix well. Cover and cook on low for 4 to 5 hours, or until potatoes are tender and heated through. Yield: 14 servings.

Amy Aberson

Make-Ahead Potatoes

10 lg. potatoes, peeled & quartered
1 c. (8 oz.) sour cream
1 (8 oz.) pkg. cream cheese, softened
6 T. butter, divided
2 T. diced minced onion (opt.)
1/2 to 1 tsp. salt
Paprika

Place potatoes in a Dutch oven or large kettle; cover with water and bring to a boil. Reduce heat; cover and cook for 20 to 25 minutes, or until potatoes are tender. Drain and place in a bowl; mash. Add sour cream, cream cheese, 4 tablespoons butter, onion and salt; stir until smooth, and cream cheese and butter are melted. Spread in a greased 9x13x2-inch pan. Melt remaining butter; drizzle over potatoes. Sprinkle with paprika. Refrigerate or bake immediately, covered, at 350° for 40 minutes; uncover, and bake 20 minutes longer. Yield: 12 servings.
Note: If potatoes are made ahead and refrigerated, let stand at room temperature for 30 minutes before baking.

Carol Kleyer

Party Potatoes

Mashed potatoes (enough for 8 to 10 people)
8 oz. sour cream
8 oz. cream cheese
2 T. onion flakes
1/4 tsp. garlic salt
1/4 lb. margarine, melted

While mashing potatoes, add sour cream and cheese; add onion flakes, garlic salt and margarine. Bake 30 minutes at 350°.
Note: This may be frozen, or made the day ahead and refrigerated.

Kari Dykstra

Burdens are not to make us bitter, but better.

Broasted Potatoes

6 lg. potatoes, peeled & quartered

Mix:
1/4 c. flour
1/4 c. Parmesan cheese
3/4 tsp. salt & pepper

Melt:
1/3 c. butter or margarine

Add:
Garlic powder (opt.)
Seasoning salt (opt.--if using, omit salt)

Dip potatoes in butter, shake potatoes in flour, cheese and seasoning mixture. Drizzle remaining butter over potatoes. Bake in large, buttered, jellyroll pan 1 1/4 hours at 350°. Turn potatoes halfway through cooking time.

Mary Ann Winchell

Screaming Potatoes

2 lb. clean, scrubbed, new potatoes
1/2 T. salt
2 T. water
1 T. margarine

Place potatoes in bottom of large skillet. Add water, butter and salt. Cover tightly and place over low heat. Cook 40 to 50 minutes, occasionally giving the pan a shake. Do not lift the lid while it is cooking, or you'll ruin it.

Michelle Bomgaars

Shake N' Bake Potatoes

6 med. potatoes, peeled & quartered
1 env. Shake 'N Bake (original flavor)
Milk

Dip potatoes in milk and coat with Shake 'N Bake. Salt to taste. Bake on cookie sheet that has 1/8-inch cooking oil. Bake at 400° for 30 minutes. Turn 2 or 3 times. Serve with sour cream.

Karen Bos

Sweet Potato Casserole

3 or 4 med. sweet potatoes
2 eggs
1/3 c. milk or evaporated milk
1 stick oleo
3/4 c. sugar
1 tsp. vanilla
1 c. brown sugar
1/2 c. flour
1/3 c. soft butter
1 c. pecans

Peel and cook sweet potatoes. Mix eggs, milk, oleo, sugar and vanilla. Add to the potatoes. Put mixture in 2-quart casserole dish. Top with crumbled topping. Bake at 350° for 30 minutes.
Topping: Mix brown sugar, flour, butter and nutmeats.

Elnora McGilvra

Western Potato Rounds

2 lg. unpeeled baking potatoes
Vegetable oil
1 c. (4 oz.) shredded Co-Jack cheese
6 bacon slices, crisply cooked, drained & crumbled
1/3 c. green onion slices
1/4 c. barbecue sauce

Preheat oven to 450°. Cut potatoes into 1/4-inch-thick slices. Spray both sides of slices with oil. Bake 20 minutes, or until lightly browned. Remove from oven. Combine cheese, bacon and onion. Brush potato slices with barbecue sauce; sprinkle with cheese mixture. Return potato slices to oven and bake 3 to 5 minutes, or until cheese is melted.

Raegen Blom

Baked Asparagus

2 (14 oz.) cans asparagus, or 28 oz. home-grown or wild, cooked
5 hard-boiled eggs

1 (4 1/2 oz.) can mushrooms
1 T. parsley
1 T. pimento
Bread or cracker crumbs

WHITE SAUCE:
3 T. flour
3/4 c. milk

3/4 tsp. salt
1/4 c. asparagus liquid
1 c. American cheese, grated

Make white sauce; add grated cheese. Stir until melted and thickened. Fold in half of mushrooms, parsley and pimento. In a 2 to 2 1/2-quart dish, layer asparagus, eggs and mushrooms. Add white sauce and cover with buttered crumbs. Bake at 350° until bubbly, about 30 minutes.

Greg Van Beek

Baked Beans

1 (48 oz.) jar Randall's white beans or pork & beans
1 c. brown sugar
1 c. catsup
2 T. dry mustard
2 T. vinegar
A little dried onion
Fried bacon

Mix together and bake in oven for 1 hour at 350°.

Cindy VanDer Weide

Bean Casserole

1 lg. can baked beans
1 can butter beans
1 lg. can kidney beans
2 T. dry mustard
6 slices bacon
1 lg. onion, sliced
1 c. brown sugar
1/2 c. chili sauce

Fry bacon; add onions and sauté. Mix all ingredients together. Place in a casserole dish. Bake in 325° oven for 1 hour.

Laura Haverdink

Calico Beans

1 lb. hamburger
1 sm. onion
1 c. ketchup
2 T. mustard
3/4 c. brown sugar
2 T. white vinegar
1/4 lb. bacon, fried crisp (opt.)
1 (16 oz.) can kidney beans, drained
1 (15 oz.) can butter beans, drained
1 (21 oz.) can pork & beans

Brown hamburger in a large fry pan and then add rest of ingredients. Put in a crock-pot for 1 hour on high and 3 hours on low.

Sharon Plendl

Calico Beans

1 lg. can Bush baked beans*
1 can kidney beans*
1 can butter beans*
1 can baby lima beans*
1 c. brown sugar
1 T. vinegar
1 sm. onion, chopped & browned
1/2 lb. bacon, cut up & browned
1 lb. ground chuck, browned

*Drain most of liquid--but not all completely.
Put all ingredients in a slow-cooker for 2 1/2 to 3 hours, or in oven for 1 1/2 hours at 325°.

Wanda Hofmeyer

Green Bean Casserole

1 can mushroom soup
3/4 c. milk
1/8 tsp. pepper

2 (9 oz.) pkg. frozen cut green beans
1 1/3 c. French-fried onions (2.8 oz. can)

In 1 1/2-quart casserole, combine soup, milk and pepper; mix well. Stir in beans and 2/3 cup onions. Bake at 350° for 30 minutes, or until hot. Stir. Sprinkle with 2/3 cup onions. Bake 5 minutes more, or until onions are golden. Yield: 6 servings.
Variation: Can use 2 (14.5-ounce) cans cut green beans, drained.

Wanda Hofmeyer

Green Beans Supreme

Shred and set aside 4 ounces processed cheese food (about 1 cup, shredded). Cook 2 (10-ounce) packages frozen French-style green beans, or use 2 to 3 cans of same. Heat 2 tablespoons margarine in a saucepan over low heat and add 2 tablespoons minced onion; cook until transparent.
Remove from heat and blend in a mixture of:

1 T. flour
1/2 tsp. salt
1/2 tsp. paprika

1/4 tsp. dry mustard
1/4 tsp. Accent
1/2 tsp. Worcestershire sauce

Heat until mixture bubbles. Remove from heat. Add gradually, stirring constantly, 1 cup evaporated milk. Return to heat and bring rapidly to boiling, stirring constantly; cook 1 to 2 minutes longer. Drain beans and add to sauce, blending well. Put mixture into baking dish. Sprinkle with cheese and 2 tablespoons fine, dry bread crumbs. Broil 5 minutes, or until crumbs are lightly browned and cheese is melted. Yield: 5 to 6 servings.

Clarine Van Klompenburg

Broccoli Casserole

1 stick margarine
2 (10 oz.) pkg. frozen chopped broccoli, or fresh broccoli, chopped

4 oz. shredded cheese (a kind that melts easily)
30 Ritz or butter crackers

Crush crackers and melt butter. Mix together with cheese and broccoli. Bake at 350° for 1/2 hour.
Note: You may want to cover for part of baking time so it doesn't dry out.

Dawn Beukelman

Broccoli Dish

2 c. cooked Minute Rice
3/4 c. Velveeta cheese, cut up
2 T. melted butter

1 can cream of chicken soup
1 pkg. frozen broccoli

Mix and put in buttered casserole. Cover. Bake 1 hour at 350°.

Wanda Hofmeyer

Broccoli-Cauliflower Bake

1 lg. pkg. broccoli, cooked
1 lg. pkg. cauliflower, cooked

2 c. cut-up cheese
2 cans cream of mushroom soup

Top with bread crumbs tossed in melted butter. Bake until hot, about 25 to 30 minutes, at 350°.

Eunice Koopmans

Broccoli-Rice Casserole

1 (20 oz.) pkg. broccoli
 & cauliflower
1 c. Minute Rice (uncooked)
1 (8 oz.) jar Cheez Whiz

1 can cream of chicken soup
1/2 c. milk
4 T. oleo, melted

Cook vegetables. Combine all ingredients in casserole and bake at 325° for 1 hour.

Joyce Baker

California Vegetable Dish

1 c. cooked Minute Rice
1/2 stick margarine
1/2 c. onion
1/2 c. celery

20 oz. California Blend
 vegetables
1 sm. jar Cheez Whiz
1 can cream of mushroom soup

Sauté butter and onion. Add vegetables and simmer until thawed. Add Cheez Whiz and soup mix with rice, and put in greased 9x13-inch dish. Bake 45 minutes at 350°.

Amy Krogman

Christmas Cauliflower

1 lg. head cauliflower, broken into flowerets
1/4 c. green pepper, diced
1 (7.3 oz) jar sliced mushrooms, drained
1/4 c. butter or margarine
1/3 c. all-purpose flour
2 c. milk
1 c. (4 oz.) Swiss cheese
2 T. pimentos, diced
1 tsp. salt
Paprika

In a 3-quart saucepan, cook cauliflower in a small amount of water for 6 to 7 minutes, or until crisp-tender, drain well. In a medium saucepan, sauté green pepper and mushrooms in butter for 2 minutes. Add flour; gradually stir in milk. Bring to a boil, boil for 2 minutes, stirring constantly. Remove from the heat. Stir in cheese until melted. Add pimentos and salt. Place half of cauliflower in a greased 2-quart baking dish. Top with half of sauce; repeat layers. Bake, uncovered, at 325° for 25 minutes, until bubbly. Sprinkle with paprika. Yield: 8 to 10 servings.

Chris Van Beek

Corn-Broccoli Casserole

1 egg
1 (10 oz.) pkg. frozen broccoli, partially thawed
1 (8 1/4 oz.) can creamed corn
1 T. grated onion
1/4 tsp. salt
Dash of pepper
3 T. butter, melted
1 c. chicken stuffing (Stove Top)

Grease 1-quart casserole. Combine egg, broccoli, corn, onion, salt and pepper. Stir in melted butter and stuffing mix. Bake 30 to 40 minutes at 350°.

Wilma Ruisch

Cheesy Baked Carrots

4 c. sliced, cooked carrots
3 T. butter
1/4 c. chopped celery
1/4 c. chopped onion
2 T. flour
1/2 tsp. salt
1/2 tsp. dry mustard
1/8 tsp. pepper
1 c. milk
1 c. cubed American cheese
1 c. crushed corn flakes
3 T. melted butter

Place carrots in well-buttered casserole. Sauté celery and onion in 3 tablespoons butter until tender, about 5 minutes. Add flour, salt, pepper and mustard. Cook about 1 minute, stirring constantly. Add milk, bring to a boil, cook until thick, about 1 minute. Remove from heat. Add cheese. Stir until melted. Pour over carrots. Mix corn flakes and melted butter. Sprinkle over cheese sauce. Bake 45 minutes at 350°, or until cheese is bubbly.

Ruth De Koter

Corn Casserole

1 can cream-style corn
1 can whole kernel corn
8 oz. sour cream
1 box Jiffy cornbread mix
1 stick oleo

Use half of liquid from corn. Melt oleo. Mix all together. Bake in greased casserole for 1 hour at 375°.

Wanda Hofmeyer

Corn Dish

1 can corn, drained
1 (3 oz.) pkg. cream cheese
2 T. sugar

Heat and eat.

Sadie Van Peursem

Vegetable-Rice Hot Dish

1 c. Minute Rice
1 (16 oz.) pkg. frozen California Blend vegetables
1 can cream of chicken soup
2 T. diced onion
1/2 c. diced celery
1/2 c. (or more) diced Velveeta cheese
1/2 c. milk

Mix all ingredients together and bake at 350° for 1 hour.

Evonne Wielenga

Vegetable-Rice Dish

1 pkg. chopped broccoli or California Blend
1 c. Minute Rice
1 can cream of mushroom soup
1 c. milk
1 c. grated Cheddar cheese
Chopped onion, to taste

Mix all ingredients together, except broccoli or vegetables. Then toss in vegetables. Put in 1 1/2-quart casserole. Bake 45 minutes at 350°.

Marcia Cleveringa

Notes & Recipes

Sandwiches & Soups

Sandwiches

Barbecues

4 lb. ground beef
2 onions
2 tsp. dry mustard
2 tsp. chili powder
1 1/3 c. catsup
Salt & pepper
2 c. water

Brown ground beef and onion. Add remaining ingredients.

Cindy VanDer Weide

Sloppy Joes

4 lb. hamburger
1 lg. onion, chopped
2 stalks celery, chopped
1 pepper, chopped
2 (8 oz.) cans tomato sauce
1/4 c. barbecue sauce
1 T. prepared mustard
1 c. catsup
1/4 tsp. garlic powder
2 T. Worcestershire sauce
4 T. brown sugar

Brown and drain hamburger, onion, celery and pepper. Add the remaining ingredients and simmer for a couple of hours.

Mary Ann Winchell

Taverns

1 pt. water
1 lg. onion
3/4 c. catsup
2 T. dry mustard
2 T. chili powder
2 lb. ground beef, browned
Salt
Pepper

Boil onion in water until done. Add other ingredients and cook for 20 minutes.

Lynn Herzog

Barbecue Beef Buns

SAUCE:
1/4 c. brown sugar
3/4 c. beef broth
1/4 c. vinegar
1 sm. onion, chopped

Dash of Worcestershire sauce
Dash of chili powder
1/2 c. barbecue sauce
1/2 c. catsup

Cook 1 (3- to 4-pound) roast until done. Simmer sauce ingredients together and mix with roast beef, which has been cut up.

Rachel Hubers

Chipped Beef on Toast

1/4 c. oleo
1/4 c. flour

2 c. milk
5 oz. dried beef

Melt oleo; stir in flour until smooth. Stir in milk and heat until thick. Stir in dried beef, which has been cut in small pieces. Stir and cook for about 1 minute, until heated through. Serve over toast.

Marilyn Kruid

Canadian Bacon Buns

1 stick softened oleo
1 tsp. chopped onion
3 tsp. mustard
1 T. poppy seeds

12 to 20 slices Canadian bacon
12 to 20 slices American or Velveeta cheese
12 to 20 buns, depending on size

Mix oleo, onion, mustard and poppy seeds together. Spread this mixture on buns. Put Canadian bacon and cheese on buns and wrap in foil. Bake at 325° for 20 minutes.

Evonne Wielenga

Oven Ham and Cheese

2 T. prepared mustard
1/4 c. oleo
1 T. minced onion
1 T. poppy seed

1 lb. sliced ham
24 slices cheese
2 doz. buns

Make a spread of the first 4 ingredients. Spread on bun. Top with a ham and cheese slice. Top with other half of bun and wrap in foil. Bake at 325° for 12 to 15 minutes.

Elvera Van Horssen

Canned Meat Sandwich

1 qt. canned meat
1 lb. hamburger
1 can cream of chicken soup
1/2 pkg. Lipton beef-onion soup

Brown and drain hamburger. Combine the rest of the ingredients with hamburger. Heat everything together and serve on buns.

Denise Vander Stelt

Haystacks

30 slices bread

Cut circles from each slice.

FILLING:
1 c. cut-up chicken
3 hard-boiled eggs
1/4 c. minced onion
1/2 c. mayonnaise

Put filling on slice of bread; then one slice of bread, place more filling on. End with bread.

TOPPING:
2 jars Old English cheese spread
1/2 c. butter
1 beaten egg

Put this in double boiler; melt. Frost the 10 haystacks with this mixture. Bake for 15 to 20 minutes at 300°. Yield: 10.

Note: You can make these ahead of time and put into refrigerator or freezer.

Jo Kuiken

The Ultimate

1 (3 oz.) pkg. cream cheese
3/4 c. mayonnaise
1 c. (4 oz.) shredded Cheddar cheese
1 c. (4 oz.) shredded Mozzarella cheese
1/2 tsp. garlic powder
1/8 tsp. seasoned salt
10 slices Italian bread, 1/2" thick
2 T. butter or margarine

In a mixing bowl, beat cream cheese and mayonnaise until smooth. Stir in cheeses, garlic powder and seasoned salt. Spread 5 slices of bread with the cheese mixture, about 1/3 cup on each. Top with remaining bread. Butter the outside of sandwiches. Cook in a large skillet over medium heat until golden brown on both sides. Yield: 5 servings.

Jennifer Vander Schaaf

Cheese Spread

1 T. white sugar
1 T. butter
1/2 tsp. salt
1 T. flour
3 T. vinegar
1 egg, beaten
1/2 c. cream or evaporated milk

Mix and cook until thick, in a double boiler. Add 2 hard-boiled eggs (chopped fine), 1/2 pound Velveeta cheese (cubed), and onion, if desired. Stir in while cooked custard is hot. Cool.

Wanda Kuiken

Cheese-Dried Beef Spread

1 lb. Velveeta cheese, cubed
1 can evaporated milk or whipping cream
1 beaten egg
12 to 14 slices dried beef

Stir Velveeta cheese and milk until melted, in top of double boiler. (Stir frequently so it doesn't scorch.) Add egg and dried beef (tear this into small pieces). Spread on bun halves and serve open-faced. Store in covered jar, in refrigerator, if any spread is leftover.

Brenda Herbst,
Tonya Venema

Dried Beef Spread for Sandwiches

2 c. tomato juice
2 T. tapioca
2 1/2 c. grated cheese
1 1/4 c. dried beef
1/8 tsp. black pepper
1/4 tsp. prepared mustard
1/4 tsp. Worcestershire sauce

Cook tomato juice and tapioca until clear, about 15 minutes. Stir in cheese while hot. Add cut-up dried beef, pepper, mustard and Worcestershire sauce.

Mrs. Anna De Jager (William)

Egg Salad

1 T. melted butter
1 T. flour
1/2 c. evaporated milk
1 T. sugar
2 T. vinegar
1/2 tsp. salt

Mix all ingredients together and add a beaten egg. Cook until thick and add 1/2 pound of Velveeta cheese. Stir until melted. Chop up and stir in 4 to 6 hard-boiled eggs. May add pickle relish for flavor.

Elaine Vander Broek

Egg Salad Spread

6 eggs, boiled & chopped
8 oz. cream cheese
3/4 c. Miracle Whip
1 T. sugar
Salt, to taste

Mix together and chill. Serve on open-face rusk buns. Yield: 1 1/2 to 2 dozen sandwiches.

Elvera Van Horssen

Egg Salad

1 T. butter
1 T. flour
2 T. sugar
1 beaten egg
1/2 tsp. salt
3 tsp. vinegar
1/2 c. cream

Mix together.
Add:
1 T. minced onion
2 grated, hard-boiled eggs
8 oz. cream cheese, mashed
1/2 sm. can or jar pimento

Mix all together.

Tonya Venema

Soups

California Blend Vegetable Soup

1 1/2 qt. water
3 chicken bouillon cubes
2 T. parsley flakes
3 carrots, diced
3 potatoes, diced
1 sm. onion

Boil until done. Add 1 (16-ounce) package broccoli and cauliflower (frozen); boil a little longer. Turn off burner. Add 2 cans cream of chicken soup and 1 pound Velveeta cheese, cubed. Stir until melted. Reheat and serve.

Jonna Wierda

Cheese-Vegetable Soup

6 c. water
3 chicken bouillon cubes
1 bag baby carrots
2 c. diced potatoes
1 pkg. winter mix vegetables
2 cans cream of chicken soup
1 lb. Velveeta cheese

Cook until tender, the water, bouillon cubes, carrots and potatoes. Add 1 package winter-mix vegetables. Cook for about 10 minutes. Remove from stove; add 2 cans cream of chicken soup. Return to low setting on stove. Add 1 pound Velveeta cheese. Cook until cheese melts.

Jeanne Van Roekel

Delicious Vegetable Soup

2 qt. water
2 lb. stew meat or cut-up roast
2 c. carrots, sliced
2 c. potatoes, cubed
1/4 tsp. pepper
2 beef bouillon cubes
1 (46 oz.) can V8 juice
2 c. celery, sliced
1 c. onion, diced
2 tsp. salt
1 T. Accent
1/2 c. barley

Brown meat lightly. Add the remaining ingredients. Cover tightly and place in a 350° oven for 4 to 5 hours. Stir occasionally.

Jo Kuiken

Vegetable Soup
(Soup Supper Recipe)

2 gal. water
2 lb. beef & 1 soup bone
1/2 c. chopped onion
3 c. tomato juice
1 1/2 c. rice
3 to 4 c. carrots, diced
1 1/2 c. celery, chopped
2 boxes frozen mixed vegetables
2 c. potatoes, diced
2 beef bouillon cubes

Boil meat until done. Cut meat off bones into small pieces. Simmer all of the ingredients together until flavors are well blended. Yield: 2 gallons.

Committee

Zingy Vegetable Soup

1 soup bone or beef roast, or
  1 qt. canned beef
1 (46 oz.) can V8 juice
1 (10 oz.) can tomato soup
2 1/2 qt. water
1/2 c. barley (medium)
1 c. diced onion
2 c. celery, chopped
Green beans (opt.)
2 c. carrots
2 c. corn
2 c. cubed potatoes
3 beef bouillon cubes
1/2 tsp. pepper

Cook soup bone. Strain broth and use. Combine remaining ingredients and simmer in a crock-pot or large kettle on low heat, until vegetables are tender.
Dee Ann Cleveringa

Pea Soup
(Soup Supper Recipe)

2 gal. water (soft water works best)
1 lb. split peas
2 lb. whole dried peas
4 potatoes, small cubes
6 pork hocks, or 2 lb. pork roast
Salt & pepper, to taste
2 onions, chopped

Soak whole peas overnight. Use soft water for the soup. Boil meat until well-done. Remove from bones and cut into small pieces. Do not use the skin. Simmer together with other ingredients until flavors are well blended. Yield: 2 gallons.
Committee

Baked Potato Soup

4 to 6 med. potatoes
3 T. butter
1 c. diced onion
2 T. flour
6 c. water
2 T. chicken base
1/4 c. cornstarch
1 1/2 c. instant potatoes
3/4 tsp. pepper
1/2 tsp. basil
1/8 tsp. thyme
2 c. half & half
1 1/2 c. milk

Bake potatoes and set aside to cool. Melt butter in a 6-quart pot. Sauté onions until light brown. Add flour and mix well. Add everything, except milk and half & half. Bring to a boil. Reduce heat and simmer for 5 minutes. Cut potatoes in half and scoop out contents. Add potatoes, half & half and milk. Bring to a boil, and then simmer another 15 minutes, until thick. Top with grated cheese and serve.

Michelle Bomgaars

Golden Creamy Potato Soup

3 c. diced potatoes
1 c. water
1/2 c. celery, diced
1/2 c. carrots, diced
1/4 c. onion
1 tsp. parsley flakes
1 bouillon cube (chicken)
Salt & pepper

Simmer all ingredients in saucepan for 20 minutes. Gradually add 1 1/2 cups milk mixed with 2 tablespoons flour. Cook until thickened. Add 1/2 pound Velveeta cheese; melt. Cook slowly--do not boil.
Note: Can double the recipe.

Suzanne Haverdink

Potato-Noodle Soup

6 c. boiling water
1 1/2 c. diced carrots
6 c. diced potatoes
1 c. diced celery
1 can cream of mushroom soup
3 tsp. salt
1/2 tsp. pepper
12 oz. egg noodles
1 c. chopped onion
1 1/2 c. butter
1/2 c. flour
1 T. chicken base or bouillon
6 c. milk
1 lb. Velveeta cheese
5 strips bacon, fried & diced

Add boiling water to carrots, potatoes, celery, salt, pepper, onion, noodles and 4 cups milk. Cover and simmer for 10 minutes. Do not drain!
Make a sauce of butter, flour and 2 cups milk. Remove from heat and stir cheese until melted. Add bacon and sauce to undrained vegetables. Heat through, but do not boil.
Note: You may add more milk to get a desired thickness.

Mike Klemme

Broccoli-Cheese Soup

1 pkg. frozen, cut broccoli
3 1/2 c. milk
1 pkt. chicken noodle soup mix
1 T. minced onion
1 tsp. parsley flakes
1 can Cheddar cheese soup
2 c. shredded Cheddar cheese

Put all ingredients, except the shredded Cheddar cheese, in crock-pot. Mix together. Simmer for several hours, until broccoli is tender, stirring occasionally, to prevent sticking to the crock-pot. When broccoli is done, add the shredded Cheddar cheese. Stir into soup mixture until cheese is melted.

Dawn Beukelman

Cauliflower-Cheese Soup

2 c. water
1/2 c. shredded carrots
1/2 c. chopped onion
1/4 c. diced celery
1 med. potato (1/2" cubes)
1 (16 oz.) bag frozen cauliflower, cut into flowerets
1 can cream of chicken soup
1 can cream of mushroom soup
2 soup cans milk
1 c. boiled (baked) ham, cubed
1 lb. Velveeta cheese, cubed

In a covered saucepan, cook carrots, onion, celery, potato, cauliflower flowerets and 2 cups water until tender-crisp. Do not overcook. Drain. Add soups, milk, ham and cheese. Continue to heat on low until cheese is melted and soup is hot. Do not boil! Yield: 2 quarts.

Evonne Wielenga

Cheese Soup

2 qt. water
4 chicken bouillon cubes
6 cubed potatoes
2 bags California Blend vegetables
2 cans cream of chicken soup
2 lb. Velveeta cheese

Bring water, bouillon cubes and potatoes to a boil for 25 minutes. Add vegetables and boil for 15 minutes. Lower heat to warm setting. Add soup and Velveeta. Stir all together.

Cindy VanDer Weide

Cheese Soup

1 1/2 qt. water
6 chicken-flavored bouillon cubes
1 c. celery
1/2 c. onion
10 diced potatoes
1 (1 lb) bag California Blend vegetables

Boil potatoes, water, bouillon cubes, celery, onion and vegetables until done, about 10 to 15 minutes.
Add:
2 cans cream of chicken soup
1 lb. Velveeta cheese, cubed

Heat until melted and hot. Serve.

Winova Van Regenmorter

Chicken Soup

1 chicken
1 c. rice
2 chicken bouillon cubes
1 can cream of chicken soup
3 stalks celery
3 carrots, sliced
Onion

Boil chicken; take meat off bones. Boil vegetables until done. Simmer.

Joyce Baker

Chicken Soup

1 pt. chicken, cooked & cut up
1 qt. chicken broth
1 qt. water
Scant 1/2 c. rice
Onion, to taste
1 c. mixture of carrots & celery
2 chicken bouillon cubes
1 (1"-diameter) bunch spaghetti noodles, broken & uncooked
Salt & pepper, to taste

Combine all in soup kettle or crock-pot; simmer on low several hours, until tender, and rice and vegetables are cooked.

Dee Ann Cleveringa

Chicken Soup
(Soup Supper Recipe)

2 gal. water
1 (5 to 6 lb.) chicken
1/2 c. diced onion
2 c. rice
1 c. celery, chopped
Salt & pepper, to taste
2 chicken bouillon cubes

Cook chicken in water until done. Remove meat from bones to dice. Add all other ingredients to broth and cook until well blended. Yield: 2 gallons.

Committee

Fiesta Chicken Soup

6 boneless, skinless chicken breasts, cut up
4 (14 1/2 oz.) cans chicken broth
2 cans kidney beans, undrained
2 c. salsa
2 c. frozen whole corn
1 c. instant rice
1 c. shredded Monterey Jack cheese (set aside)

Cut up chicken and fry until done. In a large saucepan, combine chicken, chicken broth, kidney beans, salsa and corn. Bring to a boil. Reduce heat and simmer, uncovered, for 5 to 10 minutes. Stir in rice; cover and remove from heat. Let stand 5 minutes. Top individual servings with Monterey Jack cheese.

Priscilla Jansma

Chicken and Wild Rice Soup

3 (10 3/4 oz.) cans chicken broth
2 c. water
1/2 c. wild rice
1/2 c. green onions, finely chopped
1/2 c. butter
3/4 c. flour
1/2 tsp. salt
1/8 tsp. pepper
1/4 tsp. poultry seasoning
2 c. half & half
1 1/2 c. cubed, cooked chicken
8 slices bacon, cooked crisp & crumbled

In a large saucepan, combine broth and water. Add wild rice and onion; simmer for 35 to 40 minutes, or until rice is tender. In a medium saucepan, melt butter; stir in flour, salt, pepper and poultry seasoning. Cook over low heat, stirring constantly, until mixture is smooth and bubbly. Add half & half; cook 2 minutes, until mixture thickens slightly, stirring constantly. Add remaining ingredients and heat thoroughly. Garnish with additional bacon, if desired.

Lori Van Gorp

Wild Rice Soup

1/2 c. wild rice
1 qt. half & half
2 cans cream of potato soup
1 can cream of celery soup
1 lb. Velveeta cheese, cubed
3 to 8 slices bacon, cooked (can use 1 pkg.)
1/4 c. onion or 1 tsp. onion flakes
1 c. cooked carrots (can use 1 can diced carrots)

Cook wild rice as directed on box. Add the rest of the ingredients and simmer. Add garlic and onion salt to taste.
Note: Can substitute chicken for bacon.

Jonna Wierda

Chili Soup

1 lb. hamburger, browned & drained
2 T. Tabasco sauce
Garlic salt, to taste
Pepper, to taste
2 lg. (Hi-C size) cans tomato soup (+ 2 to 3 sm. cans, if you feel it needs to be thicker)
1 (16 oz.) can fancy red kidney beans
1 qt. V8 juice

Brown hamburger with Tabasco sauce, garlic salt and pepper. When browned, add remaining ingredients and simmer for 2 to 2 1/2 hours, covered.

Dawn Beukelman

Chili
(Soup Supper Recipe)

2 lb. ground beef
1 c. onion, chopped
4 c. kidney or chili beans, & juice
4 c. tomatoes
1 can tomato soup
1/2 to 1 tsp. garlic salt
1 T. chili powder
1 tsp. salt

Brown ground beef and onion. Add remaining ingredients. Cover and simmer for 1 1/2 to 2 hours. Yield: a good 3 quarts. **Committee**

Hillbilly Chili

2 lb. ground beef
1 lb. ground pork
28 oz. (2--14 oz. cans) Mrs. Grimes' chili beans
28 oz. tomatoes, cut up
1 (8 oz.) can tomato paste
2 cans Hunt's Special Sauce
1/2 lb. bacon, sliced thin & browned
2 T. chili powder
1/2 T. black pepper
1 T. seasoning salt
1 T. cumin
1 yellow onion
1/2 green pepper
1 (18 oz.) can pork & beans
1/2 c. brown sugar
1/2 c. honey
1 (32 oz.) can tomato juice
1 clove garlic, minced
1 (4 oz.) can mushrooms, drained

Fry bacon until crunchy; drain. Add beef and pork. Brown together. Combine all ingredients, except beans, in a large pot and bring to a boil, stirring occasionally. Turn heat to low; add beans. Simmer at least 1 hour.
Chris Van Beek

Mexican Chicken Chili

1 lb. chicken breast fillets
1 T. olive oil
12 c. water
2 T. chicken bouillon
8 oz. tomato sauce
1 lg. potato, diced
1 sm. onion, diced
1 1/2 tsp. chili powder
1 tsp. cumin
15 oz. corn
1 carrot, sliced
1 celery stalks, sliced
15 oz. diced tomatoes
15 oz. red kidney beans
4 oz. diced chilies
2 cloves garlic, pressed
Dash of cayenne pepper
Dash of basil
Dash of oregano

Sauté chicken breasts in olive oil in a large pot until done. Remove chicken and let cool. Do not rinse pot. Shred chicken into bite-size pieces and return to pot. Add the remaining ingredients and turn heat on high. Bring to a boil; reduce heat and simmer for 4 to 5 hours. Stir every 20 to 30 minutes. Chili should reduce substantially to thicken and darken. Serve hot, with a dollop of sour cream, and sprinkle with grated cheese. **Michelle Bomgaars**

Mexican Soup

2 lb. ground beef
1/2 c. onion
1 pkg. taco seasoning
1 sm. can tomato paste
1 (10 oz.) pkg. mixed vegetables, frozen
1 can Mrs. Grimes' chili beans
2 c. water

Brown hamburger and onion together; drain grease off. Mix other ingredients together and cook until well blended. Serve with tortilla chips and shredded cheese.

Diane Munro

Hamburger Soup

1 qt. tomatoes & juice
2 c. diced potatoes
1 c. diced carrots
1 c. diced onion
1 c. diced celery
1/4 c. rice
1 beef bouillon cube
1 1/2 qt. water, or to thickness desired
Celery salt
Salt
Pepper
1 lb. hamburger, browned

Add above ingredients to your browned hamburger. Simmer for 45 minutes to 1 hour. After it has simmered for 45 minutes, use the salt, pepper and celery salt to season to taste.

Audrey Vander Stelt

Love Soup

1/3 c. beef bouillon granules
1 T. chili powder
1/4 c. onion flakes
1/2 c. split peas
1/2 c. ABC macaroni (or ring macaroni)
1/4 c. barley
1/2 c. lentils
1/2 c. rice
Approx. 1 1/4 c. heart-shaped pasta, to fill jar to top

Place ingredients in layers, in a quart canning jar, or divide recipe in half and use pint jars. Place in jar in order given. Cover with a lid (decorate with a square of pinked material). Finish with flowers or ribbon.

To Use: Brown 1 pound hamburger in a large soup kettle. Drain. Remove heart pasta from top of jar and reserve. Add the remaining ingredients from jar to 12 cups of water. Add 1 large can of whole tomatoes (chopped) with juice. Simmer for 45 minutes. Add heart pasta for the last 15 minutes. Enjoy!

Note: This recipe is for a quart-sized soup starter. When reheating, add another small can of tomatoes.

Imo Mulder

Notes & Recipes

Kids

Three-Layer Bars

FIRST LAYER:
3/4 c. flour
1/2 tsp. baking powder
1/2 tsp. salt
1 c. sugar

1/2 c. margarine
2 eggs, beaten
1 tsp. vanilla
1/4 c. cocoa
1 T. Crisco

SECOND LAYER:
1 pt. marshmallow creme

THIRD LAYER:
12 oz. milk chocolate chips
1 c. peanut butter
1 c. Rice Krispies

First Layer: Beat first 7 ingredients for 1 minute, then add next 2 ingredients and beat for 30 seconds. Bake in greased 9x13-inch pan at 350° for 15 to 20 minutes.

Second Layer: Drop marshmallow creme by spoonfuls on brownie layer and bake for 3 minutes. Spread marshmallow creme and cool. Melt chips and peanut butter together; add Rice Krispies and spread on marshmallow layer. Refrigerate to set.

Jason De Weerd

Almost Candy Bars

In large bowl, cut 1/2 cup margarine or butter into 1 package Pillsbury Plus devils food cake. Mix with fork until crumbly. Sprinkle into ungreased 10x15-inch baking pan. Press lightly. Sprinkle with 1 cup butterscotch chips and 1 cup chocolate chips. Pour 1 (14-ounce) can sweetened condensed milk over. Bake at 350° for 20 to 30 minutes.

Dustin VanDer Weide

Cream Cheese Bars

1 box yellow cake mix
1 egg

1 stick oleo, melted

Mix and pat in 9x13-inch pan.
Then mix:
2 eggs, beaten
8 oz. cream cheese

2 2/3 c. powdered sugar

Spread over cake mixture. Bake in 350° oven for 30 to 40 minutes.

Katie Dykstra

Chocolate Scotcheroos

1 c. sugar
1 c. corn syrup
1 c. peanut butter
5 1/2 c. Rice Krispies
1 c. chocolate chips
1 c. butterscotch chips

Combine sugar and corn syrup in saucepan. Cook over moderate heat until sugar is dissolved. Do not boil. Remove from heat, stir in peanut butter. Add Rice Krispies, stir until well coated. Put in greased 9x13-inch pan. Melt chips together over low heat. Spread on top of bars.

Tara and Traci Smits

Marble Bars

1 c. white sugar
1 c. white syrup
3/4 c. peanut butter
5 to 6 c. Rice Krispies
6 oz. chocolate chips

Microwave sugar and syrup for 3 minutes and 30 seconds. Stir and add peanut butter until melted. Slowly add Rice Krispies, mix well. Add chocolate chips last, stir only enough to marble. Pour into 9x13-inch pan. Refrigerate until set.

Jessie De Weerd

No-Bake Bars

4 c. Cheerios
2 c. Rice Krispies
2 c. peanuts
2 c. M&M's
1 c. light corn syrup
1 c. sugar
1 1/2 c. creamy peanut butter
1 tsp. vanilla

In a large bowl, combine first 4 ingredients; set aside. In a saucepan, bring corn syrup and sugar to a boil. Cook and stir until sugar is dissolved. Remove from heat, stir in peanut butter and vanilla. Pour over cereal mixture and toss to coat evenly. Spread into a greased 10x15-inch pan. Cool.

Casie VanDer Weide

Pecan Squares

CRUST:
3 c. all-purpose flour
1/2 c. sugar
1 c. oleo
1/2 tsp. salt

FILLING:
4 eggs
1 1/2 c. light corn syrup
1 1/2 c. sugar
3 T. oleo
1 1/2 tsp. vanilla
1 1/2 c. chopped pecans

Crust: Blend crust ingredients together and press into a greased 10x15-inch pan. Bake at 350° for 20 minutes.
Filling: Combine ingredients for filling and spread over hot crust. Bake at 350° for 25 minutes.

Shawndra Beukelman

Chocolate Chip Cookies

1 c. white sugar
1 c. brown sugar
1 c. shortening
1 c. vegetable oil
1 egg, beaten
1 T. milk
1 tsp. vanilla
1 tsp. salt
1 tsp. cream of tartar
1 tsp. baking soda
3 1/2 to 4 c. flour
1 pkg. chocolate chips

Mix in order given. Bake in 350° oven until light brown, about 8 to 10 minutes. Yield: about 4 dozen cookies.

Jenny De Weerd

Chocolate Chip Cookies

2 c. shortening
1 1/2 c. brown sugar
2 1/2 c. sugar
4 eggs
2 tsp. baking soda
2 tsp. salt
3 tsp. vanilla
5 c. flour
1 lg. bag chocolate chips

Mix until smooth. Add flour slowly and mix well. Add chocolate chips and mix. Bake 10 to 12 minutes at 350°. Yield: 8 dozen cookies.

Samantha VanDer Weide

Chocolate-Peanut Butter Cookies

2 c. sugar
1/2 c. milk
1/2 c. butter
4 T. cocoa
3 c. quick oatmeal
1/2 c. peanut butter

Mix sugar, milk, butter and cocoa together in a saucepan. Bring to a full boil and remove from heat immediately. Pour this mixture over oatmeal and peanut butter. Beat until well mixed and drop by teaspoon on waxed paper.
Jodi Wielenga

"Cookie Cutters"
(Cookies)

1 1/2 c. powdered sugar
1 c. butter, softened
1 tsp. vanilla
1/2 tsp. almond extract
1 egg
2 1/2 c. all-purpose flour
1 tsp. baking soda
1 tsp. cream of tartar

FROSTING:
3 c. powdered sugar
1/3 c. butter, softened
1 1/2 tsp. vanilla
2 T. milk

Mix powdered sugar, margarine or butter, vanilla, almond extract and egg. Stir in remaining ingredients, cover and place in refrigerator for at least 2 hours. Heat oven to 375°. Grease cookie sheet lightly. Roll out dough on lightly-floured surface. Cut with cookie cutters. Bake 7 to 8 minutes, or until edges are light brown. Cool.

Frosting: Mix powdered sugar and butter. Stir in vanilla and milk. Beat until smooth and of spreading consistency. Use food coloring for desired colors.
Aaron Van Beek

Golden Brown Chocolate Chip Cookies

1 c. white sugar
1 c. brown sugar
1 c. Crisco shortening
1 c. cooking oil (vegetable)
1 egg
1 T. milk
1 tsp. vanilla
1/4 tsp. burnt sugar flavoring
1 tsp. cream of tartar
1 tsp. salt
1 tsp. baking soda
4 c. flour (unsifted)
12 oz. chocolate chips

Preheat oven to 350°. Mix white sugar and brown sugar together. Then add shortening. Add next all remaining ingredients. Make sure to add flour cup by cup. Roll into balls and flatten with a glass dipped in sugar. Bake on an ungreased pan for 8 to 10 minutes.
Afton Vander Zwaag

No-Bake Cookies

2 c. sugar
1/4 c. cocoa
1 tsp. vanilla
Pinch of salt

1/2 c. milk
1 stick oleo
1/2 c. peanut butter
3 c. oatmeal

Combine sugar, cocoa, milk and oleo in a pan. Cook until it starts to boil. Add vanilla, salt, peanut butter and oatmeal. Drop on waxed paper.

Jalen Van Wyk

Cookie Sandwich

1 c. oleo
1 c. white sugar
1 c. brown sugar
3 eggs
2 tsp. baking soda with 1 T. water dissolved in it

1 T. vanilla
1 (6 oz.) pkg. chocolate chips
1 tsp. cream of tartar
1 tsp. salt
4 c. flour
Ice cream

Preheat oven to 350°. Cream together oleo, sugars, eggs, baking soda, water and vanilla. Stir in dry ingredients. Bake at 350° for 10 to 15 minutes. Once cool, scoop ice cream between 2 cookies. Freeze. Enjoy!

Michaela Van Klompenburg

Banana Bread

2 mashed bananas
3 T. milk
2 eggs
1 tsp. vanilla
1/2 c. oleo, melted

2 c. flour
1/2 tsp. baking powder
1/2 tsp. baking soda
1 c. sugar

Combine bananas, milk, eggs, vanilla and oleo. Add sugar, then dry ingredients. Beat until smooth and well blended. Pour mixture into buttered 4x8x3-inch loaf pan. Bake at 350° for 1 hour, or until toothpick in center tests clean. Store in tightly-covered container.

Note: This recipe can be doubled.

Reid Hundt

Monkey Bread

3 cans buttermilk biscuits
1/2 c. sugar
1 tsp. cinnamon
1/2 c. brown sugar
3/4 c. butter

Quarter biscuits and coat with sugar and cinnamon mixture. Layer biscuits in well-greased bundt pan. Boil brown sugar and butter for 1 minute. Pour over biscuits and bake at 325° for 30 minutes. Cool 10 minutes before taking out of pan.

David Dykstra

Chocolate Chip Coffee Ring

1/2 c. butter or margarine, softened
1 c. sugar
2 eggs
8 oz. sour cream
1 tsp. vanilla

2 c. flour
1 tsp. baking powder
1 tsp. baking soda
1/2 tsp. salt
3/4 c. chocolate chips

TOPPING:
1/2 c. flour
1/2 c. brown sugar
1 1/2 tsp. cocoa

1/4 c. butter or margarine
1/4 c. chocolate chips
1/2 c. chopped pecans

Cream butter and sugar until fluffy. Beat in eggs. Add sour cream and vanilla; mix and set aside. Combine flour, baking powder, baking soda and salt; add to creamed mixture. Stir in chocolate chips. Pour into a greased 8-cup fluted tube pan (bundt pan).

Topping: Combine flour, sugar and cocoa; cut in butter until mixture resembles coarse crumbs. Stir in pecans and chocolate chips. Sprinkle over batter. Bake at 350° for 55 to 60 minutes. Cool in pan for 20 minutes.

Jessica VanDer Weide

Peanut Butter Balls

1 (18 oz.) jar peanut butter
1 lb. powdered sugar
1/2 c. melted butter
3 c. Rice Krispies

Roll in balls. Cool, then dip in 2 (24-ounce) melted almond bars and 1 bar paraffin wax. Refrigerate.

Katie Dykstra

Tootsie Roll Candy

2 T. butter
1/2 c. white syrup
2 sq. melted chocolate
1 tsp. vanilla
3 c. powdered sugar
3/4 c. dried milk

Mix and knead. Roll out into 3/4-inch roll and cut off lengths. Let stand awhile and then wrap. Keeps soft for 6 months.

David Cleveringa

Caramel Popcorn
(Microwave)

1 c. brown sugar
1 stick oleo
1/4 c. white syrup
1/2 tsp. salt
1/2 tsp. baking soda

Put all ingredients, except baking soda, in 1 1/2- to 2-quart baking dish. Boil in microwave for 2 full minutes. When done, add baking soda. Pop 3 to 4 quarts popcorn. Put in paper grocery bag. Pour on syrup and shake. Cook 1 1/2 minutes. Shake. Cook 1/2 minute.

Katie Dykstra

Marshmallow Popcorn Balls

7 to 8 qt. popped popcorn
1/4 c. sugar
1/4 c. butter
1 pkg. marshmallows

Melt last 3 ingredients. Pour over popcorn. Spray hands with cooking spray and shape into balls.

Casie VanDer Wiede

Puppy Chow

2 c. chocolate chips
1 c. peanut butter
2 to 3 c. powdered sugar
1 stick margarine
1 (12.3 oz.) box Crispix cereal

Melt chocolate chips, peanut butter and butter together. Put cereal in a large bowl. Pour chocolate mixture over the cereal; mix thoroughly. In a large paper bag, put powdered sugar. Add Crispix mixture and shake until well-coated.
Enjoy!

Maggie Vander Stelt

Heath Candy Bar Cake Dessert

1 white cake mix with pudding
1 box chocolate instant pudding
2 c. water
2 egg whites

Mix and bake 30 minutes at 325°. Cool and frost.

FROSTING:
1 c. powdered sugar
1/3 c. melted butter

Mix together and add 8 ounces Cool Whip. Shave a Heath candy bar on top.

Jessica VanDer Wiede

Ho Ho Bars

2 boxes Little Debbie cake rolls
2 pkg. instant white chocolate pudding
3 c. milk
1 (8 oz.) ctn. Cool Whip
Heath or other candy bar

Cut snack cakes in half the long way. Put frosting-sides down, in a 9x13-inch pan. Mix pudding and milk together. When thick, pour over Little Debbies. Wiggle the pan so pudding goes between cake. Refrigerate until set. Top with Cool Whip. Shave candy bar over the top. Cover and refrigerate.

Amber Vlietstra

Ice Cream Bar Dessert

12 ice cream sandwich bars
1 jar Mrs. Richardson's hot fudge topping
Cool Whip
Butterfinger bar, crushed (opt.)

In an 8x8-inch pan, place 6 ice cream sandwich bars to cover the bottom of the pan (you will have to cut 2 of them in half). Spread half of the fudge topping on top of the ice cream bars. Then place remaining 6 ice cream bars in a layer on top of this layer. Top with a layer of Cool Whip sprinkled with crushed Butterfinger bar. Freeze.

Shawndra Beukelman

Chicken Roll-Ups

2 c. cooked chicken, diced
1 (8 oz.) pkg. cream cheese
2 to 3 cans crescent rolls
1/2 stick melted oleo
Crushed corn flakes
1 sm. can mushrooms (opt.)

Fill crescent rolls with chicken mixture made with chicken, cream cheese and mushrooms. Roll in melted oleo and corn flakes. Bake at 350° for 20 minutes, or until brown.

Emily Hundt

Dave Dogs

Hot dogs
Bacon

Put a hot dog on roasting stick. Take a slice of bacon and wrap around hot dog. Use 2 toothpicks to keep bacon on hot dog. Put stick and dog over the campfire and roast until done. Be patient and turn often. Enjoy!

Bryce Vander Stelt

Pizza Braid

2 pkg. crescent rolls
4 T. pizza sauce
Sliced pepperoni &/or hamburger, browned & drained
1 to 2 c. shredded Mozzarella or pizza cheese

Unroll crescent rolls and place on a flat baking sheet to form a large rectangle. Press open edges together with your fingers, or use a rolling pin. On long sides of rectangle, use a pizza cutter to cut 3-inch-long strips every inch or so into the rectangle and toward the opposite side. Do this on both of the longer sides. Spread pizza sauce to cover the center section of the dough. On top of the pizza sauce, place 1, or more, layers of pepperoni and/or hamburger (and any other fillings you like on pizza). Top with a layer of Mozzarella or pizza cheese. Fold the inch-wide strips you cut earlier over the fillings and toward the opposite side, twisting once and pressing the edges of the strips together to hold the filling inside. Bake at 350° for approximately 15 minutes, until top is golden brown.

Time Saving Tip: Brown and drain hamburger ahead of time, and store in small Ziploc bags in the freezer. This way the hamburger is ready to use when you need it.

Shawndra Beukelman

Stromboli

2 loaves frozen bread dough
Basil
Parsley
Oregano
1/2 lb. Mozzarella cheese
1/4 lb. pepperoni
1/4 lb. sliced ham

Unthaw bread dough and partially rise. Roll out each loaf to a 12x12-inch rectangle. Sprinkle each loaf with basil, parsley and oregano. Put half of the Mozzarella cheese, sliced thin or grated, half of pepperoni and half of sliced ham; roll up and pinch bottom and ends together. Let rise 1 hour. Put loaves on a greased cookie sheet. Cover loaves with aluminum foil and bake at 350°, for 20 minutes covered and 10 minutes uncovered, until brown. Remove from oven and butter tops. Slice and eat. Dip in pizza sauce.
Michael Vander Stelt

Swiss, Turkey and Ham Bake

2 T. butter
1/2 c. cornflake, cracker or bread crumbs
2 c. cubed, cooked turkey
1 c. cubed, cooked ham
1 (8 oz.) can water chestnuts, drained & sliced
1 1/2 tsp. parsley flakes
1 can cream of celery soup
1/4 tsp. salt
1/8 tsp. pepper
1/2 c. shredded Swiss cheese
Paprika

Place butter in small bowl. Heat in microwave on FULL POWER 20 to 30 seconds, or until melted. Mix in crumbs; set aside. Combine turkey, ham, water chestnuts, parsley, soup and seasonings in 2-quart casserole. Cook in microwave on FULL POWER 7 to 9 minutes, or until heated through and temperature of 150° is reached. Stir halfway through cooking time. Top with cheese and sprinkle with paprika as desired. Cook in microwave on FULL POWER 45 seconds to 1 1/2 minutes, or until cheese is melted. Yield: 6 servings.
Lisa Muilenburg

Upside-Down French Toast

1/2 c. brown sugar
1/2 tsp. cinnamon
1/2 c. melted margarine
3 T. milk
3 eggs, slightly beaten
2 tsp. sugar
A dash of salt
Texas toast

Sprinkle brown sugar, cinnamon and margarine in a 9x13-inch pan. Mix milk, eggs, sugar and salt together. Dip slices of Texas toast in the mixture and arrange dipped slices of bread on sugar mixture. Pour remaining egg mixture over the bread. Refrigerate until baking time, or overnight. Bake at 350° for 20 minutes.
Jana Sneller

Quiche

8 eggs
4 c. milk
1 1/2 c. flour

1 tsp. salt
1 tsp. dry mustard

Beat together; pour into pan.
Add:
Ham
Onion

Mushrooms
3 c. shredded cheese

Bake at 350° for 30 to 40 minutes, until lightly browned.

Austin Van Klompenburg

Finger Jello

4 env. Knox gelatin
3 (3 oz.) pkg. flavored Jello

4 c. boiling water

Mix in large bowl until Jello is dissolved. Pour into 9x13-inch pan and refrigerate.

Joel De Weerd

Snicker Salad

1 (3 oz.) pkg. vanilla instant pudding
1 c. milk

8 oz. Cool Whip
2 apples, cut up
3 Snickers candy bars, cut up

Mix pudding and milk. Fold in Cool Whip. Cool. Just before serving, add apples and Snickers.

Darren Wielenga

Nacho Cheese Dip

1 (15 oz.) can Hormel chili (without beans)

1 lb. Velveeta cheese, cubed

Mix all ingredients in a medium microwave-safe bowl and heat in microwave until cheese is melted; stir. Serve with chips and possibly salsa.

Matt Kleyer

Vegetable Pizza

2 pkg. crescent rolls
1 lg. pkg. cream cheese
1 sm. pkg. cream cheese
2/3 c. mayonnaise
1 T. dill weed
1/2 tsp. garlic salt

Spread crescent rolls on 10x15-inch pan. Bake rolls in 400° oven for 10 minutes. Cool. Mix ingredients and spread on crust. Then add favorite vegetables, such as carrots, celery, broccoli, onions, cauliflower and radishes.

Katie Dykstra

Bubble Solution

1 c. water
1/2 c. liquid dish soap
1 T. sugar

Mix ingredients together. Use pipe cleaner or heavy wire to make wands.

Dustin VanDer Weide

Finger Paints
(Kid's Delight)

1/2 c. cornstarch
3/4 c. cold water
1 env. unflavored gelatin
1/4 c. cold water
2 c. hot tap water
1/2 c. Ivory soup (liquid)

Mix first 2 ingredients in saucepan. In meantime, soak gelatin in 1/4 cup cold water. Stir hot water in the starch mixture and cook over medium heat until mixture comes to a boil and is smooth. Remove from heat and blend in softened gelatin. Add soap, stir until dissolved. This makes 3 cups. Divide in portions in jars or bowls. Food coloring may be used for color. Add a few drops of coloring for the desired shade. For white, use white tempera powder. Store paint in jar with tight lid. Store in cool place.

Brody De Jager

Playdough

2 1/2 c. flour
1/2 c. salt
3 T. cooking oil
1 T. alum
2 c. boiling water

Mix flour, salt, oil and alum. Put food color of your choice into boiling water. Add to mixture; mix thoroughly. Store in plastic bag or containers in refrigerator. Will last a long time. Mom and dad, sit down and create with your kids some evening!

Breanne Cleveringa

Uncooked Playdough

3 c. flour
1 c. salt
1 c. water
1/4 c. oil
2 T. vinegar

Mix all ingredients well. Add more water if necessary. Knead! This dough keeps indefinitely in a plastic bag in the refrigerator. May need to add water occasionally.

Samantha VanDer Weide

Coal Plant

6 T. salt
6 T. bluing
6 T. water
1 T. ammonia
6 to 8 charcoal briquettes
Sm. evergreen sprigs (opt.)
Food colors

Mix first 4 ingredients. Place coal in shallow pie pan and place evergreen sprigs over them Pour mixture over all, and drop food color on scattered spots. Set aside, do not shake or disturb, and watch what happens.

Carissa Cleveringa

Notes & Recipes

Miscellaneous & This 'n That

Miscellaneous

Crunchy Chocolate Sauce

1 c. chopped walnuts or pecans
1/2 c. butter (no substitutes)
1 c. (6 oz.) semi-sweet chocolate chips
Ice cream

In a skillet, sauté nuts in butter until golden. Remove from heat; stir in chocolate chips until melted. Serve warm over ice cream (sauce will harden). Store in the refrigerator. This sauce can be reheated in the microwave. Yield: 1 1/2 cups.
Note: This recipe can be doubled, but don't double the nuts.

Elvera Van Horssen

Homemade Noodles

3 eggs
1 tsp. salt
Flour

Add enough flour to make stiff; roll out with rolling pin. Cut into strips with pizza cutter. Put with chicken or beef soup.

Carolyn De Jager

Canning

Freezer Cucumbers

2 qt. peeled, sliced cucumbers (8 c.)
1 onion, sliced thin
2 T. pickling salt
1 1/2 c. sugar
1/2 c. white vinegar

Combine cucumbers, onion and pickling salt; refrigerate for 24 hours. Drain. Blend the sugar and vinegar to cucumbers and let stand in refrigerator for 24 hours. Put in freezer containers and freeze.
Note: Can be served in vinegar-sugar syrup.

Melissa De Jager

Baby Dill Pickles

2 qt. water
1 qt. vinegar
1 c. sugar
1 c. canning salt (scant)

Use very small pickles. Put 1 dill head or 1/2 teaspoon dill seed, bud of garlic and 1/4 teaspoon alum in pint jars. Bring the juice to a boiling point, put over the jars of pickles and seal. Put jars in water bath and cook for 15 minutes. Remove at once.

Edith Kuiken

Pickle Relish

1 gal. ground-up lg. cucumbers
8 sm. onions
3 green peppers

Add:
1/2 c. pickling salt
1 qt. ice cubes

Let stand 3 hours. Drain thoroughly.
5 c. sugar
5 c. vinegar
1 1/2 tsp. turmeric
1/2 tsp. ground cloves
2 tsp. mustard seed
1 tsp. celery seed

Add vegetable mixture. Bring to a boil again. Put hot mixture into sterile jars and seal.

Wanda Hofmeyer,
Colette Hofmeyer

Berry Jam

3 c. berries
5 c. sugar
1 pkg. Sure-Jell

Mash berries and sugar and let stand 20 minutes; stir occasionally. Dissolve Sure-Jell in 1 cup water. Boil 1 minute. Add to fruit-sugar mixture and stir for 2 minutes. Put in jars and store in refrigerator or freezer.

Dorothy VanDer Weide

Rhubarb Juice

4 c. rhubarb
1 c. pineapple juice
1/2 c. sugar

Cover stalks of rhubarb with water and boil 5 minutes. Pour off juice and add other ingredients. Put in jars and bring to a boil. Process 15 minutes.

Marlene Van Beek

Rhubarb Jam

5 c. rhubarb, chopped
1 c. water
5 c. sugar

1 can blueberry pie filling
2 (3 oz.) pkg. grape Jello

Cook rhubarb in water until tender. Add sugar and cook a few minutes, stirring constantly. Add pie filling and cook 6 to 8 minutes. Remove from heat and add Jello. Stir until completely dissolved. Put into containers and keep in refrigerator or freezer.

*Hattie Dykstra,
submitted by Helen Oolman*

Rhubarb Jam

5 c. rhubarb, cut fine
1 c. water
4 c. sugar

1 c. strawberry pie filling
2 (3 oz.) pkg. strawberry Jello

Cook rhubarb in water until tender. Add sugar and cook a few minutes longer, stirring constantly. Add pie filling and cook 6 to 8 minutes longer. Remove from heat and add Jello. Stir until completely dissolved. Pour into jars and seal. Store in refrigerator or freezer.
Variations: You may substitute cherry pie filling and cherry Jello, or blueberry pie filling and raspberry Jello.

Vicki Schrock

Rhubarb Jam

7 c. diced rhubarb
4 c. sugar

1 can blueberry pie filling
2 (3 oz.) pkg. raspberry gelatin

Boil rhubarb, sugar and pie filling for 10 minutes. Remove from heat. Add Jello and stir well. Put in jars and seal. Or, put in pint containers and store in freezer.
Variations:
•For Rhubarb-Strawberry Jam, use 4 cups diced rhubarb, 3 1/2 cups sugar and 1 (16-ounce) package strawberries. Boil gently for 15 to 20 minutes. Stir constantly. Add 1 package strawberry Jello.
•For Rhubarb-Raspberry Jam, use raspberries instead of strawberries, and 5 cups of sugar instead of 3 1/2 cups.

Al and Marlene Van Beek

"The Best" Jam

6 c. rhubarb
4 c. sugar
1 (6 oz.) pkg. raspberry Jello
1 can blueberry pie filling
1/2 c. water

Boil rhubarb in water until tender. Add sugar and boil for 5 minutes. Add Jello and pie filling. Freeze or can jam.

Kari Van Klompenburg

Strawberry Jam

10 c. strawberries, washed & hulled
5 c. sugar

Boil for 10 minutes. Add 2 cups sugar. Boil 5 minutes more. Set in shallow pan. Stir often, all day. Pack next morning in hot, sterilized jars and seal.

Al and Marlene Van Beek

Strawberry-Rhubarb Jelly or Jam

5 c. rhubarb, cut up
4 c. white sugar
2 sm. pkg. strawberry Jello
2 c. strawberries

Combine rhubarb and sugar and let stand 1 hour. Then add a little water and boil 1/2 hour, or until rhubarb is very mushy. Remove from heat. Immediately stir in Jello and strawberries. Stir until Jello is totally dissolved. Put in jars and seal, or put in plastic containers and freeze.
Very good.

Colette Hofmeyer

Cooked Salsa

3 c. onion
15 c. tomatoes, peeled & diced
6 (6 oz.) cans tomato paste
Dash of sugar
Dash of cumin
6 c. peppers: 5 1/2 c. green peppers for mild, or 4 c. for hot
1/2 c. jalapeño peppers for mild, or 2 c. for hot

1/3 c. fresh chopped cilantro

Bring to boil for 30 minutes. Put in jars and seal at 10 pounds pressure for 8 minutes.

Mike Klemme

Salsa Sauce

12 skinned tomatoes, chopped
5 to 6 white onions, chopped
1/2 c. jalapeño peppers (can be canned)
5 cloves minced garlic
2 c. diced green peppers
1 T. salt
1/4 c. sugar
1 c. cider vinegar
2 (6 oz.) cans tomato paste

Put in large pan. Boil. Simmer for 30 minutes. Put in sterile pint jars, 1/2-inch from top. Process in hot water bath for 25 minutes. Yield: 8 to 9 pints.

Kathy Dykstra

Spaghetti Sauce

2 lg. onions
2 cloves garlic
1/3 c. oil
12 tomatoes
2 c. water
2 beef bouillon cubes
4 tsp. leaf basil
2 bay leaves
2 tsp. salt
1 tsp. oregano
1 (12 oz.) can tomato paste

Sauté garlic and onion until soft. Stir in tomatoes (chopped). Cook 5 minutes. Add remaining ingredients; cook 1 hour, stirring occasionally, until thickened. Yield: 3 quarts.

Marlene Van Beek

This 'n That

Crystal Garden

3 or 4 pieces charcoal
4 T. water
4 T. salt
4 T. baking soda
4 T. laundry bluing

Put charcoal in a bowl and cover with water. Let stand about 30 minutes. Remove from water and place charcoal in a shallow dish--a styrofoam meat tray works well. Mix water, salt, baking soda and bluing in a small jar; shake it well, then pour over the charcoal. Within a few hours, snowflake-like crystals begin to form. When crystals begin drying, add small amounts of salt and water along the edge of the dish. If you move the dish and crystals break, add more of the original mixture. When the garden grows to the size you want, stop adding water and salt. It's interesting to watch the crystals form.

Marilyn Kruid

Edible Play Dough

1/2 c. creamy peanut butter
1/2 c. honey
3/4 c. oatmeal

3/4 c. powdered milk
2 1/2 c. powdered sugar
2 T. hot water

Mix well. Sprinkle a little powdered sugar on table so play dough won't stick. Kids can make animal shapes, etc., but usually can't wait to eat it!
Note: Can add food coloring, if desired.

Rose Dykstra

Natural Insect Trap

1 c. sugar
1 c. vinegar

1 banana peel

Combine all ingredients in gallon milk jug. Add water until half-full. Hang in fruit trees, or elsewhere, to keep worms out of fruit and flies under control.

Dee Ann Cleveringa

Index

Appetizers, Snacks & Beverages

Appetizers
Crab Appetizers
Deviled Eggs
Low-Fat Pimento Cheese
    Spread 1
Cheese Puffs
Cheesy Bacon Bites
Ham-Pickle Roll-Ups
Oyster Crackers 2
Puppy Chow
Ritz Cracker Snacks
Grandma Lisa's Cheese Ball 3
Taco Cheese Ball
Taco Tartlets
Walking Taco
Tidbit Smokies 4
Vegetable Pizza 5

Snacks
Caramel Corn
Old Dutch Caramel Corn 5
Microwave Caramel Corn
Caramel Chex Mix
"Sweet and Chewy" Chex Mix 6
Easy Bean Dip
Hamburger-Cheese Dip
Mexican Dip (2) 7
Nacho Cheese Dip
Nacho Dip
Dip for Nachos
Pizza Dip 8
Salsa Dip
Taco Dip (2)
Caramel Apple Dip 9
Creamy Caramel Fruit Dip
Dip for Apple Slices
Fruit Dip 10

Beverages
Brunch Punch 10
Easy Party Punch
Elegant Punch
Golden Fruit Punch 11
Grape Punch
Grape Slush Punch
MOC-FV Purple Punch 12
Pineapple-Banana Punch
Punch
Raspberry Punch
Fizzy Ice Cream Drinks 13
Frozen Slush Drink
Lemonade
Fresh Lemonade
Orange Julius 14
Orange Julius
Non-Alcoholic Strawberry
    Daiquiri
Eggnog
Amaretto Hot Chocolate Mix 15
Cappuccino Mix (2)
Instant Cocoa Mix 16

Bars & Cookies

Bars
Almond Bars (2) 17
Almond Bars (3) 18
Almond Tarts
Dutch Treats 19
Dutch Almond Tarts
Marla's Almond Puffs 20
Best-Ever Brownies
Brownies
Brownie Pizza 21
Brownie Pizza
Buttermilk Brownies 22
Buttermilk Brownies (2) 23
Candy Bar Brownies
Chocolate Crunch Brownies
Cream Cheese Brownies 24
Crunchy Brownies
Disappearing Marshmallow
    Brownies
Easy Bars 25
Frosted Fudge Brownies
Macaroon Brownies 26
Marbled Brownies
Milk Chocolate Brownies 27
Mom's Brownies

Triple-Fudge Brownies
Chocolate Caramel Bars 28
Chocolate Chip Coconut Bars
Chocolate Chip Bars
Chocolate Chip Bar 29
Chocolate Marshmallow Bars
Chocolate-Oatmeal Bars 30
Chocolate Revel Bars (2)
Easy Fudge Bars 31
Fudge Bars
Marshmallow Fudge Bars 32
Napoleon Cremes
Turtle Bars
Caramel Bars 33
Caramel Bars (2) 34
Tackling Toffee Caramel Bars
Caramel Rice Krispie Bars (2) 35
Krunch Bars
Scotch-a-Roo Bars
Scotcharoos (2) 36
Rice Krispie Bars
Easy Bars
Chipper Bars 37
M&M Bars (2) 38
Best Oatmeal Bars
Cola Bars 39
Delicious Bars
Double Dairy Bars 40
Double-Delicious Cookie Bars
Dump Bars
Peanut Butter Bars 41
Peanut Butter S'mores Bars
S'more Bars 42
Salted Nut Bars
Sugarless Bars 43
Super Party Bars
Twix Bars (2) 44
Applesauce Bars
Apple-Nut Squares
Apple Squares 45
Banana Bars
Carrot Bars
Cherry Bing Bars 46
Cherry Squares
Coconut-Pineapple Bars
Lemon-Coconut Squares 47
Raisin Bars

Raisin Cream Bars 48
Sour Cream Raisin Bars (2) 49

Cookies

"Can't Eat Just One"
   Chocolate Chip Cookies
Chocolate Chip Cereal Cookies
Chocolate Chip Cookies 50
Chocolate Chip Cookies
No. 1 Chocolate Chip Cookies
Cinnamon Chocolate Chip
   Cookies 51
Grandma Kate's Chocolate
   Chip Cookies
Keebler Soft Chocolate Chip
   Cookies
Our Favorite Chewy Chocolate
   Chip Cookies 52
Jordan's Cookies
Soft Batch Chocolate Chip
   Cookies
Sour Cream Chocolate Chip
   Cookies 53
$250 Dollar Cookie Recipe
Melt-in-Your-Mouth Cookies
Angel Cookies 54
Bonbon Cookies
Butter-Pecan Turtle Cookies
Best Butter Cookies 55
Best-Ever Cookies
Cookies
Forgotten Cookies 56
Coconut-Oatmeal Cookies
Neiman-Marcus Cookies
No-Bake Cookies 57
No-Bake Chocolate Cookies
Chocolate-Oatmeal No-Bake
   Cookies
Oatmeal-Cranberry-White
   Chocolate Chunk Cookies 58
Oatmeal Cookies
Oreo Cookies
Peanut Cookies 59
Peanut Butter Cookies
Peanut Butter Cup Cookies
Peanut Butter Cup Delights 60
Chocolate Star Cookies

Peanut Butter Star Cookies
Pecan Crispies 61
Snicker Cookies
Sand Cookies
Crispy Sugar Cookies 62
Old-Fashioned Sugar Cookies
Sugar Cookies
Grandma Dykstra's Tea
    Cookies 63
Thumbprint Cookies
Ten-Cup Cookies 64

Breads, Rolls, Muffins & Breakfast

Breads, Rolls, Muffins
Apple Bread
Banana Bread 65
Banana Bread (3) 66
Banana-Pecan Bread
Best Banana Bread
Bran-Banana Bread 67
Strawberry-Banana Bread
Sugarless Banana Bread
Lemon Bread 68
Oatmeal Bread
Peach Bread
Pumpkin Bread 69
Pumpkin Bread
Zucchini Bread
Boston Brown Bread 70
Cornbread
Grape-Nut Flakes Bread
Eight Dozen Buns 71
White Bread
Southern-Style Biscuits
Bubble Bread 72
Monkey Bread
Mini Cinnamon Rolls
Caramel Topping for Rolls 73
Orange-Caramel Sauce
Cream Cheese Rolls
Honey Buns 74
Banana Crumb Muffins
Morning Glory Muffins 75
Strawberry Muffins
Biscuit Bites

Cheese Biscuits 76
Cheesy Garlic Bread (2)
Bread Machine Garlic Bread
Garlic Bubble Loaf 77
Herb Bread
Olive Garden Breadsticks
Outback Bread 78
Pepperoni Pizza Bread
Pretzels 79

Breakfast
Breakfast Oatmeal Snacks 79
Ranch Granola
Orange French Toast
Popeye Toast 80
Egg and Broccoli Quiche
Egg and Sausage Casserole
Buttermilk Pancakes 81
Chocolate Pancakes
Great Pancakes
Swedish Oatmeal Pancakes 82
Belgian Waffles
Everyday Waffles
Waffles 83
Waffles 84

Cakes, Frostings & Candies

Cakes
Good Old-Fashioned Angel
    Food Cake
Apple Dump Cake 85
Carrot Cake
Creamy Coconut Cake 86
Dump Cake
Earthquake Cake
Easy Cake
Lemon Cake Supreme 87
Luscious Lemon Delight Cake
Mandarin Orange Cake 88
Moon Cake
Bundt Pudding Cake 89
Blueberry Coffeecake
Butterbrickle Coffeecake
Coffeecake 90
Coffeecake (2)
Coffeecake and Glaze 91

297

Coconut Coffeecake
Melissa's Coffeecake
Raspberry Coffeecake 92
Rhubarb Coffeecake (2)
Strawberry-Rhubarb
    Coffeecake 93
Sour Cream Coffeecake
Chocolate Cheese Cupcakes 94
Cupcakes
Chocolate Swirl Cake
Fudge Marble Pound Cake 95
Never-Fail Chocolate Cake
Microwave Chocolate Cake
Red Earth Cake 96
Snack-Attack Chocolate Cake
Strawberry Cream Cake Roll 97
Texas Sheet Cake
Wacky Cake 98
Yellow Cake with Pineapple
    Frosting
Jelly Roll Deluxe 99
Easy Rhubarb Cake
Rhubarb Cake (2)
Sweet, Tart Rhubarb Cake 100
Confetti Cake
Lazy Daisy Cake
Poke-and-Pour Cake 101
Scripture Cake
Sugarless Cake 102

Frostings

Easy Caramel Frosting 102
Never-Fail Frosting 103

Candies

Almond Toffee Crunch
Chocolate Mints 103
Caramels
Coconut Candy 104
Chocolate-Caramel Snicker
    Candy
Fantasy Fudge 105
Peanut Brittle
Peanut Butter Balls (2) 106
Peanut Butter Balls
Peanut Butter Patties
Peanut Clusters

English Toffee 107
Truffles
Wedding Mints 108

Casseroles & Meats

Chicken

Chicken-Broccoli Casserole
Chicken Casserole (2) 109
Chicken Poppy Seed Casserole
Chicken-Vegetable Casserole
Easy Chicken Casserole 110
Potluck Chicken Casserole
Chicken Hot Dish (2) 111
Make-Ahead Chicken Hot Dish
Chicken à la King
Chicken and Onion Rice Dish ... 112
Chicken-Rice Dinner
Low-Fat Chicken and Rice 113
Chicken Crêpes
Chicken Loaf 114
Easy Chicken Pot Pie
Chicken Pie 115
Alice Springs Chicken
Baked Chicken Breast
Baked Chicken Dish 116
Company Chicken
Paper Sack Chicken
Parmesan Chicken 117
Party Chicken
Easy Chicken and Pasta
One-Pan Potatoes and Chicken
    Dijon 118
Easy Chicken Crescent Rolls
Chicken Bundles 119
Chicken Crescents
Chicken Crescent Wreath
Chicken Fingers 120
Tender Chicken Nuggets
Sweet-Sour Chicken
Teriyaki-Sesame Chicken 121
Cheesy Mexican Chicken
Chicken Chalupas
Chicken Enchiladas 122
Chicken Enchilada Casserole
Spanish Chicken
Turkey Divan 123

Beef

Beef Hot Dish
Busy Day Casserole
Cheeseburger Casserole 124
Cheeseburger Pie (2)
Cheesy Potato Beef Bake 125
Crock-Pot Casserole
Easy Hamburger Hot Dish
Emergency Steak
Family Casserole 126
Farmers' Delight
Farmhouse Barbecue Biscuits
French-Style Green Bean
 Casserole 127
Hamburger and Stuffing
 Casserole
Hamburger Casserole
Hamburger Hot Dish 128
Haystack Supper
Hamburger-Potato Casserole
Mom's Hamburger Helper 129
Quick, Easy Meal
Rog's Favorite Casserole
Western Casserole 130
BBQ Meat Balls
Lazy Daisy Meat Balls 131
Norwegian Meat Balls
Porcupine Meat Balls
Meat Loaf 132
Meat Loaf
Mom's Meat Loaf
Thirty-Minute Meat Loaf 133
Beef Enchiladas (2)
Sour Cream Enchiladas 134
Easy Mexican Casserole
Nacho-Roni
Taco Bake 135
Taco Casserole (2)
Taco in a Pan 136
Taco Meat Filling
Easy-Fix Roast
Mock Prime Rib
Poor Man's Prime Rib 137
Salisbury Steak
Swiss Steak (3) 138
Tender Baked Round Steak
Beef Stew

Five-Hour Beef Stew 139
Oven Beef Stew
Old-Fashioned Goulash 140

Pork

Bacon and Cheese Puff Pie 140
Ham Balls
Ham Loaf or Ham Balls
Ham Rolls 141
Crock-Pot Scalloped Potatoes
 and Ham
Ham, Broccoli and Potato Casserole
Rice Casserole 142
Barbecued Spareribs
Dominican Pork Chops
Grilled Marinated Pork Chops ... 143
Pork Chop and Potato Bake
Pork Chop Dinner
Pork and Noodle Casserole 144
Preferred Pork Chops
Tender Pork Roast 145

Seafood

Pan-Fried Walleye
Salmon Loaf 145
Seafood-Stuffed Potatoes
Shrimp Scampi
Tuna Casserole 146
Tuna Pie 147

Lasagna, Pizza & Miscellaneous

Chicken Lasagna 147
Chicken Lasagna
Easy Lasagna (2) 148
Lasagna (2)
Old-Fashioned Lasagna 149
Sunday Lasagna
Macaroni and Cheese
Manicotti 150
Pasta Mix
Spaghetti (2) 151
Spaghetti Bake
Spaghetti Casserole 152
Bubble Pizza (2)
Chicken-Cheese Pizza 153
Crescent Roll Pizza
Crock-Pot Pizza

Pizza Casserole 154
Pizza Casserole (3) 155
Pizza Hamburger Casserole
Pizza Hot Dish
Pizza in the Round 156
Pizza Loaf
Pizza Pies
Quick and Easy Pizza 157
Upside-Down Pizza
Stromboli
Casserole Sauce Mix-Cream
 Soup Substitute 158
Campfire Bundles
Hobo Dinners
Meat Marinade 159
Sausage Gravy for Biscuits
 and Gravy 160

Ethnic

Balka-Brai
Currant Bread 161
Almond Roll
Dutch Butter Cookies
Jan Hagel Cookies 162
St. Nick Cookies
St. Nicholas Cookies 163
Stroopwaffles
Grandma's Oli Bollen 164
Zuider Zee
Poffertjes
Pigs-in-the-Blanket 165
Huss Pot
Red Cabbage and Apples
Dutch Salad Dressing 166
Specken-Dicken
German Potato Salad
German Peppernuts 167
Kheema Chaval
Kheera Ka Rayta 168
Watermelon with Yogurt
Fettuccine Alfredo
Pepperoni Stromboli 169
Chicken Enchiladas
Quesadillas 170
Swedish Meatballs
Asian Chicken Pasta 171

Desserts & Pies

Desserts
Apple Crisp
Extra-Special Apple Crisp 173
Apple Crunch
Banana Dessert
Banana Cream Brownie
 Squares 174
Blueberry Delight
Old-Fashioned Bread Pudding
Brownie Delight 175
Buster Bar Dessert (2)
Butterfinger Bar Dessert 176
Butterfinger Dessert
Butterfinger Delight
Buttery Cinnamon Skillet
 Apples 177
Holiday Cheese Tarts
Cherry Angel Food Trifle
Cherry Crunch 178
Cherry-Rhubarb Cobbler
Cherry Yogurt Parfaits
Chocolate Candy Bar Dessert ... 179
Chocolate Dessert
Chocolate Chip Sensation
Chocolate Cake Dessert 180
Chocolate Pudding Cake
German Chocolate Cake
Chocolate Cream Dessert 181
Delicious Chocolate Pudding
Chocolate Chip Cheesecake
Miniature Cheesecakes 182
No-Bake Chocolate
 Cheesecake
No-Crust Cheese Pie
Oreo Cheesecake 183
White Chocolate Cheesecake
Fruit Pizza 184
Fruit Pizza (2) 185
Fruit Pizza 186
Fruit Pizza 187
Fruit Cobbler (2)
Lazy Day Cobbler...................... 188
Cream Puff Dessert (2) 189
Puff Pastry
Custard Pudding 190

Sugarless Dessert
"Easy" Frozen Dessert
Frosty Freeze Dessert
Rich Homemade Ice Cream 191
Homemade Ice Cream Mix
Homemade Ice Cream
Hot Fudge Sauce
Caramel Ice Cream Dessert 192
Ice Cream Crispies
Ice Cream Dessert
Orange Sherbet Dessert 193
Butter Pecan Malted Dessert
Lemon Dessert 194
Lime Chiffon Dessert
Fluffy Mint Dessert
Peach Dessert 195
Elegant Peach Delight
Peaches and Cream Dessert
Peach Melba
Cornflake Pudding 196
Pumpkin Cream Dessert
Great Pumpkin Dessert
Pumpkin Pie Dessert 197
Punch Bowl Cake
Quick Refreshing Dessert
Easy Rhubarb Dessert 198
Rhubarb Crisp
Pastor Wayne's Favorite
   Rhubarb Crisp
Rhubarb Crumble Dessert 199
Rhubarb Dessert
Rhubarb Shortcake 200
Rhubarb Shortcake
Rhubarb Torte 201
Strawberry Cheesecake Pie
Yummy Strawberry Delight
Strawberry Dessert 202
Strawberry Dessert (3) 203
Strawberry-Pretzel Dessert
Strawberry-Rhubarb Angel
   Squares 204
Strawberry Shortcut
Frosty Strawberry Squares 205

Pies
Sugarless Apple Pie (2) 206
Paper Bag Apple Pie

Blueberry-Rhubarb Pie 207
Butterscotch Pie
Cappuccino Pie
Caramel Chocolate Pie 208
Chocolate-Banana Creme Pie
Chocolate Silk Pie
Cocoa Mocha Pie 209
Coconut Custard Pie
Impossible Coconut Custard Pie
Velvety Custard Pie 210
Lemon Meringue Pie
Impossible Lemon Pie
Sour Cream Lemon Pie 211
Peanut Butter Pie (2)
Peanut Butter Cream Pie 212
Piña Colada Pie
Paradise Pumpkin Pie
Impossible Pumpkin Pie 213
Pumpkin Pecan Pie
Weight Watchers Pumpkin Pie
Microwave Raisin Creme Pie 214
Rhubarb Pie
Rhubarb Cream Pie (2) 215
Rhubarb Custard Pie
Rhubarb Rumble
Fresh Strawberry Pie 216
Fresh Strawberry Pie
Grandma's Strawberry Pie
Strawberry Pie 217
Strawberry Pie
Sweetheart Pie
Creamy Yogurt Pie 218
Toll House Pie
"Good and Easy" Meringue
Flaky Pie Crust 219

Salads, Dressings & Vegetables

Salads & Dressings
Chicken Salad
Tropical Chicken Salad 221
Seafood Salad
Cookie Salad
Crazy Grape Salad 222
Creamy Fruit Salad
Easy Cherry Salad

Easy Fruit Salad 223
Easy Fruit Salad (2)
Frozen Fruit Cups
Fruit Soup 224
Hot Fruit Dish
Hot Fruit Salad
Mystery Salad 225
Peaches and Cream Delight
Piña Colada Salad
Pretzel Salad
Snicker Salad 226
Snicker Salad (3)
Watergate Salad 227
Blender Salad
Broken Window Glass Salad
Cherry Coke Salad 228
Diabetic Jello Salad
Holiday White Salad
Mimosa Mold
Easy Orange Salad 229
Orange Salad (3)
Orange Salad Supreme 230
Orange-Pineapple Salad
Golden Glow Salad
Pimento Salad 231
Peaches 'N Cream Salad
Quick 'N Easy Salad
Raspberry Cottage Cheese
   Salad 232
Spring Garden Salad
Betty's Pink Lady Salad
Strawberry Fluff
Strawberry Jello Salad 233
Strawberry Salad (4) 234
Strawberry-Cranberry Salad
Finger Jello
Classic Macaroni Salad 235
Macaroni Salad and Dressing
Macaroni Salad (2) 236
Macaroni Salad (3) 237
Pasta Salad
Rigatoni Salad
Spaghetti Salad 238
Three-Bean Salad
Broccoli Salad
Cabbage Salad 239
Cabbage Salad

Cathy's Cabbage Crunch
   Salad 240
Chicken and Cabbage Crunch
   Salad
Crispy Salad 241
Oriental Coleslaw (20
Cashew-Lettuce Salad 242
Cashew Salad
Deb's Lettuce Salad
Cathy's Spinach Salad 243
Country Salad Bowl
Garden Delight
Mandarin Lettuce Salad 244
Onion-Cucumber Salad
Pea Salad (3) 245
Chop! Chop!
Vegetable Salad (2) 246
Dilly Potato Salad
Hot Creamed Potato Salad
Potato Salad 247
Potato Salad
Potato Salad Light
L'Trio Dressing 248
Mom Van Roekel's Salad
   Dressing
Potato Salad Dressing 249

Vegetables
Cheesy Potatoes 249
Cottage Potatoes
Company Potatoes
Crunchy Potatoes 250
Grandma's Hash Brown Bake
Hash Brown Casserole
Crock-Pot Potatoes 251
Make-Ahead Potatoes
Party Potatoes 252
Broasted Potatoes
Screaming Potatoes
Shake N' Bake Potatoes 253
Sweet Potato Casserole
Western Potato Rounds
Baked Asparagus 254
Baked Beans
Bean Casserole
Calico Beans (2) 255
Green Bean Casserole

Green Beans Supreme
Broccoli Casserole 256
Broccoli Dish
Broccoli-Cauliflower Bake
Broccoli-Rice Casserole
California Vegetable Dish 257
Christmas Cauliflower
Corn-Broccoli Casserole
Cheesy Baked Carrots 258
Corn Casserole
Corn Dish
Vegetable-Rice Hot Dish
Vegetable-Rice Dish 259

Sandwiches & Soups

Sandwiches

Barbecues
Sloppy Joes
Taverns 261
Barbecue Beef Buns
Chipped Beef on Toast
Canadian Bacon Buns
Oven Ham and Cheese 262
Canned Meat Sandwich
Haystacks
The Ultimate 263
Cheese Spread
Cheese-Dried Beef Spread
Dried Beef Spread for
    Sandwiches
Egg Salad 264
Egg Salad Spread
Egg Salad 265

Soups

California Blend Vegetable
    Soup 265
Cheese-Vegetable Soup
Delicious Vegetable Soup
Vegetable Soup 266
Zingy Vegetable Soup
Pea Soup
Baked Potato Soup 267
Golden Creamy Potato Soup
Potato-Noodle Soup
Broccoli-Cheese Soup 268

Cauliflower-Cheese Soup
Cheese Soup (2) 269
Chicken Soup (3)
Fiesta Chicken Soup 270
Chicken and Wild Rice Soup
Wild Rice Soup
Chili Soup 271
Chili
Hillbilly Chili
Mexican Chicken Chili 272
Mexican Soup
Hamburger Soup
Love Soup 273

Kids

Three-Layer Bars
Almost Candy Bars
Cream Cheese Bars 275
Chocolate Scotcheroos
Marble Bars
No-Bake Bars 276
Pecan Squares
Chocolate Chip Cookies (2) 277
Chocolate-Peanut Butter
    Cookies
"Cookie Cutters"
Golden Brown Chocolate Chip
    Cookies 278
No-Bake Cookies
Cookie Sandwich
Banana Bread 279
Monkey Bread
Chocolate Chip Coffee Ring
Peanut Butter Balls 280
Tootsie Roll Candy
Caramel Popcorn
Marshmallow Popcorn Balls
Puppy Chow 281
Heath Candy Bar Cake
    Dessert
Ho Ho Bars
Ice Cream Bar Dessert 282
Chicken Roll-Ups
Dave Dogs
Pizza Braid 283
Stromboli

Swiss, Turkey and Ham Bake
Upside-Down French Toast 284
Quiche
Finger Jello
Snicker Salad
Nacho Cheese Dip 285
Vegetable Pizza
Bubble Solution
Finger Paints
Playdough 286
Uncooked Playdough
Coal Plant 287

Miscellaneous & This 'n That

Miscellaneous
Crunchy Chocolate Sauce
Homemade Noodles 289

Canning
Freezer Cucumbers 289
Baby Dill Pickles
Pickle Relish
Berry Jam
Rhubarb Juice 290
Rhubarb Jam (3) 291
"The Best" Jam
Strawberry Jam
Strawberry-Rhubarb Jelly or Jam
Cooked Salsa 292
Salsa Sauce
Spaghetti Sauce 293

This 'n That
Crystal Garden 293
Edible Play Dough
Natural Insect Trap 294

ORDER BLANK

NAME _____

ADDRESS _____

CITY & STATE _____ ZIP _____

How many copies? _____ Amount enclosed _____
    Price per book $10.00
    Postage & handling 4.00
    Total $14.00
Please make checks payable to:
                Maurice 1st Reformed Church
Mail orders to: Diane Munro
                 403 5th St. NW.
              Orange City, IA 51041

ORDER BLANK

NAME _____

ADDRESS _____

CITY & STATE _____ ZIP _____

How many copies? _____ Amount enclosed _____
    Price per book $10.00
    Postage & handling 4.00
    Total $14.00
Please make checks payable to:
                Maurice 1st Reformed Church
Mail orders to: Diane Munro
                 403 5th St. NW.
              Orange City, IA 51041

EXCELLENT FUND-RAISING IDEAS

In addition to printing cookbooks for fund-raising organizations, JUMBO JACK'S COOKBOOKS also offers the proven successful fund-raising products shown below. The products shown below are just a few of the many items you might select for your next fund-raising project, or perhaps in conjunction with your cookbook project. Any of these will be beautifully imprinted with your organization's logo and name.

If you are interested in helping your organization make money with these successful fund-raising products, just mark the products you'd like more information about, and give us your name and address.

Name _____

Address _____

Phone _____

Tear out this page and mail it to: JUMBO JACK'S COOKBOOKS
P.O. 247 • AUDUBON, IOWA 50025

❏ OVEN MITT

❏ TOTE BAG

❏ HOT PAD

❏ APRON

❏ COOKBOOK

❏ T-SHIRT

❏ MUG

❏ PLACE MAT

Or, if you prefer, give Jeanne a toll free call at 1-800-798-2635, ext. 231
FAX: 1-712-563-3118 • COLLECT: 1-712-563-2635

We hope you are enjoying using this cookbook and find it useful in your kitchen. This book was printed by JUMBO JACK'S COOKBOOKS. If you are interested in having cookbooks printed for your organization, please write us for prices and details.

A cookbook is a good way for YOUR organization to make money.

If you are interested in more information, just tear out this page and mail it to us with your name and address, or just call us toll-free 1-800-798-2635.

UP TO 90 DAYS INTEREST FREE!

Featuring the 3-ring easel binder

We also do hardback covers, square back wire covers, and other types of binding.

Yes - please send me more information!

Name _____

Organization _____

Address _____

City _____ State _____ Zip _____

Phone _____

Or, if you prefer, give Val (ext. 238), Mitzi (ext. 225), or Mike (ext. 224) a call: Toll free: 1-800-798-2635; Collect: 1-712-563-2635; or fax us: 1-712-563-3118.

JUMBO JACK'S COOKBOOKS
AUDUBON MEDIA CORPORATION
AUDUBON IA 50025 • 1-800-798-2635